Michael Jackson
Grasping the Spectacle

Edited by

CHRISTOPHER R. SMIT
Calvin College, Grand Rapids, Michigan, USA

ASHGATE

Published by
Ashgate Publishing Limited
Wey Court East
Union Road
Farnham
Surrey, GU9 7PT
England

Ashgate Publishing Company
Suite 420
101 Cherry Street
Burlington
VT 05401-4405
USA

www.ashgate.com

British Library Cataloguing in Publication Data
Michael Jackson : grasping the spectacle. – (Ashgate popular and folk music series)
 1. Jackson, Michael, 1958–2009 – Criticism and interpretation.
 I. Series II. Smit, Christopher R.
 782.4'2164'092–dc23

Library of Congress Cataloging-in-Publication Data
Michael Jackson : grasping the spectacle / edited by Christopher R. Smit.
   p. cm.—(Ashgate popular and folk music series)
 Includes bibliographical references and index.
 ISBN 978-1-4094-4144-1 (hardcover) — ISBN 978-1-4094-4696-5 (pbk.)
1. Jackson, Michael, 1958–2009—Criticism and interpretation. 2. Jackson, Michael, 1958–2009—Psychology. 3. Popular music—Social aspects—United States. 4. Popular culture—United States. I. Smit, Christopher R.

 ML420.J175M523 2012
 782.42166092—dc23
 [B]
                                                                    2012009613

ISBN 9781409441441 (hbk)
ISBN 9781409446965 (pbk)

Printed and bound in Great Britain by the
MPG Books Group, UK.

For Moses. Keep startin' somethin'.

MICHAEL JACKSON

Contents

List of Figures and Tables

Figures

Tables

List of Contributors

Amy C. Billone is Associate Professor of English at the University of Tennessee, Knoxville. In 2005, she wrote the *Introduction*, *Notes* and *For Further Reading* sections of the Barnes and Noble Classics edition of J.M. Barrie's *Peter Pan*. Her book of literary criticism *Little Songs: Women, Silence and the Nineteenth-Century Sonnet* was published with the Ohio State University Press in 2007.

Diana York Blaine is Associate Professor at the University of Southern California where she teaches rhetoric, feminist theory, and literature. She has published on William Faulkner, Thomas Pynchon, the Jon Benet Ramsey murder case, the *Dr. Phil* show, and the "Mummies of the World" exhibit.

David Dark is the critically acclaimed author of the *Sacredness of Questioning Everything* and *Everyday Apocalypse*. A frequent speaker, Dark has also appeared on C-SPAN's Book-TV and in the award-winning documentary, *Marketing the Message* (2006).

Margo Jefferson is the Pulitzer Prize winning theater, arts, and cultural critic for the *New York Times*. Prior to joining *The Times*, Ms. Jefferson taught American literature and criticism at Columbia University.

Carl Miller teaches literature at the University of Alabama, where his courses include British and American modernism and postmodernism, existential literature, and children's literature. He saw *Captain EO* at Epcot as a child on his first vacation back in 1986.

Ruchi Mital is a writer and filmmaker. She graduated from NYU with an honors degree in English and American Literature. An MA candidate in Media Studies at The New School, she is focusing on documentary filmmaking and theory. Her first film received an honorable mention at the US Super 8 Film Festival.

Sherrow O. Pinder is Associate Professor of Political Science and Multicultural and Gender Studies at California State University, Chico. She is the author of three books. Pinder's edited book, *American Multicultural Studies*: *Diversity of Race, Ethnicity, Gender and Sexuality Diversity in Race*, is forthcoming in 2012.

Raphael Raphael is Lecturer in Film and Media Studies at the Center on Disability Studies at the University of Hawaii at Manoa. He is working on a book about the cultural work of the American freakshow and is co-editing three forthcoming books on issues in transnational genre and culture and representations of disability. He serves as media specialist in Eurasia for the not-for-profit corporation International School Services.

Jesse Schlotterbeck is Assistant Professor of Cinema at Denison University, and received his Ph.D. in Film Studies from the University of Iowa. His dissertation critically surveys the musical biopic from the 1960s to the present. Recent publications include entries in *Movies in American History: An Encyclopedia and World Film Locations*: Los Angeles.

Julie-Ann Scott is Assistant Professor of Communication Studies at UNCW where she teaches courses in performance studies and directs two traveling theatre troupes. Her research centers on personal narrative as performance of identity. Her work can be found in journals such as *Text and Performance Quarterly* and *Narrative Inquiry.*

Christopher R. Smit is Associate Professor of Media Studies at Calvin College in Grand Rapids, Michigan. His most recent book is *The Exile of Britney Spears: A Tale of 21st Century Consumption* (Intellect, 2011). His essays, chapters, and reviews on popular music, critical theory, aesthetics, and disability can be seen in a wide variety of journals and volumes. For more on his academic work, popular writing, and music, please visit smitwork.com.

Zack Stiegler is Assistant Professor of Communications Media at Indiana University of Pennsylvania. His work has appeared in *Journal of Radio and Audio Media*, *Journal of Popular Music Studies*, *Javnost: The Public*, *Sociology Study,* and *Journal of Communications Media Studies.*

Brett M. Van Hoesen is Assistant Professor of Modern and Contemporary Art History and a Faculty Associate in the Gender, Race, and Identity Program at the University of Nevada, Reno. Her recent publications include contributions to the *International Encyclopedia of Revolution and Protest,* the international feminist art journal *n.paradoxa*, and *Nka*, the journal of contemporary African art.

Julian Vigo is an independent scholar and filmmaker who has taught comparative literature, anthropology, philosophy, and media studies in universities throughout the Americas, Europe, and Africa. Also a yogi, permaculturalist, dj, artist, and activist, Vigo works on human rights and farming projects in Haiti, India, Pakistan and Indonesia.

Christopher Wiley is Lecturer in Music and Director of Undergraduate Studies at City University London, UK. He is the author of full-length articles appearing in *Music and Letters* and *Comparative Criticism*, and of shorter essays in *Biography*,

Scope, and *Musical Stages*; in-press publications include book chapters in *A Companion to Malcolm Arnold* and *Music of Joss Whedon's Worlds*, as well as an article re-evaluating the role of biography in the New Musicology.

General Editor's Preface

The upheaval that occurred in musicology during the last two decades of the twentieth century has created a new urgency for the study of popular music alongside the development of new critical and theoretical models. A relativistic outlook has replaced the universal perspective of modernism (the international ambitions of the 12-note style); the grand narrative of the evolution and dissolution of tonality has been challenged, and emphasis has shifted to cultural context, reception and subject position. Together, these have conspired to eat away at the status of canonical composers and categories of high and low in music. A need has arisen, also, to recognize and address the emergence of crossovers, mixed and new genres, to engage in debates concerning the vexed problem of what constitutes authenticity in music and to offer a critique of musical practice as the product of free, individual expression.

Popular musicology is now a vital and exciting area of scholarship, and the *Ashgate Popular and Folk Music Series* presents some of the best research in the field. Authors are concerned with locating musical practices, values and meanings in cultural context, and draw upon methodologies and theories developed in cultural studies, semiotics, poststructuralism, psychology and sociology. The series focuses on popular musics of the twentieth and twenty-first centuries. It is designed to embrace the world's popular musics from Acid Jazz to Zydeco, whether high tech or low tech, commercial or non-commercial, contemporary or traditional.

Professor Derek B. Scott
Professor of Critical Musicology
University of Leeds

Communication Arts and Sciences Department of Calvin College, thank you for your financial assistance. Special thanks to my research assistants Jacqueline Ristola, Amy Hinkle and Eden McCune. You have all done wonderful work.

To my partner Dr. Elizabeth VanArragon, many thanks for your support and confidence. And to our son, yes, you can play "Big Fat Bass" on my iPhone.

General Editor's Preface

The upheaval that occurred in musicology during the last two decades of the twentieth century has created a new urgency for the study of popular music alongside the development of new critical and theoretical models. A relativistic outlook has replaced the universal perspective of modernism (the international ambitions of the 12-note style); the grand narrative of the evolution and dissolution of tonality has been challenged, and emphasis has shifted to cultural context, reception and subject position. Together, these have conspired to eat away at the status of canonical composers and categories of high and low in music. A need has arisen, also, to recognize and address the emergence of crossovers, mixed and new genres, to engage in debates concerning the vexed problem of what constitutes authenticity in music and to offer a critique of musical practice as the product of free, individual expression.

Popular musicology is now a vital and exciting area of scholarship, and the *Ashgate Popular and Folk Music Series* presents some of the best research in the field. Authors are concerned with locating musical practices, values and meanings in cultural context, and draw upon methodologies and theories developed in cultural studies, semiotics, poststructuralism, psychology and sociology. The series focuses on popular musics of the twentieth and twenty-first centuries. It is designed to embrace the world's popular musics from Acid Jazz to Zydeco, whether high tech or low tech, commercial or non-commercial, contemporary or traditional.

Professor Derek B. Scott
Professor of Critical Musicology
University of Leeds

Acknowledgments

I certainly need to acknowledge the art of Michael Joseph Jackson.

Editing a book of essays about Jackson has been quite a nostalgic experience. In 1982, when the world-of-music-changing *Thriller* record was released, I was eight years old. My dad and I went to Kmart and purchased the cassette tape that would get played in my Sony Walkman and my Panasonic boombox: in eight months' time I would have to replace it with another cassette, the first one completely worn out. And so I thank my father, Richard Smit, for helping me purchase my first Michael Jackson product. The one that started it all. By 1983 I was completely devoted to the Jackson project: I had posters on my walls, buttons on my fake Thriller-era jacket, all of his music from when he was a kid on, a sequined glove that I had made. And yes, I had the doll.

The last CD I purchased by Jackson, before the trials began, was 1987's *Bad*. I had moved on to other music by that point, mostly hair metal, and so the purchase of this CD was really a gesture, a sort of consolation to a dwindling interest in the work of Michael Jackson. I didn't like the CD that much. It wasn't what I had fallen in love with five years before. It was too aggressive, and at the same time not so: even at the age of thirteen, I knew there was some posturing going on, some fakeness.

I stopped paying attention to Jackson until 1993, when the allegation of child molestation surfaced, soon after the famous interview with Oprah Winfrey. My attention to him this time was not adolescent, but professional. By then I had started studying media and culture as a graduate student in the Media Studies department of the University of Iowa, and was also interested in the sociology of disability. My deep thanks to Dr. Joy Hayes, Dr. Ralph Cintron, and Dr. Bruce Gronbeck for explicitly and inadvertently helping me traverse the terrain that would eventually lead to my particular take on disability and culture. In particular, it is Dr. David Depew who helped me decipher the political/cultural values of aesthetics that have always guided my work including this collection of essays.

So, by 1993, Jackson became fascinating in a wildly different way. Actually, in a quite sad way. And the story just kept getting worse, so that by the time news of his death came in 2009, it was almost a relief for me. Selfish, I know. But nonetheless, his death became a sort of permission to do some restorative yet honest work on this fascinating person.

My hope is that this book achieves that goal in providing new and exciting interpretations of the life and art of Michael Jackson.

I wish to thank the authors in this collection whose work has been tireless. Thanks also to all the folks at Ashgate for their editorial assistance. To the

Communication Arts and Sciences Department of Calvin College, thank you for your financial assistance. Special thanks to my research assistants Jacqueline Ristola, Amy Hinkle and Eden McCune. You have all done wonderful work.

To my partner Dr. Elizabeth VanArragon, many thanks for your support and confidence. And to our son, yes, you can play "Big Fat Bass" on my iPhone.

Introduction

Chasing the Spectacle of Michael Jackson

Christopher R. Smit

> The whole life of those societies in which modern conditions of production prevail presents itself as an immense accumulation of spectacles. All that once was directly lived has become mere representation.
>
> Guy Debord, *The Society of the Spectacle*

As a final document, *Michael Jackson's This Is It* (2009) works. Indeed, it works well. It offers the fan all that she or he may desire in this, the "final" goodbye from their desired object. The dance moves are exquisite, the determined, if not workaholic, authority of Michael Jackson is impressive. The music, as always, perfect. There is no sad goodbye, no overly emotional tributes, no voiceover, no pity. Also absent are allegations of inappropriateness, glorified moments of the strange "Wacko Jacko," or any other glances at the dark side of Jackson. The film stays positive, at times honorific. There are images of young Jackson with his brothers, the perfect amount of nostalgia. The film pays homage to the important songs, videos, and moments in a life spent performing. The glove is put on one more time, the zippers zipped, and the leather cleaned up for the light show. All is good again. The spectacle performs one last time.

And yet to say that this is a "final" document, an end to anything, is a mistake we must not make. Instead, we must realize that the spectacle of Jackson was never tempered by time or space, by memory, projections or representations, by substance or style. Instead, the spectacle of Jackson moved freely, as environments do. It was pliable at times, rigid at others. It was always visible, never forbidden, always consumable. And that is how it will remain now that he has died. And in many ways, the spectacle will now grow beyond anything it ever was while he was alive. In death, the spectacle finds energy.[1] It fuels new music in the 2010 release of

---

[1]   Indeed, the commercial evidence of this has already been laid out; Sony has paid the Michael Jackson estate $200 million for a 10-record deal over the next seven years; the popular franchise Cirque du Soleil has produced an entire performance based on Jackson's music entitled *Michael Jackson: Immortal*; and certainly the Jackson family will continue to capitalize on the life and death of their brother and son. These types of productions have already begun to garner harsh criticism from fans. In the most striking example of this backlash thus far, fans in Wales demonstrated against a tribute concert there in October 2011; arguing that the $31 memorial T-shirts and $15 commemorative mugs were capitalizing on the death of Jackson, fans opted not to purchase tickets for the star-studded event. Only half

Michael and new questions in the awful 2010 documentary film *Alive! Is Michael Jackson Really Dead?*

Followed closely, mediated declarations of Jackson's death on June 25, 2009 illustrate this posthumous growth of the spectacle. And while the major networks, CNN, Fox news, C-SPAN, and others, offered grand headlines (*The King of Pop Dies: A Legend Is Gone*) it was our posts, blogs, discussions, and comments on Facebook and Twitter that fanned the flames most successfully. Glancing over the posts is observing postmodern performances of lament, dedication, and bereavement. Like more traditional observances of death, these snippets of thought, quickly made, often swam in memories and images shared by a community: "I'll never forget the first time I saw him moonwalk."; "The Thriller video was historical, and I'm so glad I got to see it when it premiered!"; "I saw him perform in 1965, my parents took me." Similar sentiments might have been communicated over a dedication service in a funeral home, over coffee at a church function memorializing a friend or family member. And yet, none of the folks posting were part of his family; none of us shared any authentic intimacy with Jackson. All we knew was wrapped up in Debord's proclamation of representation. All we knew was the spectacle. And so our lamenting became a spectacular performance of lament. Our sorrow became the spectacular performance of sorrow matched only by the performance of death itself.

In this way, Jackson becomes a conduit of sorts. His death and life offered spaces of postmodern enactment not only for him but also for us, the consumers. The different stages of his career create landscapes upon which we are given spaces to remember, test out, and predict cultural value. This is the life of the spectacle: active involvement in mere representation. And while the physical, biological realities of Jackson's death remain permanent, they are also mysteriously absent from the manner in which we understand his death and life. Put another way, the death of Jackson is only partial, due mainly to the representative presence of the spectacle that remains.

The work in this book, pulled from a variety of scholarly perspectives, points to these and other peculiarities of the celebrity that was and is Michael Jackson. Although interested in different elements of the spectacle of Jackson, the essays collected here all point towards new understandings of how celebrity, consumption, history, race, gender, sexuality, and physicality work when their origin is deeply entrenched in the image of spectacle.

Knowing Michael Jackson

To say that Michael Jackson was a spectacle is to also say that he was text, something worked on in order to gather meaning. An illustration from *Michael Jackson's This*

---

of the arena was filled. For more on this see Ravi Somaiya, "Michael Jackson, Celebrated and Sold," *New York Times*, October 10, 2011, C1.

Is It helps here. In the beginning of the film, viewers are offered brief testimonials by dancers preparing to audition for Jackson and his final concert production, two weeks of shows in London. Through excitement, giddiness, admiration, and often tears, these young people express in their own words who Jackson is, whom he represents, for them. Most if not all of the dancers talk about how Jackson has always been an important person in their lives, an inspiration. Every single dancer speaks to the grandeur of their hero.

What is unclear during this sequence is whether or not these dancers have met Jackson yet. The audience is unaware of their actual relationship with this hero that they are crying over. Later on in the film it becomes clear that indeed they had not met Jackson or his producer yet. They were waiting to do so.

What is remarkable about these early shots becomes clearer in a deeper analysis of the practice of "knowing" Michael Jackson. Put differently, because of the essentially spectacular, represented nature of Jackson, was it ever possible to "know" him? I ask this question from the point of view of the consumer rather than a familial one. Of course, his family knew him as a brother, husband, father. Yet, as our grief observed pointed to above, there is a sort of intimacy that characterizes our communication about the star. Certainly, the dancers express this closeness, perhaps most clearly in their emotional reactions. But again, they had never met Jackson. Like the viewer, they were absent from any sort of real interaction with the performer. As such, the film performance (albeit documentary in nature) becomes performances of our own thirst to be close to the spectacle of Michael Jackson. But more importantly, they become for us a performance of "knowing." And in this, the dancers illustrate an important element of the spectacle: that it is, in the end, unknowable, separate from what we understand as reality.

Originally published in 1967, Guy Debord's *The Society of The Spectacle* was written as a direct assault on what had become in his mind a culture deeply invested in the unreal. Working in the vernacular of Walter Benjamin, M.M. Bakhtin, and influencing several predecessors including Umberto Eco, Marc Augé, and Jonathan Crary, Debord's treatise on spectacle aimed at outlining the personal, social, and global effect of representation itself.[2] Indeed, it is what he called "the perfect separation" that clearly marks the lack of "knowing" witnessed in the dancers' testimonials. He points out early in his book that:

---

[2]   See Walter Benjamin, *Walter Benjamin Selected Writings 1935–1938* (Cambridge, MA: Harvard University Press, 2002); Mikhail M. Bakhtin, *Rabelais and His World*, trans. Helen Iswolsky (Bloomington, IN: Indiana University Press, 1984); Mikhail M. Bakhtin, *Art and Answerability*, ed. Michael Holquist and Vadim Liapunov, trans. Vadim Liapunov (Austin: University of Texas Press, 1990); Umberto Eco, *Travels in Hyperreality* (Orlando: Harcourt Brace & Company, 1986); Marc Augé, *Non-places: And Introduction to an Anthropology of Supermodernity* (London: Verso Press, 1995); Jonathan Crary, *Suspensions of Perception: Attention, Spectacle, and Modern Culture* (Cambridge, MA: MIT Press, 2001).

The phenomenon of separation is part and parcel of the unity of the world, of a global social praxis that has split up into reality on the one hand and image on the other. Social practice, which the spectacle's autonomy challenges, is also the real totality to which the spectacle is subordinate. So deep is the rift in this totality, however, that the spectacle is able to emerge as its apparent goal.[3]

Such articulations work to undermine the action or feeling of authenticity itself. In the case of the dancers, and by association the viewers, we now see that even in the potential of knowing Jackson "in the flesh," there remains an impossibility of connection, dialogue, or otherwise. Because Jackson himself exists as spectacle, he is for all intents and purposes separate from any sort of reality that we as a culture are determined by. Indeed, many of the authors in this book begin their analysis with the proclamation that Jackson, in many ways, constructed his own reality system.

The film continues this paradigm as it represents the representation of Jackson performing on stage while background video screens, showing historical images of the star, employ the memory of the audiences who will attend these final productions. Indeed, the entire concert itself is based in a sort of re-representation, one that at first creates a sort of philosophical confusion not only for the critic thinking about the movie, but the audience viewing it as well. In her review of the film for the *New York Times*, Manohla Dargis argues that "Death returned Michael Jackson's humanity, and so does *Michael Jackson's This Is It* ...".[4] I point this out as confusion within the context of the separation between spectacle and reality discussed by Debord. According to her article, the film brings out portions of Michael Jackson that we have never known, showing him in light of a newly formed triumph and security brought on by this desire to give his fans what they really wanted. One final performance. Put into the implications we are trying to draw here, she is also claiming a sort of knowledge of Jackson, the likes of which we are beginning to rethink as an impossibility.

The Layers of the Spectacle

If we conceive of the film as a sort of map of meaning, the processes of spectacle, representation, separation, and the alienation of reality, become a little bit easier to follow. Note that there are many layers in this map, all of which might be better understood as layers of representation. The helpfulness of this concept is tested, however, when we attempt to find the origin of the map, the genesis of the performance/representation itself. It helps, I think, if we embody Michael Jackson.

[3]   Guy Debord, *The Society of the Spectacle*, trans. Donald Nicholson-Smith (New York: Zone Books, 1995), 13.
[4]   Manohla Dargis, "Michael Jackson's This Is It (2009)," *New York Times*, October 29, 2009, C1.

In other words, if we, for the time being, try to conceptualize Jackson as the body of Michael Joseph Jackson (though we have never truly known this body) there is at least some possibility of separating the spectacle of Jackson from his essential, physical self. Indeed, as many of the essays collected here argue, this identification of body-reality is itself a complicated element of Jackson's career. Through plastic surgery, body modification, mystery, and performance, Jackson presents a physicality that challenges all norms and practices of everyday life. These predicaments and conditions are discussed by Raphael Raphael and Julie-Ann Scott below as part of a continual conversation about the normative versus deviant physicality in which Michael Jackson was a regular illustration. Was Jackson a disabled body? Did consumers or the performer bring on this potential disability? How might we best understand the role physicality plays in our conception of the Michael Jackson spectacle? In the end, these are all answered by contemplating the body, the origin.

In addition to this first and important layer of the spectacle presented by the film, we must also consider questions of identity itself. For beyond the physical elements of this body that is being offered to us, we must also understand that there are also mythological, psychological, and cultural values embedded within this self that we are trying to grasp. Part I of this collection is devoted to understanding these complicated areas of Jackson's career, including previously published work by the critic Margo Jefferson. Jefferson walks the reader through the history embedded, even though subconsciously, in the life and art of Jackson in a way that rejects any sort of easy explanation of stardom or celebrity. Julian Vigo offers a rereading of Jefferson's work, looking more deeply into the issues of African American identity. Pushing this complexity further, chapters below by Amy C. Billone and Sherrow O. Pinder point to several key elements in the creation and sometimes destruction of the identity of Michael Jackson.

And so, as we identify the layers of the film, we also identify the layers of Jackson himself. Once we move beyond the origin level of the spectacle, we see that indeed the most important layer of the film and of Jackson is, and always has been, the layer of music and video creation. As mentioned earlier, the film consists primarily of rehearsals for a series of concerts that never happened. Each song performed has an accompanying meaning dictated by auditory and visual cues from Jackson's catalog of popular hits. As such, his performance of *Thriller*, for example, finds an enormous video screen in the background of the stage displaying images of zombies and other elements of the macabre, all of which operate in terms of association for the audience. This performance on stage is thus contextualized by another performance, that of the original 14-minute *Thriller* video which originally aired in 1983. Add to this the obvious musical cues, which are a re-performance of the original track included on the official album release of the same title.

Michael Jackson, with the help of MTV, anchored the contemporary bridging between popular music and video, of sound and image. As such, to know Michael Jackson's music was to know Michael Jackson's image. The consequences of this are quite dramatic, if not completely invisible in today's popular music market. To be considered a good popular musician now finds itself inexplicably attached to being a good, popular, or at least interesting image as well. Pushing further, Jackson's performances of music were consequently never free of representation, indicating perhaps one of the more complex conundrums of the film itself. As viewers watch Jackson performing, they are invited to contemplate a whole menagerie of performances attached to history, cultural memory, and social meaning. Take for example his performance in the film of "Billy Jean," in which we hear a performance of the song originally released in 1982, we see a repeat performance of Jackson's performance on the "Motown 25" television show in 1983, and are asked to also remember images from the popular music video of the song as well.

It doesn't take long to realize that the demands of this performance in the film actually duplicate the demands made from any performance by Jackson, including those which might at first not appear to be performances at all; public appearances, photo shoots, pictures taken by paparazzi, news interviews, and so on. All of these events are performances which Michael had to constantly be re-envisioned through, from his childhood on. And so his music and music videos, his films, and his public performances, all can be regarded as re-performances of one kind or another. Part II of this book looks closely at the performance element of both Jackson's music and video work. Chapters by Jesse Schlotterbeck, Brett M. Van Hosen, Christopher Wiley, Carl Miller, and Ruchi Mital respectively employ expertise in art history, media studies, musicology, and cultural studies in order to unpack more significant elements of Jackson's musical and image-based performances.

A third and perhaps final layer of the film and Jackson no doubt is created upon his death, and is carefully placed at the end of this collection of essays. David Dark, Diana York Blaine, and Zack Stiegler work through the known and unknown ramifications of the death of Michael Jackson. Because his death is so recent, these essays are offered as the beginning of longer conversations that we will have as a culture in the years to come. Included in that conversation will be our reactions to how the death is handled by the film *This Is It*. The death of its subject is the never-ending context of the film, and so it is unavoidable. And while the film chooses not to mention the actual death, it is always there. It is in fact the energy of the film. The urgency of the performances, the subtlety of the conversations, the pressure of the preparations being made, are all pointing towards an end. And as mentioned above, the spectacle gets more powerful at the moment of death. As such, the death of Michael Jackson will always be the final layer through which we will observe all other elements of his career.

Grasping the Spectacle

> The spectacle is the acme of ideology, for in its full flower it exposes and manifests the essence of all ideological systems: the impoverishment, enslavement and negation of real-life. Materially, the spectacle is "the expression of estrangement, of alienation between man and man."[5]

The layer of death, which admittedly adds a similar energy to this collection of essays, is perhaps the most complicated element to address both for authors and readers. Regardless of the human quality of loss, in Jackson's case something felt at the cultural level as well as the familial, there nonetheless remain unanswered questions about the manner in which a mass-produced entity is memorialized by the masses themselves. It is this dilemma that pushes this collection beyond observations made by several critics, including Debord, who often point to the finality of the spectacle. More succinctly, he and others often see the end result of spectacle as being a violent push towards not only the separation of reality and representation, but of humanity from itself. Above, quoting Hegel, Debord offers a lament of the alienating power of the spectacle. He argues that a death of community is the only logical end to the all-encompassing power of mere representation.

Rather than produce a final document, the death of Michael Jackson seems to have offered a cultural moment in which representation and spectacle actually create a new sort of postmodern intimacy which moves beyond simple performance into what most authors in this book point to as being authentic reaction and feeling. Think again of the dancers interviewed at the beginning of *This Is It*. Even before the death of their hero, these folks perform an intimacy that mimic a sort of dialogical connection, one that can easily be noticed in the explanations of Martin Buber and Emmanuel Lévinas.[6] Both philosophers articulated a sophisticated connection between the I and the other, one bathed in responsibility, admiration, and honor. Pushing further, both saw the inescapable connections of human beings as something not based in domination, but rather reciprocal action. And while one might still argue that Jackson was never able to concretely act in or on the lives of his audience, reactions to his death nevertheless speak to a sort of connection, one that could be understood as dialogical in essence.

Again, consider the laments on Facebook and Twitter: all of these proclamations work toward an illustration of a different outcome for spectacle, one that does not find any place in the society of the spectacle. Even the death of Elvis Presley pointed to this years before; the outcry of emotions for Elvis by American audiences moved beyond public grief into a more personal one. And so is the case

---

[5]   Debord, *The Society of the Spectacle*, 151.

[6]   See Martin Buber, *Between Man and Man* (New York: Routledge, 1947); Martin Buber, *I and Thou* (New York: Scribner and Sons, 1958); Emmanuel Lévinas, *Time and the Other*, trans. Richard A. Cohen (Pittsburgh, PA: Duquesne University Press, 1987).

with Jackson. Furthermore, these personal reactions gather together a community, an audience, of the performance of spectacle itself. To know the performance of Jackson is to take part in a performance of community.

The arguments made in the essays that follow both recognize and critique this new community as well as the spectacle that created it. In doing so, they do not claim an end to it, but instead try to grasp it as it continues to grow, live, and repeat itself.

PART I
Mythology and Identity

Chapter 1

Freaks
(from *On Michael Jackson*)

Margo Jefferson

Written before his death, Jefferson's book On Michael Jackson *is without a doubt the most cited study on the star. Stemming from a background in journalism, her investigative approach is brilliantly blended with a real interest in cultural and political ramifications of African-American aesthetics. This excerpt from her book begins this collection because it sets the tone of the larger conversation being had in the following pages. Indeed, issues of history, physicality, gender, race, sexuality, and the performance of these things, is at the heart of her work, all of which are being reworked and investigated by the authors writing for this collection.*[1]

Every mind is a clutter of memories, images, inventions and age-old repetitions. It can be a ghetto, too, if a ghetto is a sealed-off, confined place, or a sanctuary, where one is free to dream and think whatever one wants. For most of us it's both—and a lot more complicated. A ghetto can be a place of vitality; a sanctuary can become a prison. Michael Jackson escaped the ghetto of Gary, Indiana, and built the sanctuary of Neverland. It's become a circuslike prison, emblematic of his mind.

Think of Michael Jackson's mind as a funhouse, and look at some of the exhibits on display: P.T. Barnum, maestro of wonders and humbuggery; Walt Disney, who invented the world's mightiest fantasy-technology complex; Peter Pan ("He escaped from being human when he was seven days old"); a haggard Edgar Allan Poe (he was the only character besides Peter Pan that Michael Jackson planned to play in a movie); the romping, ever-combustible Three Stooges; a friendly chimpanzee named Bubbles who has his own wardrobe of clothes; and a python lying coiled between placid white llamas.

Tears roll down the gnarled lizard cheeks of E.T. as he dreams of home; Charlie Chaplin sits alone on a stoop, his Little Tramp chin in his hands. A knife gleams in a darkened alley; a panther stalks through and disappears; ghouls and werewolves dance in a crumbling mansion; Captain Eo wears silver when he comes down from outer space to save children from the evils of our planet. Now lines of song-and-dance men kick, strut and turn in perfect unison. Children of all nations float happily through the night sky like Wynken, Blynken and Nod, then come down to earth and sing of peace in high, sweet voices; a colossal statue of Michael Jackson himself in military dress bestrides the world to the rapturous attack chords of "Carmina Burana."

Here is Elvis Presley, who is one of himselves; Diana Ross, who is one of himselves; Elizabeth Taylor, who is one of himselves; wee, nut-brown Emmanuel Lewis and pert, milky-white Macaulay Culkin, both parts of himself; Joseph Jackson, the father who believes in whippings but not beatings; Katherine Jackson, the mother who is always supportive and always elusive. See photos from childhood onward and videos of Michael; they are mirrors reflecting each stage of his life.

Let's begin our tour.

Phineas T. Barnum? A model for Michael. The ringmaster of American entertainment. Fantasy, fakery and touches of uplift. No one knew better than Barnum how to thrill audiences, give them raw sensation and a stirring, not especially accurate education. Barnum's first spectacular success came in 1835, when he bought the rights to exhibit an ex-slave named Joice Heth at his Connecticut theater. Servitude had left her a near cripple; the showman saw promise in those gnarled limbs and stooped shoulders. Barnum put her in a clean gown and a fresh white cap, sat her down and introduced eager crowds to the 161-year-old nurse of George Washington. "To use her own language when speaking of the illustrious Father of his Country, 'she raised him' " his advertisements proclaimed.

When Heth died the next year, Barnum ordered a public autopsy. An unexpectedly honest doctor revealed that, far from being born in 1674, Heth was no more than eighty years old. Barnum professed astonishment. He'd been conned by Heth and her ex-master, he declared. Then his business partner upped the ante and declared that Barnum had found Heth on a plantation and trained her himself to pass for Washington's nurse. The public enjoyed both tales, and Barnum enjoyed spreading both tales. People wanted to believe *and* know they'd be conned, as long as they didn't know when or how.

In 1842, Barnum opened his American Museum on lower Broadway in New York City. It cost twenty-five cents to get in, not an inconsiderable sum in those days: "One ticket guaranteed admission to lectures, theatrical performances, an animal menagerie and a glimpse of human curiosities, living and dead." An exhibit features Madame Clofullia from Europe. Madame was born in Switzerland. In a photograph she stands quietly in her black ruffled gown, resting a hand gently on her husband's shoulder. There is a bunch of white lace at her throat. But it is partially hidden by her long, dark, bushy beard. An angry museum patron takes her to court. She is a man, he protests. The suit is free advertising for Barnum. He takes a group of physicians to court with him; together they offer medical proof that Madame Clofullia is biologically female. She goes on working at the museum.

It isn't always easy to find genuine human wonders like Madame Clofullia. As a man of the theater, Barnum knows how to turn a startling visual effect into an adventure yarn. Put a tattooed man in a loincloth and he becomes Prince Constentenus of Greece. The prince was kidnapped by the Khan of Kashagar: that is why he has 185 tattoo patterns on his body, each one cruelly carved into his flesh with needles.

Michael Jackson read Barnum's autobiography fervently (at least one of the eight versions) and gave copies to all his staff, telling them, "I want my career to be the greatest show on earth." So he became both producer and product. The impresario of himself. Who among us can't recall at least one of the stunts that followed: Michael sleeping in a hyperbaric chamber like a handsome young pharaoh in his tomb or the lovely Snow White in her glass casket? He was obsessed with the Elephant Man; he claimed he saw the movie thirty-five times, never once without weeping all the way through! He made repeated attempts, offered millions of dollars, to buy the bones from The British Museum. He appeared in public wearing a surgical mask: he could have been the doctor in an old horror film, looming over the evil or tragic man about to have his identity and destiny changed forever. Then we see him without the mask, onstage, at an awards ceremony, in court, and realize he has been that man for a long time.

He became a one-man conglomerate with global reach: his own records and videos; the Beatles' catalog; Pepsi commercials; world tours. He was transnational. He re-enacted his supremacy in video after video. "If you wanna be my baby / don't matter if you're black or white." If you want to dance with me, don't matter if you're Indian, Russian, African or Native American. You can morph into anything (pudgy Eskimo into buff, white American lad with straight, honey-blond hair; American lad into slim brown-skinned lass with dark brown frizzy hair); you can be any age, race or gender. Global idealism is at one with global marketing. If you want to buy my records, don't matter who, what or where you are.

Barnum's museum exhibits, ethnological curiosities and circus sideshows also set the pattern for our daytime talk shows. The difference between then and now? Barnum's people were supposed to be freaks of nature, outside the boundaries of The Normal. Ours are marketed as lifestyle freaks. Psychology and sociology have played as big a part as biology; that's the point of those long confessional interviews with the host and those fraught exchanges with the audience. Nighttime shows like *Fear Factor* are recreational sideshows. Eating slug sandwiches and jumping into sealed tanks turn the old carnival tricks (sword swallowing, biting chickens' heads off) into middle-class pranks. Everyday people indulge their whims and get their hit of fame. More and more, they involve playacting and wish fulfillment: this week you make deals Donald Trump respects; you're the "average Joe" the right woman picks over the handsome stud; your "extreme makeover" turns you from a dog to a babe.

More and more of these shows are updates of the old talent contest. Now, though, the backstage tale, the life story, matters as much as the performance. Maybe more. It's about watching the struggle to be the best that you can be, even when you're preposterous; it's about living out your dream. These stories follow—or long to follow—the arc of Michael's early life. You start small, but you have the talent; you work night and day; you make your way to the big city at last, audition for the right talent scouts and producers. You win a contract and your shot at fame. *Star Search. American Idol. So You Think You Can Dance.*

But Michael Jackson became world-famous because he was a world-class talent. His 1983 performance of "Billie Jean" at the televised tribute *Motown: Yesterday, Today, Forever* placed Michael Jackson against the backdrop of his show-business childhood. The other performers were aging; they looked like they were barely surviving liquor and drug crises, feuds, plain old illness and career lapses. Michael looked like a pristine creation, untainted by that past.

Michael was in profile as the bass line of "Billie Jean" rumbled up: legs apart, knees bent in demi-plié, one hand lightly touching his fedora. A hoofer cavalier in high-water pants. Eight counts of pelvic thrusts turned him into a soul-man cavalier. A quick kick and thigh slap on each side, then he faced the audience and—smack on the beat—threw his hat into the wings. Song-and-dance man. Then he mimicked a fifties bad boy, giving his hair a quick comb.

All the elements of the persona we would come to know were on display. The wardrobe that joined severity (black pants, fedora, loafers) with glitter, sparkle and eccentricity (sweater jacket and shirt, white socks, single white glove). Passion that stirred the audience, yet felt private and mysterious. The intense theatricality and how he stretched small gestures into long lines of movement. Every choreographer has signature moves and combinations. Here was the core of Jackson's style: the angled feet and knock-knees of the Funky Chicken (gritty) and the Charleston (more soigné); various runs and struts; the corkscrew kicks forward (as fast as judo kicks); the spin turns; the moonwalk and the sudden crouch when, instead of falling to his knees, he rises on his toes. It's a ballet moment. And a small variation on that move shifts the tension. When he rises with feet and knees together, he looks powerful. With knees together and feet apart, he looks vulnerable, even stricken.

"Billie Jean" is a song about anxiety and guilt, desire and resentment; fathering a child and being a child. In the bridge, when he sang of how Mama warned him, "Be careful what you do / because a lie becomes the truth," he jumped straight into the air three times. The genie in the bottle is a young man who can't control his energies. In the repeat bridge, as he recalled "the smell of sweet perfume / She brought me to her room," he jumped from foot to foot with his knees up, like a boy having a tantrum.

And finally, as he sang, the expressive arms: arms outstretched, hands pleadingly open (musical theater melodrama); then an emphatic fist or sudden wrist curl; an index finger piercing the air (chitlin' circuit bravado). He brought one hand across his face when he sang "his eyes were like mine," about the mystery child; we saw his round dark eyes through spread-out fingers (Motown mime). He ended stage center, right arm in the air, looking drained but exalted. He created the show; he *was* the show. Idea man, song-and-dance man, money man. But by the mid-1980s he had a lot of us paying more attention to the freak than to the artist. The producer in him knew something had to be done. The outlet he chose was the daytime talk show, media home for our culture's freaks. The place that invites them in to explain and display their lives to regular folk; justify, flaunt, challenge and beguile. In 1993, when the public questions about Michael Jackson's whitening skin had become clamorous, he appeared on *The Oprah Winfrey Show* to explain that he had vitiligo, a disease that drained the pigment from his skin, leaving white blotches. That's why he had to even it out with thick white makeup.

His was a downward spiral after that. By 2003, when he stood on a hotel balcony high above a crowd of cheering fans and held up his new baby for them to see, people thought he had gone mad—or mad enough to be staging a *Fear Factor* publicity stunt. Actually, if you look closely at the picture, he is holding the baby firmly; there's no real danger of his dropping him. Still, why hold a baby over a balcony for cheering throngs, like royalty showing off a new prince to its subjects? By then only true Michael fanatics considered him the King of Pop.

****

Come this way. Here are real biological freaks, born, but also self-made. Barnum had a long-running hit with his "Siamese" twins, Chang and Eng (the term a remnant of period Orientalism. Of all the conjoined twins billed as "Siamese" in nineteenth-century circuses and carnivals, they were the only ones actually born in Siam). Onstage, Chang and Eng talked about their lives, sang and let themselves be stared at. Their words showed they were people. But they were creatures, too, mutations, signs that evolution is a game of chance and nature is a trickster.

Chang and Eng had immigrated to the States. But an entrepreneur who wanted exotic specimens from faraway lands couldn't often find the genuine article. So the Joice Heth model prevailed. Shameless fakery with, if possible, a strong dose of the topical. When the Civil War began, Barnum had just put an English circus performer in black makeup and a furry tunic, given him a jungle backdrop and asked the public "What Is It?" In 1875, he put an African-American in the part: William Henry Johnson played the "What Is It?" well into the next century.

"Is it a Lower Order of MAN? Or is it a higher order of MONKEY? None can tell! Perhaps it is a combination of both. It is beyond dispute THE MOST MARVELLOUS CREATURE LIVING, it was captured in a savage state in Central Africa, it is probably about 20 years old, two feet high, intelligent, docile, active, sportive and PLAYFUL AS A KITTEN. It has a skull, limbs and general anatomy of an ORANGOUTANG and the COUNTENANCE of a HUMAN BEING."

This is the language of the sideshow with touches of natural-history-museum rhetoric. And, in fact, the claims of science began to challenge those of show business. William Henry Johnson was still playing the missing link between man and ape in 1906, when a group of anthropologists arrived in New York with Ota Benga, a central African Batwa who had been brought to the States two years earlier as part of the Pygmy Village at the St. Louis World's Fair. The scientists put Ota Benga in the monkey house at the Bronx Zoo.

Barnum's love of humbug across racial lines inspired a new generation of show-business entrepreneurs. If circus owners couldn't find genuine dark-skinned specimens, they found physically handicapped white Americans to play them. Anthropologists popularized the idea that being non-white meant being at the low end of the evolutionary scale. Some turned their universities into showplaces. Others went into show business and took their specimens onto the vaudeville circuit.

By the 1880s, Americans were mastering the globe, in fact and fiction, from wars to world fairs.

Here's what's astonishing about Michael Jackson today: he contains trace elements of all this history. Some he calculated, some went beyond him. Some trapped him as surely as Ota Benga got trapped behind the bars of the Bronx Zoo. From the mid-eighties on, he turned himself into a "What Is It?" With genius and generosity as an artist; with solitary and fearsome zeal as a man.

Was he man, boy, man-boy or boy-woman? Mannequin or postmodern zombie? Here was a black person who had once looked unmistakably black, and now looked white or at least un-black. He was, at the very least, a new kind of mulatto, one created by science and medicine and cosmetology. Biology defines a mulatto as the sterile offspring of an animal or plant species. Michael Jackson's sperm count, I'm relieved to say, is one of the few things we know nothing about. We are reasonably certain he chose not to produce offspring by traditional means: here again, science joined nature to do his bidding.

Ah, but the art! He got it all back with his wondrous art. Art orders contradictions and unwelcome longings; glorifies what's perverse or infantile, lavish and dream-bright, suave, abject, incurably romantic. It gives shape and rhythm to inchoate fantasies. Finds a common fund of myth, dreams and nightmares; an archive of shared history. A shared body of sound and movement, too: melodies and beats; phrasings that quicken the blood and shock the nervous system.

When people praise Michael Jackson today, recall his gifts and why they loved him, they always mention the 1983 *Thriller* video. That's because it's a short masterpiece, a perfectly thought-through and executed horror tale. It is the tale of the double, the man with two selves and two souls, like Dr. Jekyll and Mr. Hyde, like Poe's William Wilson or Dorian Gray and his portrait. The everyday man and his uncanny double. Which is his true self? "Everything which ought to have remained secret and hidden, but which has come to light." The everyday man broods and agonizes. Why does he feel a connection to this dreadful menacing other? Why is he drawn to an alien, even criminal life? How does he keep this second self concealed? Does he really want to conceal it, especially from the woman whose love he has sought and won?

Thriller begins as Michael, wearing red leather, walks along a deserted street with a fresh-faced, ponytailed girl in a felt skirt, white blouse and saddle shoes. They are 1950s vintage teenagers. (We rarely saw such Negro boys and girls next door in the 1950s.) "You know I like you," he tells her, shyly but winningly. "And I like you," she says eagerly. "Will you be my girl?" he asks. "Oh, yes," she answers. But there's something he wants to say to her. A shadow crosses his face. "You know I'm not like the other guys," he says, to which she responds, "I know. That's why I like you."

And then, right before her eyes, the transformation. The defacement. He turns from a beautiful young man into a hairy, red-eyed werewolf. She shrieks, turns away and starts to run. He chases her, pins her down; we watch her eyes widen as she stares up at him and waits—often the last moment in a horror film—as the camera focuses on the wide-open eyes of the victim. They're our eyes, of course, but we get to keep watching. So does the girl in *Thriller*. She's us. She keeps getting pulled back to safety so that she can keep watching and loving Michael as he doubles and divides. And then, and then … And then we're in a movie theater, watching it all on the screen. Michael and his girl are sitting in the audience. She shivers and hides her face on his shoulder; he munches popcorn and grins at the screen. There's a touch of greed in his eyes.

They leave the theater and begin the long walk home. They approach a deserted mansion. And suddenly monsters begin to appear. Limbs crack through the earth; shadowy figures rise and stalk through the trees. Skeletons and demons gather on the mansion grounds. It's Walpurgisnacht in suburbia. It's movie night too. They dance in unison to a heavy drumbeat, rattling their limbs, sliding across the ground, shoulders scooping up and down, forward and back. The voice of Vincent Price— those ornamented syllables, that cavernous vibrato—can be heard intoning—no, rapping: "The hounds of hell await whosoever shall be found without the soul for getting down." The ghouls and demons rising from the dead, we are told, represent "the funk of forty thousand years."

The girl flees into the mansion and slams the door. To no avail. Heavy fists break through the walls; bodies splinter the door. They move closer and closer; she twists herself into an agonized ball and … Silence. "Come on," Michael says with a sweet smile. (She looks up tremulously.) "I'll take you home." He helps her to her feet and, arm round her waist, guides her toward safety. Then turns back to us for one last moment. Red is the color of demons. His smile widens and hardens; his eyes flash yellow. The video ends. The credits roll. Good or evil, human or monster, victim or criminal; on-screen Michael will swap selves forever.

Life is another matter. Moving from art to life, Freud talks about fears we cannot dispel or overcome. The best we can do is repress them. But they return in disguise. They look different, unfamiliar, but we know them; they draw us back in. How could Dr. Jekyll live and work if Mr. Hyde weren't there to act on his beastly, murderous impulses? Dorian Gray could not go on if the portrait weren't there in the attic—and if he couldn't forget about it most of the time.

Art makes all of this bearable, even thrilling. But when art crosses back into life and fantasy becomes biography, we're appalled. That's what happened to Michael Jackson in the 1990s. Even as his music and dance were mattering less and less, his looks, his marriages, his masked children, the first round of sexual abuse charges, the out-of-court settlement, all took center stage. With the onset of the new millennium, there were now reissues of old hits and new charges of sexual abuse. We brought those images to his criminal trial of 2005. By now he had achieved full-blown uncanniness; his double, whoever or whatever it was, seemed to have triumphed. As Freud says: "You can also speak of a living person as uncanny, and we do so when we ascribe evil intentions to him. But that is not all. We must feel that his intentions to harm us are going to be carried out with the help of special powers." But who is Michael Jackson's double? Is it the brown-skinned self we can no longer see except in the old photos and videos? Is he a good man or a predator? Child protector or pedophile? A damaged genius or a scheming celebrity trying to hold on to his fame at any cost? A child star afraid of aging, or a psychotic freak/pervert/sociopath? What if the "or" is an "and"? What if he is all of these things?

****

Over here, please. We call our next funhouse exhibit "Have You Seen My Childhood?" This little fellow is Tom Thumb. Not the one in *Grimm's Fairy Tales* who outwits thieves and cuts his way through a wolf's belly. No, this is Charles Stratton. He began working for Phineas T. Barnum when he was just five years old. He was a two-foot midget. Barnum taught him to sing, dance and act, then named him General Tom Thumb. At his full height of 33", audiences loved to see him play virile military heroes like Napoléon: he'd march about the stage waving a wooden sword ten inches long; after a tour of Europe he even staged a battle with Queen Victoria's poodle.

The child star and the freak were one and the same. General Tom, the midget child imitating heroically grand soldiers (instead of heroically sexy soul men, as Michael did). It had drama and sentiment. It had the wink of the dirty joke (a sword much smaller than Napoléon's, but far longer than the average erect penis!). However, Tom Thumb grew up on the inside, heeded the demands of his brain, muscles and hormones. At the age of twenty-six he married another show-business midget, "Queen" Lavinia Warren. He aspired to be normal. So did she. And their wedding was mobbed. Fans wanted to look at them and try to imagine just how they would go about becoming man and wife.

People see freaks and think: "How do they do it? What kind of sex lives are available to Siamese twins, hermaphrodites, bearded ladies, and midgets?" There is a certain morbid speculation about what it would be like to be with such persons, or worse, to be them. A lot of child stars fail as adult actors because they cannot convince their public or themselves that they can be desirably sexual. Tom Thumb and Queen Lavinia retired once they had married. General Tom moved into adulthood. Michael Jackson married, had children and moved away from adulthood.

Here's another little man. Bigger than Tom Thumb, but still, only five feet one inch tall. And though he lived to the age of seventy-seven, he kept his black hair to the end-never a trace of gray or white. He is James Barrie, who wrote *Peter Pan*. Peter was a boy who wanted never to grow up; Barrie was a grown-up who longed to be a child and spend his life with children, not other grown-ups. Especially boys like him and his brother David. He married, but the women he loved most were friends and protectors. His childhood ended when he was six and his brother David died. He saw that his mother could not be consoled; she had lost the son she loved best. His child-hood never ended because he remained six. He tried to revise his life by forever being the boy who was loved by other boys and loved by their mothers.

Neverland is a happy presexual island ("for the Neverland is always more or less an island") ruled by boys. Grief and loss are at its root. Peter Pan ran away from home when he was seven days old ("he escaped by the window") and settled in Kensington Gardens. "If you think he was the only baby who ever wanted to escape, it shows how completely you have forgotten your own young days." The birds taught him to fly, and he settled in with the fairies and had a fine time dancing and playing his pipes night after night. Eventually he became half human and half bird, "a betwixt-and-between." Sometimes, though, he would visit his house and watch his mother weep; the window was always open. He liked that she missed him, and he wanted to keep his options open. But one night when he arrived expecting a welcome, the window was locked. When he looked in, she was asleep with her arm around another child. "When we reach the window, it is Lock-Out Time. The iron bars are up for life." Devastated, he turned his back on her, flew to Neverland, and turned himself into the island's boy-king. From that day on, he helped other children flee their parents to a life of pleasure and adventure. "I'm youth, I'm joy," he crowed to his enemy, the wicked, unloved Captain Hook. Hook and his pirates were the only adults on the island. Peter and his band of Lost Boys killed them all. But they never discussed fathers. Mothers, he told Wendy, were not to be trusted.

When Jane Fonda told Michael that she wanted to produce *Peter Pan* for him, he began to tremble. He identified so with Peter, he told her; he had read everything written about him. Did he know that the book's original title was *The Boy Who Hated His Mother*? As Michael wrote in his autobiography: "I don't trust anybody except Katherine. And sometimes I'm not so sure about her."

We have to move on now. As we go, please study this replica of P.T. Barnum's first mansion. He commissioned it from the same architect who had built King George's royal pavilion in Brighton. Its "Hindoo" style reflected Chinese, Japanese, Indian and Moorish design (real or imagined). Barnum gave it the mythical name "Iranistan." Once more he had started a tradition: Iranistan, Disneyland, Graceland, Neverland.

Here are old pictures of Michael at Disneyland in the 1970s. He looks so happy standing next to Mickey Mouse. He watched cartoons for hours, he told interviewers; "I loved being a cartoon," he said about *The Jackson 5ive* series that turned The Jackson Five into animation idols. It seemed so infantile at the time. ("Do you realize this is someone whose inner life is *Tom and Jerry*?" a psychoanalyst friend said wonderingly.)

Who knew that he was after the power of Walt Disney's imagination and brand, his ability to make magic and money from any kind of setting or creature—a park, a mouse, a duck, an elephant, the heroine of a fairy tale that's been told a thousand times? In 1981, Michael's father sold him fifty percent of Hayvenhurst, the family estate. He made it into a private amusement park. When he moved out of his parents' house, he filled his new place with toys and animals, televisions, movie screens and mannequins. His next? A mansion that was an amusement park and a shelter for children: a Disney-like property with its proper constituency. He placed himself at the center of this universe as the only human who was also a mythical creature, the missing link (but elevated, not degraded) between humans and animals, grown-ups and children, real life and fairy tales.

Follow me from a master builder of popular culture to some of its star performers. Michael put together his own legacy. He revered the black forerunners: James Brown, Jackie Wilson, Diana Ross, Sammy Davis Jr. If his white forerunners were Hollywood stars of an older generation, he revered them too. But if they were rock and pop stars, they had to be dealt with differently. They'd gotten all the props and the perks. They'd been crowned the prime movers, the brainy creators, the ones with the depth, the flash and the vision.

Elvis the King. Heavy hangs the head that wears the crown, true. But lucky and blessed is the man the world crowns king. If you have to claim it for yourself—if you feel you're from a family, a tribe, a clan denied its proper due—do what you have to do, but get that crown. The old Negro spiritual says "all God's chillun got crowns." Not in this world they don't—certainly not the Negroes who made the spirituals. White America made Elvis the King of Rock and Roll. (Yes, he had black fans, too, but they didn't count with the power brokers.) All the culture's resources were there for him. The big-time *Billboard* and *Variety* pop charts, not the provinces of" "race music" or "rhythm and blues." The royal road to movie stardom: sex appeal that went from bad boy across the tracks to good boy next door. Hot moves, a sexy voice and a tender reverence for the Lord's gospel music too. Talent? Deluxe voice? Charisma? You bet.

As for The Beatles, why are they here? Didn't John Lennon say The Beatles were bigger than Jesus? Michael learned to be as big as The Beatles. He learned to be bigger when he outbid Paul McCartney and purchased the Beatles' catalog (a clever twist on the old money, power and race equation that had white performers outselling black ones with cover versions of black hits). And Michael, too, tried to make himself bigger than Jesus: in the *Brace Yourself* video of 1995 he is an enormous stone statue flanked by armies, come to save the world from the sins of war and inhumanity, come to halt the devastation of the planet, come to rescue innocent victims and children.

But look, here's an entertainer with no name, just another show-business trouper. She knew her stuff though. Michael saw her at the Apollo Theater in the early 1960s, when he and his brothers were still on the chitlin' circuit. He never forgot her.

I had seen quite a few strippers, but that night this one girl with gorgeous eyelashes and long hair came out and did her routine. She put on a *great* performance. All of a sudden, at the end, she took off her wig, pulled a pair of big oranges out of her bra, and revealed that she was a hard-faced guy under all that makeup. That blew me away. I was only a child and couldn't even conceive of anything like that. But I looked out at the theater audience and they were *going* for it, applauding wildly and cheering. I'm just a little kid, standing in the wings, watching this crazy stuff. I was blown away.

What a moment: blown away, swept away to someplace else. Children work so hard at learning what's expected of them, what grown-ups want from them. Or what grown-ups say they want. Kids learn by mimicking adult behavior and following adult instructions. If you think a gender switch shocking, try making sense of what some parents do versus what they say.

So, to be young, gifted and a witness to an act that violates all models of adult behavior in your life might be scary, but it's a thrill too. "Life ain't so bad at all, if you live it off the wall." A transvestite is like a cartoon. It keeps changing shape. It breaks the rules of cause and effect. It excites and incites the audience. A transvestite crosses gender zones. A transvestite masters the art of the betwixt and between. A transvestite works against nature, fights off time. But who wants to see an aging transvestite? Who wants to see an aging star, for that matter, especially a female whose face (worked over too much or not enough) has become a freak version of its younger self? It's no wonder that Michael Jackson has been compared to Gloria Swanson in *Sunset Blvd.*: to Norma Desmond, a travesty looking very much like an aging transvestite, a freak.

Little freak, who made you? Dost thou know who made you? Genes made you. Disease and illness made you. Religion made you. Show business and science made you. History made you: the norms and needs of your time and place made you. Your family and your psyche made you.

Chapter 2
Michael Jackson and the Myth of Race and Gender

Julian Vigo

Critiquing Margot Jefferson's study on Michael Jackson, which argues that Jackson's physicality was anchored in strong, knowable structures, Julian Vigo proposes an alternative reading of Jackson's body based on her interest in post-colonial criticism, cultural studies, and gender. She firmly rejects Jefferson's hope to anchor Jackson within a concrete system of realities and instead pushes the reader to understand Jackson as a postmodern body, one which challenges traditional binaries of race, gender, and ability. Below you will find concise analysis of not only Jackson's life, but also his music videos and dancing.

To be different is to lead a life of pain and persecution

Nip/Tuck

Many influential writers and theorists, including Jean Baudrillard and Bernard-Henri Lévy, have attempted to deconstruct the persona of Michael Jackson. Likewise there are the various media sources whereby pop psychologists and social pundits have discoursed upon the figure of Jackson in deconstructing his "race," body, and sexuality. Usually these comments serve to buttress a myriad of newly generated "syndromes" or social behaviorisms pathologized in the past 25 years whereby Jackson is simultaneously public figure and pathology. However, no treatment of Jackson has ever been so extensive and postmortem in the clinical sense of the word as how Jackson's body was textually treated after his death in 2009. Jackson's body was, in a tradition reminiscent of nineteenth-century anthropology, diagnosed from afar—ETV, Geraldo Rivera, morning television shows and every media personality with a clip-on microphone espoused Jackson's illnesses: how he was "emotionally" a 14-year-old child who wanted to recreate himself as Peter Pan in both thought and physical incarnation; that he was bulimic; that he had body dysmorphic disorder; that he tried to look like Diana Ross; and that he bleached his skin, among a myriad of other speculations. Jackson's life and body were analyzed *ad nauseum* to the point where his personal and legal troubles were revisited in a scene reminiscent of a very dark version of *A Christmas Carol*. How could people not be interested in discovering the "truth" about Jackson, since his entire life was a media spectacle undertaken by his parents and the entertainment industry to obfuscate and even destroy the very notion of a singular essence of his person? Since Jackson's death, there has been an incessant—even obsessive— dissection of Jackson's life with each authority and specialist lending a newer, specific meaning to his body in all its dimensions and polymorphic positionings. Jackson's body has become this self-fetichized object upon which media and the people have latched in attempting to understand who this person was.

Herein I propose an alternative reading of Michael's body whose performativity went far beyond dance and approached the realm of somatic change which included a blurring of the lines between male and female, between black and white and between human and animal. In the end, Jackson's body defied definition: he was sexless as he interpreted the roles of both man and women; his sexuality was represented as either non-existent or hyperactive, between the media sensationalism of his not possessing a sexuality whatsoever to his preying upon children; and likewise Jackson defied race as he was neither black nor white, paradoxically because he was both black and white. Jackson modeled his body after the coincidences of its condition and of its health (and disorder). From this he sculpted his identity into and around these narratives creating a body that put into question his markings within a culture obsessed with "race" and a society where identity is singular or, at the most, hyphenated. Jackson's body reveals his struggle with identity as it is hinged between the somatic and the performative denying any sort of fixed corporeality and the various traditions and language of identity. A product of a social landscape wherein labeling is everything, where names reveal and where play and gesture are secondary to identity, Jackson created a new language for the body and performance as his body denied both his physical and social heritage. While Jackson's music, dance and video reveal a body that makes high art from street dance and which creates a musical discourse of racial equality that denies the centrality of color and ethnicity, Jackson's bodily transformations went even further in much the style of Barney's Cremaster *in vivo* or Orlan's autobiographical scriptings on the skin.

In her study, *On Michael Jackson*, Margo Jefferson describes Jackson as feminine, as womanly, as effacing his blackness and *his nature*. Attempting to understand how Jackson invented himself as a performer and as a human—in part as a consequence of his childhood, in part because of his extraordinary relationship to his fans—Jefferson's book focuses upon the specifically American history of transformation of freakery within our culture, putting Jackson front and center of this cultural and historical metamorphosis.

Jefferson contends that Jackson shifted the metaphors of black self-hatred around, pushing it into the past while ironizing the paradoxical relationship between "black" and "white": "What's the point of calling someone an Oreo (black on the outside, white on the inside) when he isn't even trying to be black on the outside?"[1] Throughout her attempt to deconstruct Jackson's "freakery," Jefferson reconstructs yet another freakery: that of the "new kind of mulatto" which she reveals as far

---

[1]   Margo Jefferson, *On Michael Jackson* (New York, 2006), 82.

from "new."[2] Jefferson's work elides the social history of the "mulatto," of ethnic hybridity in a country where racial purity is nothing other than a fiction and where the "mulatto" is certainly more the rule than the exception. Indeed, Jefferson's central argument collapses upon itself since although she is correct in asserting that Jackson did not *pretend* to be white because he somatically changed his body to be *neither*, she mistakenly assumes a seamlessness in the language of science and ethnicity. Jefferson's study skips from social to biological discourses of "race" without clarifying their interconnectivity and the way in which a language of "race" is created by the very social discourses she propounds. When she writes: "Biology defines a mulatto as the sterile offspring of an animal or plant species," Jefferson slides across the scientific specificity of this term, "mulatto," dropping her sentence into the vulgar mire of nineteenth century racializations in which the term "mulatto" in popular culture is uniquely related to the production of something *in between*.[3] Jefferson attempts to nail down, throughout the entirety of her book, these very dichotomized, outdated identities. She is asking nineteenth-century questions in an era when the identifications of "pure race" (biological or sociological) are now seen as conservative attempts to re-racialize a subject whose body and culture was already in the throes of post-racialism: Was Jackson black *or* white, man *or* woman, gay *or* straight? Questions that elide how Jackson's somatic and performative lives broke down these very barriers by eluding them and by reinventing his race, gender, sex and arguably his humanity.

The paradox of Jackson is that all parts of his life were rendered public; the popular dissections of his life produced both factual and fictive representations of his body which collectively all came to hold as much truth as they did fiction. Consequently, Jackson's public persona is entirely based upon an unknown mixture of truth and fabrication that ranges from the biographical to the somatic, each reflecting the confusing nature of essence and singularity in the obfuscation of his body. As a result of his enormous fame and the painful coincidence of a family that consistently exploited his talents and his body, he was propelled from an early age to perform various sorts of on and offstage *confessionals* about his skin, his plastic surgeries, his hair, his skin disease (vitiligo), his sex, his sexuality and even his religious beliefs. According to Jefferson, Jackson was a performer in denial of the *real*. However, I posit that Jefferson's volition to create and believe in a *real* results in her not seeing that Jackson was a product of this rupture between life and performance, between the real and the artificial. The lines between each of these constructions are always blurred and the reality of Jackson's body was as much about acting, performing and mutating the organic, as the theatre of Jackson's musical performances and videos was about harnessing a certain "naturalness" of movement, expression of love and reframing physical, sexual gestures that otherwise would be "out of place," or even vulgar. There was a certain symbiosis between the *realness* of movement and emotion that Jackson's

---

[2] Ibid., 14.

[3] Ibid.

music and performances evoked and the conterminous unreality of his physical appearance. I would argue that there is a conscious deconstruction of the pathos within Jackson's performativity and the very body he created both as private subject and public spectacle. It is in this nexus of public and private where we can no longer decipher or tease out one from the other, just as in the simultaneous conscious amalgamation of fact and fiction about Jackson's life.

In the chapter above, her comparison of Jackson to P.T. Barnum's collection of freaks from the early nineteenth century is telling. Reminding the reader that the freak in early American culture was the "African," Jefferson illustrates how Barnum would typically put an actor of European origin in blackface and exhibit him with the title "What is it?" Identity was, in its very essence, already performative and mimetic. Later this act was changed and an actual African American, William Henry Johnson also known as "Zip the Pinhead," represented the "missing link"—fact and fiction are blurred and racial identity is as real in early stage representations as it is fictional performances.[4] Freakery in early American cultures was not about representing the truth of visibility but rather about *exploiting the fictions of visibility*. Despite ironizing this juncture between real and invented, however, Jefferson returns to the typical dichotomies of "normal" and "freak," transposing nineteenth-century notions of strangeness onto late twentieth- and early twenty-first century American culture:

> Barnum's museum exhibits, ethnological curiosities and circus sideshows also set the pattern for our daytime talk shows. The difference between then and now? Barnum's people were supposed to be freaks of nature, outside the boundaries of The Normal.[5]

Comparing Jackson to this travelling freak show of old, remember that Jefferson attempts to create parallels between these nineteenth-century relics and contemporary television shows like *Fear Factor* or *Extreme Home Makeover*. She suggests these shows are "updates" of older talent competitions where "the backstage tale, the life story, matters as much as the performance."[6] Jefferson suggests that Jackson is not an irreducible part of the dichotomies that have made him up—Jackson as either child or pervert, either humanitarian or predator, either a child star or a psychotic man fearful of aging. Jefferson asks: "What if the 'or' is an 'and?' What if he is all of these things?"[7]

As much as I find this part of Jefferson's critique insightful in forcing the reader to abandon the traditional modalities for reading "either/ors," Jefferson nonetheless creates moral dichotomies between real and imitation and between nature and fakery, ultimately classifying Jackson as a mimetic fraud who hides behind a mask

---

4   Ibid., 12.
5   Ibid., 8.
6   Ibid.
7   Ibid., 18.

of cosmetic surgery, skin lightening, and increasing "effeminization," despite Jefferson's list of endless rock stars who have followed this path of gender-bending since the beginning of rock and roll. We should recall that both Little Richard and Elvis Presley threatened the status quo: both artists' bodily movements and costumes were considered "over the top" during the entirety of their careers as their dance moves imperiled static notions of masculinity where "manly hips" simply didn't move, as in the case of Elvis Presley, and where make up and wild hair designs were a constant source of gossip surrounding Little Richard. Though Jefferson brackets Little Richard's performances as somehow part of "black masculinity" to include his trademark screams during his concerts ("You're gonna make me scream like a white lady"), she starkly separates Jackson's odyssey into gender-bending from Little Richard's. I find this separation suspicious given there is no real distinction between these artists which she claims "few black men followed." If anything, Little Richard made similar performances possible for the multitudes of gender-blending artists who were his contemporaries and those who followed: James Brown's hairdos, Freddie Mercury's costumes and onstage flamboyance, Sylvester's falsetto bravado and David Bowie's similarly extravagant and transgendering use of make-up and gestures. Jackson simply did not innovate gender or racial bending and the history of American music prior to Jackson is riddled with similar performances that were admittedly less intense and more infrequently performed. Nonetheless, as in the history of queer performance upon popular culture, the multiplicity of performers who played with gender and race is simply not negligible.

Jefferson's study takes this concept of the freak from the confines of scientific discourses of medical pathology and from the popular narratives of social exclusion current in American culture and moves it towards the biographical, attempting to demonstrate how Jackson's childhood was a form of freakery. Likewise, in subsequent chapters not published in this collection, she shows how Jackson's entry into Motown and his subsequent move to Encino, California, allowed him to know similar child freaks who, like him, had lost their childhood to show business—Brooke Shields, Elizabeth Taylor, Liza Minelli, Tatum O'Neill. These people became part of Jackson's menagerie of friends throughout various parts of his adulthood and resultantly, Jackson's existence tended toward two extremes: the distension of hyper-performativity and "adult-like" professionalism on stage and in the studio and antithetically, his reclusion and performativity of childhood acts in his private life where water balloon fights were part of his quotidian existence. Jefferson portrays Jackson's "loss of childhood" as its own sort of freakery in a world where this six year-old boy went on to embody forever the boy who "was loved by other boys and by their mothers."[8] Jefferson takes this childhood embodied in the adult body of Jackson even further by comparing his physical form to that of *Sunset Blvd.*'s Norma Desmond who was a "freak version of its younger self … A travesty looking very much like an aging transvestite, a

---

[8]   Ibid., 21.

freak."[9] But is this rendering of the freak accurate in a culture where being a freak is a societal marginalization of difference to include race, gender, sexual, mental, and physical disability as this difference? Jefferson makes little effort to tease the problematic historical discourse of freakery from the present, for the late twentieth century freak was often a role model for others to follow. In short, freakery is no longer about a cruel excision of the individual from the social core or the abjection of a specific ideal; instead, freakery in recent years has very much been about embracing difference and rendering it both spectacle and normal.

In the chapter "Alone of All His Race, Alone of All Her Sex," Jefferson conflates black masculinity with hyper-masculinity as if these two modalities are mutually interdependent. Despite the fact that most successful black musical artists had in fact exploited the play between masculinity and femininity (that is, Little Richard, Rick James, and Prince) until the era of hip-hop and that there was a recent resurgence of this gender play with artists like Kanye West, Jefferson remains stuck in an outdated theoretical approach to "black masculinity" where somehow there is a homogeneous construction thereof. Consequently, her interpretation of Jackson's crotch-clutching is laden with the weight of an extremely overused, if not entirely problematic, interpretation of black masculinity that she views as always—or at least is intended to be—macho:

> In retrospect, the crotch clutch seems at once desperate and abstract. It is as if he were telling us, "Fine, you need to know I am a man, a black man? Here's my dick: I'll thrust my dick at you! Isn't that what a black man's supposed to do? But I'm Jackson, so just look but you can't touch."[10]

Jefferson, it seems to me, fails to see how Jackson was consciously subverting race and gender in his performances for which the "crotch clutch" was never about blackness, and hardly about sexuality. In reviewing his *Dangerous World Tour* performance shot in Bucharest in1992, I am reminded that Jackson's one gesture that was never about race or sexuality was precisely his crotch thrust. In his yellow unitard over black pants I recall how children often wear underclothes on the outside of their clothes in attempting to emulate any number of super heroes. In this performance by Jackson, all reference to sexuality was annulled by the neutering of sex organs through the mere absurdity and playfulness of costume. In a similar way, Jackson's employment of mobster fashion with an external unitard combined with the *pastiche* mob violence of a Broadway show tune annuls the sexuality of the crotch grab while heightening the sexuality of every single mobster-esque gesture—from the faux fireworks which symbolize machine gun fire to the violent turns and twists of each spin.

This curious mixture of "insideout" wear is both costume and play for Jackson—the crotch grab becomes an innocent act of desexualization rather than

---

[9]   Ibid., 27.
[10]   Ibid., 102.

of sexualization. We see this again in his Budapest concert where onstage Jackson's body retains a purity of movement and where the thrusts, the twists, his primal screams and high-pitched "heees" are much more about being in the presence of this icon and his movements rather than witnessing sexualized gestures. Certainly there is more sexuality onstage in this concert demonstrated by what Jackson *does not do* than what he does. Jackson's concert opening contains more sexual reference and play of "pent up sexual energy" masked as desire than all of the crotch grabs of this concert combined. Jackson plays with stasis and rhythm of the opening moments of his consent, creating all the plays of sexuality—and even the sexual act as metaphor—as each opening move is choreographed as part his dance: he is propelled onstage by an underground catapult and as he lands, he stands perfectly still for two minutes looking towards his right, his aviator sunglasses masking his interiority, his long hair resting on his shoulders likewise is motionless, and his arms slightly bent and his fists cocked as if ready for action. The crowds scream hysterically as this icon rendered life-statue remains motionless, completely fixed, and their screams become admonishments to wake him from his inaction reminding him to move. Little by little these screams turn to chants of "Michael, Michael." His frozen body teases the crowd as if a challenge for them to break him with their adulation and cries, until two minutes have elapsed and then suddenly he quickly jerks his head left and the crowd escalates its screams. Just as quickly he moves both hands up to the temples of his sunglasses and once again remains still as he reduces his rhythm ever so slowly taking off his sunglasses. The crowd grows even wilder with their cries and by the time he has fully removed his glasses, the tears and screams are insurmountable. It is then that he immediately propels his body into his speed of light spin followed by his signature leg kick which initiates the song "Jam." Jackson has brought his audience to a climax with little more than stasis, a slow removal of sunglasses and a spin. Sexual energy is both present and absent in this concert opening—it is confused within the elated screams of men and women alike, it is confused by this deity plummeted to earth rendered human for whom sexuality is but a tool for his performance.

Jefferson creates a solipsism between black masculinity as either real *or* symbolic, viewing these conditions as somehow always separable. However, for Jackson, the symbolic and real are entirely inseparable and play off one another attaining their meanings from this very type of reflexivity just as they do in "real life." For instance, Jefferson theorizes the penis as purely sexual in Jackson's performances and then as quickly as she engages this idea, she abandons it to suddenly proclaim that his crotch thrust is phallic, not sexual: "It wasn't real, it was symbolic. Not a penis but a phallus."[11] It would seem that Jefferson misses the mark on understanding how the phallic can be both symbolic and poetic—especially in the gesticular and corporeal movements of dance. For instance, Jackson was conscious about keeping his body free from too much musculature, maintaining his body fit and agile while also slender and even androgynous. His dance flows

---

[11]   Ibid., 102.

onscreen and onstage and his nubile movements allow for any dancer—be he a classical ballet dancer to one trained in the Cunningham technique—the ability to transcend the clichés of gender. Jackson strikes a pose, hand on crotch, right hand in the air, pausing while singing "Human Nature." He renders the private public while also turning the sexual on its head. Or as he once described his dance moves to Oprah, "I don't think about it … I just do it."

What is most problematic in Jefferson's reading of Jackson's body is this intent of inscribing race onto Jackson for whom race was the center of his deconstruction in song, dance and interviews. He would often throw back questions at his interlocutor saying, "I bet if everyone who has had plastic surgery were to go on vacation, Los Angeles would be empty" or "People are always changing the color of their skin … tanning." Jefferson cites Ralph Elison's *Invisible Man* regarding the task of the black artist which "was not actually one of creating the uncreated conscience of his race, but of creating the uncreated features of his face."[12] Yet, Jefferson attempts to set up an incredibly racialized reading of fluid race and gender of Jackson while conversely focusing on this notion of the "black woman" she maintains is embodied by Jackson's mother, Katherine, and Diana Ross. Jefferson points to black femininity as the core of Jackson's representation of gender as if "black femininity" were in and of itself a representational domain, or at least the specific focus of Jackson's mimetic changes which certainly seemed to mimic an imagined "raceless woman." The very same notion that the crotch represents the penis or that Diana Ross must somehow be the referent for all black femininity are positions postulated by Jefferson which impose racialization despite the lack of substance for such arguments. In short, Jefferson attempts to limit the constructions of "normative identity" (in all their alleged referents) that Jackson's performances and body actually deconstructed. Jackson was a hybrid of gender, ethnicity and sex onstage whose corporeal interpretations refused belonging or stasis. The moon walk, like so much of Jackson's choreography, touched upon the very magical realism of his performances, his constructed worlds of peace and equality on and offstage—his somatic transformations and the heterogeneity of his gestures embodied his defiance of gender, race and anthropomorphism. As Jackson coopted the moonwalk from popular American cinema or the ghettos, this dance has become the metaphor for Jackson's ability to bring the unreal into the sphere of the real and in a majestic mixture of fantasy and fiction, he somehow managed to bring the moon to earth through dance.

What started this journey of bringing the fantastic to earth, however, was born through the very medium that brought reality and fiction together: cinema. Jackson's fame was made by his music, but it was stamped and sealed by his video work. Jackson's videos brought to the fore issues of social and racial inequality in the United States as seen through cinematic tropes as he borrowed from an expansive tradition of cinematic traditions of song, dance and horror. Working through social discourses of racial, class and social injustice in American society,

---

12   Ibid., 97.

Jackson re-enacts stories of injustice: he invokes racial and species division from *I Was a Teenage Werewolf* (1957) as replayed in the video *Thriller* (1983); he reinterprets Fred Astaire from *The Band Wagon* (1953) as the lyrics tell a story of domestic violence, the video recreating a 1920s gangster scenario in *Smooth Criminal* (1988); and *Scream* (1995) takes on the aesthetics of Japanese sci-fi Anime as this song autobiographically decries Jackson's treatment by the media during the child sexual abuse accusations made against him in the early 1990s. Jackson borrows from cinematic traditions that ignore color barriers, he employs dance techniques that likewise bring together a grand history of the American musical in film and Broadway, and he creates a hybridized form of dance and visual media that bars all specificity to race by forcing the spectator to realize that no one dance move or note can be reduced to any single meaning or origin. Song and dance become metaphors for race. By bringing to the fore the rich history of American music, film, and dance in the context of historical and fictional themes of racial, gangster and biological divisions, Jackson's videos offer a paradisiacal, fictional world of racial and cultural hybridity. His videos create a domain where color no longer matters and where the outside simulation of the somatic body and the gesticulations of the dancer invoke dialogue by virtue of pure spectacle. Jackson's videos bring together such a diverse range of cinematic and performative traditions such that what he presents is a product of a cultural heterogeneity within the United States and other international settings.

For instance, the moonwalk, whose origin has been the focus of much discussion, is a dance form which was not solely invented in the tradition of African American dance or in the ghetto despite the insistence of many people. Instead, Jackson recuperates the moonwalk in its plurality of meaning and origin and demonstrates this dance's rich heritage throughout his video work and live performances. More amazing is how Jackson uses this dance form to deconstruct racial and cultural specificity by bringing the moonwalk to various settings, from his first live performance of the moonwalk at *Motown* 25, discussed above by Jefferson, to a video dealing with early twentieth-century gangster mafia culture. The various manners through which Jackson employs the moonwalk strips it of all specificity and deprives it of any type of univocality. We observe the early forms of the moonwalk from as far back as 1932 with Cab Calloway, as performed by the mime masters Etienne Decroux and Jean-Louis Barrault. We also see other performances of the mookwalk from Marcel Marceau's mime performances to the films *Cabin in the Sky* (1943), *Les Enfant du paradis* (1944) and *Showtime at the Apollo* (1955), popularized by performers such as Bill Bailey and Fred Astaire. We also are given the moonwalk in contemporary breakdance of the 1980s as represented in television and film such as *Fame* (1982) and *Flashdance* (1983). The historical plurality of this dance move's performance dilutes the specificity of meaning or ownership. Jackson capitalizes on this movement's rich history and renders the moonwalk as not black, nor white, but as specifically his own. Over the course of his lifetime, Jackson's body became a *tabla rasa* for reading cultural and racial exchanges the result of which was twofold: on the one hand, there was forever doubt cast upon the "truth" about his body, from his illness, Vitiligo, to his plastic surgeries; while on the other hand, the amorphism of his body allowed for his music and dance to be cast as universal truths. In his opening up to readings on his body, Jackson likewise posited the possibility for everyone to access his music, his dance and even to embrace their own special sort of marginalization. While making a film on the public mourning of Jackson, *To Neverland and Back* (2010), I was rather surprised how many of Jackson's fans identified with him due to their own marginalizaiton due to disability, illness, sexuality and ethnic identity.

Certainly Jefferson acknowledges how Jackson's body becomes similar to that of a cyborg in her citation of Keith Haring's famous journal entry about Jackson, which foresaw in many ways this performer's continued metamorphoses:

> I talk about my respect for Michael's attempts to take creation in his own hands and invent a non-black, non-white, non-male, non-female creature by utilizing plastic surgery and modern technology. He's totally Walt-Disneyed out! An interesting phenomenon at the least. A little scary, maybe, but nonetheless remarkable, and I think somehow a healthier example than Rambo or Ronald Reagan. He's denied the finality of God's creation and taken it into his own hands, while all the time parading around in front of American pop culture. I think it would be much cooler if he would go all the way and get his ears pointed or add a tail or something, but give him time![13]

However, throughout her analysis, Jefferson attempts to maintain the real by projecting her expectations of a real: the real "masculine," the real "black masculinity," and the implied betrayal of an "African American community." I am left wondering, after reading Jefferson's book, if she understood at all the incredible richness of Jackson's work and life simply because his work did not speak to race—it spoke to the end of race and division. Jackson even played consciously with color in each of his concerts through his choice of band members and dancers. His lead guitarists were women who would often wear huge masks which would transform them into more animalesque creatures and the dancers were always a mixture of Latino, African American, and lighter-skinned dancers. Jackson de-emphasized race by emphasizing the aesthetics thereof and by bridging the white/black dichotomies with something far more radical: the human-animal divide.

Reminiscent of Keith Haring's statement is the liminality that Jackson's body presents to the spectator—not the body of race, but rather the body of human. For much of Jackson's public and private persona was that of an animal lover; however, if we look a bit more deeply at his facial features, we notice how much of what Jackson surgeries accomplished was rendering his body more and more feline as could be seen in his 2005 trial. And certainly the Oprah Winfrey and Martin Bashir interviews revealed this performer's opulent lifestyle as a blatant

---

[13]   Keith Haring, *Keith Haring's Journals* (London, 1996), 179.

form of freakery in and of itself by showing Jackson's animal fetishes from his close relationships with animals he rescued: Bubbles the chimp, Louie the llama, Muscles the snake, and Bubba the lion. As Amy C. Billone discusses further in Chapter 3, there was always something suspect about this man who built a huge sanctuary for himself in a place he called Neverland, fashioning himself a modern-day Peter Pan, holding dozens of wild animals and somatically changing his body little by little into something that went far beyond "humanlike." Might Keith Haring have been correct in his reading Jackson as transhuman, as cyborg? Or could it be that Jackson's performances offstage had slowly become his reality, reversing a pattern which his parents had established for him as a child star living life primarily through public performances?

This division between animal and human, which metaphorically represented racial division in his work from the 1980s, came to represent in the 1990s a metaphor for divide between adults and children, between animal and man. Jackson found solace with children and animals, as he often states in interviews, simply because they did not want anything from him. The dichotomies of Jackson's double identity are best revealed through his somatic transformation from a young African American kid to a superstar who in a strange pastiche of private and public performances transgresses sex, gender and race. With Jackson we are constantly given myriad and opposing identities from his onstage and offstage personas: real/performance; childhood/adulthood; passivity (life)/ aggression (stage); live performance hypersexuality/ "real life" interview mode and asexuality. I agree with Christopher R. Smit's conclusions above in the introduction; even this notion of the *real* for Jackson is always performative and is never a real *real*—the artifice of his onstage performances, on-camera interviews and spontaneous candid moments before the camera dazzle the spectator in what could be the most sincere of confessions, or it could be one of many plastic layers of authenticity spread thick for the camera. The spectator is never given confirmation and Jackson's authenticity is grounded in a complete confusion of the real and the artifice. In analyzing Jackson's "interview persona" after his death, I have to admit to feeling uncomfortable with the massive transformation from this sweet-voiced, giggling "boy" at home who suddenly turns himself into a virile, dexterous and extroverted performer on stage. It was clear to me that Jackson's authenticity was derived from neither his private persona nor his performative figure, but instead his *realness* is maintained in his transgressions between both public and private selves.

Jackson's performances embraced all that was part of America as he stretched the limits of representability both as victim of an abusive childhood and as a superstar who went on not only to dominate the music industry for a solid decade, but to continue to support economically the entirety of his abusive family, *even after his death*. Jackson was a mutant of various identities with which he constantly struggled throughout his life: in his private life he was able to write his own identity as a product of abusive parents, as a victim of sexual violence and as a son who recognized the loss of his childhood owing to a career forced upon him, and while in public, he was the subject of scrutiny regarding his race, his bodily transformations, his sexuality and his relationships to other adults and children. Jackson's image was symbolic of what American culture was experiencing: struggles with the language of racial identity, with the novelty of somatic transformations through plastic surgery, and with the newly confronted homosexual identities tragically brought to public attention through the tragedy of AIDS in the 1980s. Synchronic with these social negotions, Jackson embodied the coincidence of his skin disease, vitiligo, which organically transformed his skin while he would go on to perform songs that denied racial—and at times human— singularity. Jackson took the cultural coincidences of somatic complexities and embraced them within his private and public personas. Jean Baudrillard contemplates this performer's body:

> Jackson is a solitary mutant, a precursor of hybridization that is perfect because it is universal—the race to end all races. Today's young people have no problem with a miscegenated society: they already inhabit such a universe, and Jackson foreshadows what they see as an ideal future. Add to this the fact that Jackson has had his face lifted, his hair straightened, his skin lightened — in short, he has been reconstructed with the greatest attention to detail. This is what makes him such an innocent and pure child—the artificial hermaphrodite of the fable, better able even than Christ to reign over the world and reconcile its contradictions; better than a child-god because he is child-prosthesis, an embryo of all those dreamt-of mutations that will deliver us from race and sex.[14]

Yet what was freakish about Jackson was that he brought the historical metaphors of hybridity—very much part of American history—to the fore and evidenced that which we all knew, but did not dare act or say. He took corporeal metamorphosis outside the simplistic container of black and white and moved it into the celestial spheres of invention and spectacle that transcended all human divisions, to end all races.

As a superstar, it was most difficult for Jackson to convey the childhood he never had living a life that economically most on this earth could never imagine. How to portray childhood cruelty from the mouth of a God who "has it all"? Jackson did manage to accomplish this task from the transmission of his childhood story in song and interview through the very recreation of his childhood *as an adult*. Jackson created a form of private and public freakery that few could understand as he entered into a child-sphere of reclusion that made the prospects of skin-bleaching appear normal to many and that sadly left his life open for those who attempted to extort and slander him. The menagerie of animals at Neverland were indices of a man-boy who refused to grow up and likewise his affection for these animals displayed both a childhood innocence (even regression) as did his anthropomorphic regard for these creatures whom he viewed *as his boyhood*

---

[14]   Jean Baudrillard, *Cool Memories: 1980–1985*, trans. Chris Turner (London, 1990), 21–2.

self. Jackson's animals were largely saved from circuses and zoos and as such spared from the life he had: that of circus performers. Inevitably, Jackson recreates the scene for the salvation of his own childhood through his salvation of these animals—to give them, in a sense, their own childhood. Jackson recreated his face through plastic surgery to resemble that of an organic other and he took back control of his body from nature and made with it his own, forcing the line separating the real and artificial to slowly fade. Viewed from an organic perspective, Jackson enacted humanistic performance and song through a transhuman body.

Jackson's performances were invested in making the artifice look real, even when the artificial was so painfully unreal, as can be noted in the introduction of his *HIStory* Tour (1996–97) when the spectator is given a 10-minute prelude to his stage entrance: a huge screen which has a virtual reality shuttling through the world of Jackson as seen from a roller coaster passing the pyramids at Giza, a large Buddha statue, New York's Chrysler Building, the Parthenon, a statue of Mercury, and then suddenly, the viewer is no longer subject but is once again spectator, floating high above in the Sistine Chapel, watching geysers of fire emerging from the earth as a space capsule floats above space, the animated cranks and wheels of Chaplin's *Modern Times* appears followed by an Egyptian obelisk covered in cameras and video screens. The anachronism and inaccuracy of these images renders them all the more mesmerizing as the spectator is being given name brands of the world's greatest wonders with absolutely no contextualization. The audience awaits Michael's landing as they scream his name and, minutes later, we finally hear his voice: "Mission control: What is my TOA?" Jackson makes one last stop on earth as there are animations of video screens along the roller coaster which we (the fans) are watching and upon these screens are fans faces screaming "Michael!" This entry is cinematic kitsch of the simulation of fandom amidst the simulation of fandom. And at long last, the video comes to an end and a real-life cockpit of the spaceship emerges from the stage and what was the "real" cinematic image is now transformed into yet another, three-dimensional real. Jackson emerges from the cockpit in a golden suit: he is not human, he is android. He peels off the first layer of body armor and then his helmet, busting out into the song "Scream" with his body still partially confined by silver leggings that are held on by dozens of straps, and of course his signature loafers.

Jackson's concerts are, in their totality, a wonderfully strange mixture of high-tech showmanship, performances of hyper-masculinity with his dancers costumed in military and mafia dress, and of course Jackson's own corporeal and gesticulative transformations between femininity, masculinity, and androgyny. What makes his shows so transformative for the viewer is how Jackson mixes an array of fantasy, mafia, and outer space themes in one performance while his songs actually touch upon very real issues that are either autobiographical or overwhelmingly common themes of humankind: from the sexual tone of the description of a groupie in "Dirty Diana" to the ecological call of "Earth Song" to his song about the non-importance of race in "Black or White" to the humanist song which invokes Ghandi's "be the change you want the world to be," "Man in the Mirror." Between the realness of his music which imagines a world of social justice—no matter how schmaltzy some might find these themes—and the extraordinary vision of technological and performative displays of excellence and other worldliness, Jackson created the perfect space on stage for realizing his Neverland *with* his fans as the concert becomes a dreamscape for imagining possibility through somatic deception. For instance, the finale of his *Dangerous World Tour* is laden with as much fakery and kitsch, bookending his world of imaginary power of the real: while singing "Change" he dawns a white spacesuit, helmet, and then straps on a rocket ship (when the body double takes over through a lovely *trompe l'oeil* of stage imaginary), and he launches off giving his fans a finale that is prohibitively unreal. While no insurance company would back Jackson to launch himself offstage, a body double "becomes" the body of Jackson while the crowds are tricked into believing that it is Jackson himself who is launching off. The dream of spectacle is realized through a fraud, and a body double becomes Jackson's boyhood dream of flying high above the screaming crowds.

Bernard-Henri Lévy maintains that Jackson did not die from a drug overdose; instead, Lévy states that "he died because of his desire not only to invent a vaccine against life, but also to want to inoculate himself with it."[15] What Jackson was, must be spoken in the present tense because although he is gone from this earth, what he represents is very much alive and part of American culture in the cultural inevitability to name or be named, to frame or be framed. Jackson was rendered an archaeological artifice his entire life, forced to answer questions that go beyond the scope of fame and enter into the framework of our postmodern circus, that of tabloid journalism. Certainly, to some, Jackson is a freak. To others he is a hero, an artist, an innovator, a peacemaker, a philanthropist. But what if he is all of the above?

The truth about Jackson is that *he was our freak, every bit as much as we were his*. His moves, his dance, his music, his media performances, his mixture of *kitsch* and humanistic discourses of world peace and love are a huge part of our cultural landscape and language both in the United States and abroad. Likewise, Jackson's body and artistic work create an order and cultural logic that shatters the univocal treatments of identity. And more importantly, Jackson proposes both physical and emotional change as part of the landscape of humanity's future. In the months following Jackson's death we heard one armchair analysis after another about *his* "body dysmorphic disorder" relating how Jackson did not accept his body. These kinds of readings struck me as both irresponsible—for how can the dead be psychoanalyzed?—and careless since the readings that every "specialist" lent to Jackson were unidirectional: each analysis was inevitably about Jackson's inability to accept himself, never about our culture's inability to accept difference. I think the dysmorphic disorder that needs further interrogation is not that of Jackson but rather that of a culture that claims to be the freest in the world whilst

---

    [15]   Bernard-Henri Lévy, "The Three Stations of the Cross in Michael Jackson's Calvary," *Huffington Post* (2009).

this very culture kills its own creatures. In his refusal to be named, Jackson died. In our refusal to let him name himself, we killed him.

Chapter 3

Sentenced to Neverland: Michael Jackson, Peter Pan, and Queer Futurity

Amy C. Billone

In her chapter on the connections between Michael Jackson and the fictional character Peter Pan, Amy Billone digs deeply into the realm of fantasy and its crucial role in Jackson's identity. By employing expertise in comparative literature and queer studies, Billone weaves through fact and fiction to challenge the very idea that sexuality could ever come to define Jackson in any precise way. In the process, her conclusions challenge the very nature of the concept "queerness," and its uses in academic discourse about time and space.

Queerness is not yet here. Queerness is an ideality. Put another way, we are not yet queer. We may never touch queerness, but we can feel it as the warm illumination of a horizon imbued with potentiality. We have never been queer, yet queerness exists for us as an ideality that can be distilled from the past and used to imagine a future. The future is queerness's domain.

José Muñoz, *Cruising Utopia*

This is it. I can feel I'm the light of the world. This is real.

Michael Jackson

In 1988, Michael Jackson purchased the Sycamore Valley Ranch in Santa Barbara County, California for a sum reported to be somewhere between 16.5 to 30 million dollars, retitling it Neverland Valley Ranch. In his 2003 documentary, *Living with Michael Jackson*, Martin Bashir visited Neverland, commenting, "As with most of his life, it has to be seen to be believed. Inspired by the children's fairy tale Peter Pan about the little boy who never grew up, it's a multi-million dollar manmade slice of make-believe." J.M. Barrie, the famous Scottish author and dramatist who invented the story of Peter Pan, described Neverland in his 1911 novel *Peter and Wendy* as being "not large and sprawly, you know, with tedious distances between one adventure and another, but nicely crammed."[1] Similarly, a Map Key available to guests at Jackson's Neverland included similarly "crammed" sites

---

[1] J.M. Barrie, *Peter Pan*, ed. Amy Billone (New York: Barnes and Noble Classics, 2005), 12.

such as four train stations, Lake Neverland, Neverland Gardens, a Teepee Village, nature preserve, the Nestle Lounge (tent), the Red Bull Lounge (tent), the Britto Art Exhibit, a Lunge/Club KISS, a Michael Jackson Museum, movie theater, basketball court, Carnival Alley, a carousel, bumper cars, a Sea Dragon, a Ferris wheel, a Zipper, the Neverland Amphitheater, a petting zoo, a Serpentarium, a crocodile, the Neverland Aviary, elephants, giraffes, orangutans, tigers, a bear, and a Massage Therapy Center.

In this essay I argue that Jackson's heightened sympathy with Peter Pan, combined with both his tremendous success and his tragic downfall, sheds crucial light on the way we need to understand queerness today. Jackson tearfully told Jane Fonda, "You know, all over the walls of my room are pictures of Peter Pan. I've read everything that Barrie wrote."[2] When Bashir asked why Peter Pan was a figure of such interest and inspiration to him, Jackson answered that Peter represented "youth, childhood, never growing up, magic, flying … what it's all about." Bashir asked if he identified with Pan and without hesitation Jackson responded "Totally … I am Peter Pan." When Bashir corrected him, clarifying, "You're Michael Jackson," Jackson replied calmly and confidently, "I'm Peter Pan in my heart." Certainly, Jackson clung throughout his career to the appeals of childhood: his repeatedly pronounced devotion to children, his invention of "Neverland," his high male voice, his apparent androgyny and asexuality. I agree with Steven Bruhm that "Michael Jackson *can be nothing but queer*, if we take 'queer' to mean sexually ambiguous, protean, corporally illegible."[3] Moreover, I understand Jackson to be a queer artist because of his boundary-crossing performances both on and off stage. Because Jackson's perpetually shifting identity, or "queerness," made progressively less sense to the public—as many of the authors in this text agree, he persistently transgressed boundaries of race, gender, sexuality and temporality itself—the very qualities that generated his staggering fame also helped bring about his tragic collapse.

In the context of the urgent questions that are currently being debated about what queerness is, what it does and what relevance it has for the intellectual, political and social world we live in, I think it is imperative that we understand the simultaneously elating and heartrending intersection between queerness and dreamscapes. I am influenced in my interpretation of queer time and space by scholars such as Judith Halberstam and José Muñoz, both of whom argue that queerness aims to reject the here and now and instead points the way toward future landscapes. But I will add a specific focus on dreams to my study of Michael Jackson and Peter Pan, exploring how future oriented fantasies can all too easily slip into the realm of nightmare when they are made manifest in the present.

Jackson was obsessed with returning to the past, yet this is a past that never was; his sympathy with Peter Pan was with a ghostchild who was also a dreamchild,

---

[2]   *Michael by the Editors of Rolling Stone* (New York: HarperCollins, 2009), 128.

[3]   Steven Bruhm, "Michael Jackson: Queen Funk," in *Queering the Gothic*, ed. William Hughes and Andrew Smith (Manchester: Manchester University Press, 2009), 158.

one who might have existed but never did. In his preoccupation with Peter Pan, Jackson was entranced both by the spatial and the temporal vertigo of queerness—he fell in love with a neverland as well as with a neverchild, a child who never was and could never be. In particular, I propose that the neverchild from the past is activated in and through the imagination as a potently future child, a child who *could* be. Jackson fiercely maintained that his dreams—his wishes—translated seamlessly into future reality. However, it was by endeavoring to reanimate the irretrievable past in his art that Jackson thrilled audiences with a dream future. The danger was that by moving (as Peter Pan did) entirely into a dreamspace, Jackson became exiled from the real world; having interchanged dreams and reality, he at last could not fall asleep without dying first. The terror and hope of queerness, then, derives in part from the troubling yet thrilling tension between dreaming and waking life.

The Fantasy and Nightmare of Neverland

How do we make sense of the nightmarish prison that Michael Jackson's paradisiacal 2,700-acre Neverland Valley Ranch ultimately became? Referring to rumors that Jackson's family was considering interring the pop star on the grounds of his once-beloved ranch, Jack Wishna, president of CP America and orchestrator of Jackson's return to the U.S. after a year abroad following the sensational 2005 trial, stressed Jackson's profound resistance to Neverland at the end of his life: "I *never, never, never* want to go back to Neverland," Jackson told Wishna. "*Never.*"[4] Wishna suspected that if someone were to bury Jackson in Neverland, "he [would] come up out of the ground like in Thriller and strangle them … I tried to get rid of Neverland for him. He would *never* set foot back in Neverland. He *never* wanted to go there, *never* wanted to sleep there—*never, never.*"[5] Even though he developed a profound aversion to the fantasyland he had created in the spirit of his role model, Peter Pan, Jackson continued to identify with the adventurous boy who will never grow up. In *Michael Jackson's This Is It*, Jackson summarized the point of his final show to performers only days before his death: "But it's an adventure. It's a great adventure. There's *nothing* to be nervous about … We want escapism. We want to take them places that they've *never* been before. We want to show them talent like they've *never* seen before."[6] Jackson's words about the purpose of his art closely resemble Peter Pan's famous statement in the moments

---

[4]   Whitney English and Natalie Finn, "It's Going to Be a Disaster: Associate Says Jackson Was Too Weak for Major Comeback," *Eonline*, July 10, 2009. [Online]. Available at: http://www.eonline.com/uberblog/b133691_its_going_be_disaster_associate_says.html. Author emphasis.

[5]   Ibid. Author emphasis.

[6]   Author emphasis.

before he almost drowns on the Marooners' Rock when he joyfully proclaims: "To die will be an awfully big adventure."[7]

Like the character of Peter Pan and the various texts revolving around him, Jackson derives his incomprehensible charm and authority at least in part because of his seemingly magical ability to change roles. As a play first performed in 1904, Peter Pan drew heavily from the pantomime tradition, a British theater genre traditionally produced at Christmas. Theatrical cross-dressing is common to pantomime: women played the part of Pan for almost 50 years. If Pan and Jackson partly captivated audiences by questioning gender roles, what is so attractive about gender crossing? Marjorie Garber argues that "in *Peter Pan* category crises are everywhere."[8] However, by making a spectacle of these crises, Barrie satisfies the fantasies of his audience: "Transgression without guilt, pain, penalty, conflict, or cost: this is what Peter Pan—and *Peter Pan*—is all about. The boy who is really a woman; the woman who is really a boy; the child who will never grow up; the colony that is only a country of the mind."[9]

Michael Jackson not only destabilizes gender categories in the manner of Peter Pan, but, as Julian Vigo has suggested in Chapter 2, he also disturbs racial categories. And the crossing of racial boundaries has added a new angle of inquiry to recent studies in queer theory. For example, Marlon B. Ross challenges Michel Foucault's famous theory of homosexuality as a kind of transparent closet which is marked on a body even at the same time it is invisible in the anatomy of the sexual deviant. As Ross sees it, the phrase "enslaved African" could easily be substituted for Foucault's "nineteenth-century homosexual" and "race" could replace "sexuality" so that his theory could be taken as "explaining the invention of race, rather than sexuality, as a total composition and thus as a species identity."[10] For this reason, Ross also challenges Eve Sedgwick's epistemological theory of the closet, which does not adequately take racial issues into account. Jackson, consequently, pushed the queerness of Peter Pan to an even more extreme level by unsettling these racial dimensions.

Jackson's remarkable ability to shift and challenge identities served not only to please audiences; it also angered and upset them. The dramatic changes in Jackson's appearance due to his excessive use of cosmetology and plastic surgery inspired intense media criticism and speculation. It was as if Jackson functioned not as the handsome model but as the painting in Oscar Wilde's *The Picture of Dorian Gray*. In Wilde's novel, the beautiful young protagonist is able to trade places with the image of himself in a painting. Dorian remains handsome and

---

[7]   Barrie, *Peter Pan,* 87.

[8]   Marjorie Garber, *Vested Interests: Cross-Dressing and Cultural Anxiety* (New York: Routledge, 1992), 182.

[9]   Ibid., 184.

[10]   Marlon B. Ross, "Beyond the Closet as Raceless Paradigm," in *Black Queer Studies: A Critical Anthology*, ed. Patrick E. Johnson and Mae G. Henderson (Durham, NC: Duke University Press, 2005), 164.

youthful while only his picture changes to reveal his age and the defacements of sin. As Jackson's body degenerated, tabloids encouraged the public's belief that his appearance reflected the corruption of his life. Once Jackson was suspected of engaging in inappropriately sexual behavior with minors, he went "from being Peter Pan to being James Barrie—from the eternal child to the man who surrounds himself with children."[11] Like Jackson, Barrie showed excessive affection for little boys, namely for the five Llewellyn Davies boys, whom he adopted after their parents died. Two of Barrie's beloved Llewellyn Davies boys, Michael and Peter (who were the original inspiration for Peter Pan), committed suicide, quite possibly in response to the shadow that Barrie cast over their lives, while the eldest brother George died at war when he was 21 years old, just after he received a passionate love letter from Barrie. The similarity with Jackson here is undeniable, and although he denied all counts and was found not guilty on all charges, he continued to be disparaged by the media and doubted by the public. His reputation would be tarnished for the rest of his life.

I in no way want to imply in this essay that queer sexuality is akin to the sexual exploitation of children. Many people believe that Jackson was indeed guilty of perpetrating sexual abuse on vulnerable young boys. According to these accounts, Jackson used his fame, power, and money to silence children as he took advantage of them in pathological ways. Attaching this act of violence to queer sexuality has the potential to do great damage to my conceptualization of queerness as a utopian ideal. Nevertheless, we need to consider carefully why Jackson could breathtakingly queer time and space in his art while he could not literally accomplish the same moves in real life. Jackson could not actually create Barrie's dreamspace of Neverland and invite countless little boys there, make them promise to never leave and seduce them into "sleeping" with him so that he could play out his own fantasies about having escaped time—that is, so he could go back joyfully to a time that never was and create exciting possibilities for an ecstatic future in which the apparent rules of time and space no longer matter. Even to appear to do so brought Jackson to court with the threat of a lifetime sentence in jail. In this process, the paradisiacal Neverland transmuted into a nightmare universe.

In spite of Jackson's failure to queer time and space in the real world, he brilliantly realized this goal in his status as a performer and in his art itself. His high male voice hardly changed when he ceased to be a child (urban myths suggested he took female hormones to make this possible); his race altered from black to white or at least in Margo Jefferson's words, "un-black"; his relation to time confused the public: was Jackson biologically stuck in childhood or trapped in a developmental stage he could not grow out of because of the abuse and celebrity that crippled him in his youth or was he a grown man simply pretending to be an eternal child? Furthermore, he perplexed people with his ambiguous gender

---

[11]   Marjorie Garber, *Bisexuality and the Eroticism of Everyday Life* (New York: Routledge, 1995), 236.

as he began to look more like a woman than a man even while he made claims to a kind of hetero-masculinity in his songs and his dances. Moreover, in his art, Jackson looks like he really is flying when he spectacularly does the moonwalk; he takes spellbound viewers and listeners beyond time as he continually changes his shape (in the video for *Thriller* he transforms from human to werewolf to a movie rendition of a werewolf to human to zombie returned from the dead to a figment of the imagination to human again and finally to a devious being with yellow eyes that only the audience can see).

Jackson the artist shows the world at large what queerness (as a boundary-crossing force) can do: the power of what he was able to achieve was recognized to such an extent globally that he became the most popular entertainer of all time. Peter Pan, the dreamchild who could be nothing other than a little boy but who was played by a grown and aging woman, earned similar mythological status. What fantasies and tragedies does this particular kind of queer artistry make evident? What connection exists between the most rapturous dreams of the world at large and debilitating nightmares? What, exactly, are the risks of moving outside or at least questioning accepted definitions of time and space?

Death, Anonymity and Fantasyland

Jackson pinpointed the euphoria and despair of queer time and space in his performances. According to Lee Edelman's theory of reproductive futurism, Western nations endorse biological reproduction and its machinery, heterosexuality, as the basis of the political future. Following this model, queer people who inhabit the political present can have no possible future. Furthermore, Bruhm studies Jackson's obsession with the Gothic in relation to queer sexual performance in both the video of *Thriller* in 1983 and *Ghosts* in 1997. He argues that Jackson's passion for the *danse macabre* or dance of the dead, a primarily medieval phenomenon, suggests that "only the dead body is the animated body; and the living body, if we can call it that, is already dead in spirit if not in tissue and organ."[12] Edelman accentuates an ontological instability which can be imagined as a "pulsion" around a death-center, and Bruhm reads this kind of circulation as allegorizing what the *danse macabre* does for a queer artist like Jackson:

> That transvestite pulsion, that engagement in physical circulation around a meaning, that insistence upon an ontology that can never be inhabited or embodied, is the rich paradoxical status of the macabre dancer, for this dancer signifies through choreography the impossibility of the subject whose teleology is to signify.[13]

---

[12]   Bruhm, "Michael Jackson's Queen Funk," 160.
[13]   Ibid., 162.

In other words, Jackson's *danse macabre* indulges in the "expressive impossibilities of the non-subject."[14]

I agree with the notion that Jackson embraces and in a sense reanimates the non-subject. However, I think Muñoz's conception of queerness as an ideality that we take from the past in order to imagine a dazzling future more accurately explains the role Jackson played as a performer than Edelman's annihilation of the future for queer subjects. Jackson reached out to a dream of a past—to the neverchild—in order to propel himself and his audience toward the "thrill" of a queer future. The danger for Jackson was that even though he was able to perform in a Neverland that exists outside of time, and even though he was able to take the public there with him in his art, he could not accomplish the same task in real life. As Muñoz emphasizes, "Queerness is not yet here ... We have never been queer."[15]

In his 1988 autobiography, *Moonwalk*, Jackson made a confession that he would repeat for the rest of his life: "I believe I'm one of the loneliest people in the world."[16] In spite of and even because of Jackson's identification with Peter Pan, Neverland became a place not of paradise but of an imprisonment he could not escape. Rabbi Shmuley Boteach visited Neverland with his family in 2000 to interview Jackson and to help him rehabilitate his image after the devastating effect of the 1993 molestation accusation. Boteach's impression as soon as he arrived at Neverland was that Jackson "had created his own private universe, a world of children's laughter, fun and games, cartoons, and candy. A world with no pain."[17] However, after staying there a few days, his opinion completely changed:

> Neverland got stale for me and even my kids pretty quickly. It's one thing to visit Disneyland. It's another thing entirely to live in it. For the first few days the rides and attractions were fascinating. But after that they lost their novelty and Neverland came to feel like a giant cage.[18]

Jackson was aware that his affiliation with Peter Pan might be a sign of affliction rather than transcendence. For example, he told Boteach that he believed people were ignorant about what happened to Bobby Driscoll, the actor who played the part of Peter Pan in Disney's famous animated 1953 film:

> I don't think people know that Bobby Driscoll went missing for about a year and nobody recognized him. His own family didn't know that he was the one

---

[14]   Ibid.

[15]   José Muñoz, *Cruising Utopia: The Then and There of Queer Futurity* (New York: New York University Press, 2009), 1.

[16]   Michael Jackson, *Moonwalk* (New York: Harmony Books, 1988), 162.

[17]   Rabbi Shmuley Boteach, *The Michael Jackson Tapes: A Tragic Icon Reveals his Soul in Intimate Conversation* (New York: Vanguard Press, 2009), 14.

[18]   Ibid., 17.

in the pauper's grave with a heroin overdose. He was a Disney giant, the voice of Peter Pan.[19]

Jackson related so profoundly to Driscoll because he had gone through a similar crisis when he outgrew his role as child star.

Before accusations of child molestation, Jackson's profound attachment to the character of Peter Pan and his celebration of eternal childhood enabled him to sustain and magnify the astonishing fame he had first gained as a child celebrity. However, Jackson was haunted throughout his life by a fear of mis-recognition and anonymity. Rather than encouraging him to grow up, the public wanted him "to stay young and little forever."[20] Jackson felt an intimate connection to all child stars. For instance, during his time as a child performer he would request that the hotel room where he was staying be decorated with pictures and cut-outs of Shirley Temple. When at last he met the adult Shirley Temple Black in 2000, he said he "left there feeling baptized."[21] "I said, 'You don't know how you've saved my life.'"[22] In all of his child performances, Jackson even had Shirley Temple's picture taped to his mirror backstage. When the most brilliant little boy performer of all time gazed into the mirror before, during and after his shows, he saw the reflection of a smiling little girl.

What happened to Jackson as he moved farther and farther away from the stardom of his childhood? On one level, he found everything that Peter Pan embodied: eternal youth and eternal life through his performances, the capacity to move the hearts of millions, to provide the sense of "escapism" for which his audience yearned. But on another level, like Pan, he found his very dreamworld to be a nightmare universe instead of a paradise; imprisoned in Neverland, Jackson was exiled from the same world that he had flown above and cast spells upon. In Jefferson's words, "Michael Jackson escaped the ghetto of Gary, Indiana, and built the sanctuary of Neverland. It's become a circuslike prison, emblematic of his mind."[23] How and why did this transformation take place? Certainly, people were distressed by the *specific* charges made against Jackson in 1993. When the same story repeated itself with much greater consequences in 2005, Jackson's credibility was severely undermined, never to be entirely regained. Two years before the first accusations against Jackson were made, Ian Hacking notes that "The explosion in child abuse literature is remarkable."[24]

At the same time, since the advent of queer theory in the early 1990s, notions of child sexual abuse have become increasingly complicated. Drawing from

---

[19]   Ibid., 228.

[20]   Ibid., 225.

[21]   Ibid.

[22]   Ibid.

[23]   Margo Jefferson, *On Michael Jackson* (New York: Vintage Books, 2006), 3.

[24]   Ian Hacking, "The Making and Molding of Child Abuse," *Critical Inquiry* 17, no. 2 (1991): 269.

Foucault, scholars such as Bruhm and Natasha Hurley maintain that "The modern-day queer is unthinkable without the modern child."[25] In "How to Bring Your Kids up Gay: The War on Effeminate Boys," Sedgwick pointedly observes that in 1973 the American Psychiatric Association formally dropped the pathologizing diagnosis of homosexuality from its next Diagnostic and Statistical Manuel (DSM-III). [26] The 1980 DSM-III contained no entry for "homosexuality" but it included an entirely new diagnosis: "Gender Identity Disorder of Childhood." According to Sedgwick:

> While the decision to remove homosexuality from DSM-III was a highly polemicized and public one, accomplished only under pressure from gay activists outside the profession, the addition to DSM-III of 'Gender Identity Disorder of Childhood' appears to have attracted no outside attention at all—not even to have been perceived as part of the same conceptual shift.[27]

The biggest problem with the re-naturalization and enforcement of gender assignment, for Sedgwick, is that it offers absolutely no resistance "to the wish endemic in the culture surrounding and supporting it: the wish that gay people *not exist.*"[28] Kathryn Bond Stockton follows Sedgwick's lead by arguing that "In essence, the DSM freed the homosexual only to embattle the child. It waged war against homosexuality precisely on a field where a war could be hidden: the proto-gay child."[29]

According to Stockton, the proto-homosexual child is thought only to exist through the concept of *Nachträglichkeit*, which Derrida claimed governed the whole of Freud's thought. The term has been loosely translated to mean among other things "deferred effect" and "belated understanding" so that "events from the past acquire meaning only when read through their future consequences."[30] Furthermore, Stockton convincingly shows how by existing only on the margins of comprehension (as we might remark about Peter Pan), all children must be understood as queer. In addition to the increasing fusion between notions of queerness and theories about the nature of childhood, questions continue to be raised about age of sexual consent. Donald E. Hall lists "Age of sexual consent"

---

[25] Steven Bruhm and Natasha Hurley, introduction to *Curiouser: On the Queerness of Children*, ed. Steven Bruhm and Natasha Hurley (Minneapolis: University of Minnesota Press, 2004), xiv.

[26] Eve Kosofsky Sedgwick, "How to Bring Your Kids Up Gay: The War on Effeminate Boys," in *Tendencies*, ed. Michèle Aina Barale et al. (Durham, NC: Duke University Press, 1993).

[27] Ibid., 157.

[28] Ibid., 161.

[29] Kathryn Bond Stockton, *The Queer Child, Or Growing Sideways in the Twentieth Century* (Durham, NC: Duke University Press, 2009), 14.

[30] Ibid.

and the "complexities of any concept of universal 'queer rights'" alongside "Monogamy" as the three issues that he believes need to be addressed "in radical, imaginative fashion."[31] Of course, these arguments do not imply that had Jackson been found guilty in the cases made against him, he would not have been guilty of serious crimes. No matter how hard he tried to escape the laws of time and space, Jackson's dreams could not be actualized in the here and now.

Fantasies, Nightmares and Queerness

If Jackson's dreams could be realized in his art but not in real life, how do the hopes and fears inspired by queerness connect to the act of dreaming? Peter Pan not only exists as a figment of children's imaginations but he himself dreams with great intensity, forgetting his dreams as soon as he has them. Because Pan himself exists as a figure in dreamland, he persistently risks dissolving into nothingness. Due to his own insubstantiality, he is tormented by nightmares. Barrie contemplates Pan's trouble with dreams: "Sometimes, though not often, he had dreams, and they were more painful than the dreams of other boys. For hours he could not be separated from these dreams, though he wailed piteously in them. They had to do, I think, with the riddle of his existence."[32] Like Pan, Jackson was an active dreamer. On one level, dreaming for Jackson was the same thing as wishing so fervently that his hopes became realized. In a compelling section of his autobiography, Jackson relates how ever since he was a little boy he "dreamed of creating the biggest-selling record of all time."[33] He used to go swimming as a child and make a wish before he jumped into the pool. He would stretch his arms out, as if he were sending his thoughts "up into space," would make a wish and would dive into the water: "I'd say to myself, 'This is my dream. This is my wish,' every time before I'd dive into the water."[34] Jackson never lost his belief "in wishes and in a person's ability to make a wish come true."[35] For instance, whenever he saw a sunset he would quietly make his secret wish before the sun disappeared: "It would seem as if the sun had taken my wish with it."[36] Indeed, *Thriller* did become and still remains the most popular album ever made. This success, Jackson says, "transformed many of my dreams into reality."[37] Peter Pan's queerness derives from his status as the dream of a child who never was but one who tempts us into

---

[31]   Donald E. Hall, *Reading Sexualities: Hermeneutic Theory and the Future of Queer Studies* (New York: Routledge, 2009), 53.

[32]   Barrie, *Peter Pan,* 115.

[33]   Jackson, *Moonwalk*, 180.

[34]   Ibid.

[35]   Ibid.

[36]   Ibid.

[37]   Ibid., 184.

a dreamfuture that can never be; similarly, Jackson's queerness involves his ability to translate dreams into reality.

Beyond dreaming as a powerful form of wish making, reverie also created the space in which Jackson's songs first took shape. Hirshey notes that Jackson finds the creative process mysterious:

> I wake up from dreams and go, "Wow, put *this* down on paper" … The whole thing is strange. You hear the words, everything is right there in front of your face. And you say to yourself, "I'm sorry, I just didn't write this. It's there already."[38]

Jackson maintained throughout his career that he owed his inspiration to dreamlife and at the same time he and many people who worked with him stressed that he would stay up all night to write and rehearse songs and performances. The bewildering combination of creating while asleep and dreaming and not being able to sleep—even choosing not to sleep so as to create—gives Jackson a perplexing relationship to nocturnal spaces. In "What Went Wrong," Claire Hoffman and Brian Hiatt write for *Rolling Stone*:

> For the most part, nights seemed to be the biggest problem for Jackson—he had complained of insomnia for years. But it was also the time when he felt a higher power was channeling creativity to him. "I didn't get a whole lot of sleep last night," he would tell Ortega. "I was up working on music. That's when the information is coming, and when it's coming, you gotta work."[39]

As evidence during the 2005 child molestation trial, court documents include interviews with two former Neverland workers "who reported that Jackson regularly took as many as 40 Xanax a night in order to sleep."[40] For the final planned concert of his life, "This Is It," Jackson told Ortega: "I want this to be the most spectacular opening the audience has ever seen … I want them to *not be able to sleep*, because they are so amped up from what they saw."[41]

Jackson's most offensive behavior in the minds of his accusers was his insistence on sharing his bed with boys presumably so as to "sleep." When Diane Sawyer asked him in 1995 if he ever had sexual contact with "this child" (that is, Jordan Chandler) "or any other child," Jackson answered "*Never* ever. I could *never* harm a child or anyone. It's *not* in my heart. It's *not* who I am. And it's *not* what I'm interested … I'm *not* even interested in that."[42] Jackson's repetition of negations in his reply recall Barrie's initial appellation for Peter Pan's secret world as the

---

[38]   *Michael by the Editors of Rolling Stone*, 128.

[39]   Ibid., 199.

[40]   Ibid.

[41]   Ibid., 198. Author emphasis.

[42]   Author emphasis.

"*Never Never Never* Land" as if the resistance to time that seems to embrace eternal innocence doubles as a false denial of its passage. He insisted to Sawyer that he refused to stop sleeping with children, again repeating his use of negations: "If you are talking about sex, then that's a nut. It's *not* me. Go to the guy down the street, cause it's *not* Michael Jackson."[43] Jackson continued to openly declare his strong belief that there was nothing more pure and loving one could do than to share a bed with children, even as late as his interview with Bashir in 2003. What was going on during these times of supposed sleep with children? What was *not* going on?

Jackson's preoccupation with the uncertain line between sleeping and waking penetrated every aspect of his life and art. By conducting word searches on all of the music Jackson recorded throughout his career I have calculated that he uses the word "dream" at least 49 times in the lyrics to his songs. As both the *Thriller* and *Ghosts* videos show, dreams and nightmares kept alternating until they finally became indistinguishable in Jackson's creative universe. What I would like to suggest in this essay is that when seen through the lens of Jackson's successes and failures, queerness presents us with a crisis not simply because it opposes every fixed aspect of identity in the real world—gender, sexuality, race, age, and so on—but because to be fully queer is to pass wholly into a kind of dreamland. Even if this Neverland is the place human beings most long to visit, should they believe it to be real, it poses some terrible threats when it is made incarnate in the present moment.

As a master of performativity, Jackson may have become the most dazzling embodiment of queerness that the world has yet known. The danger of performing so well was that "Michael Jackson" almost completely disappeared. Became anonymous. A faded picture of Shirley Temple taped to a mirror backstage. A secret wish that the sun has carried away with it after the day is done. "People who didn't know me would come into a room expecting to be introduced to cute little Michael Jackson and they'd walk right past me. I would say, 'I'm Michael,' and they would look doubtful."[44] The danger was finally to exist as mere spectacle. The tragic turn in Jackson's life may show us that when taken to an absolute extreme the exhilarating potentiality of a queer future can never be *touched*. Jackson was both blessed and doomed to become a fascinatingly immaterial dream figure.

When the rapper Nas received the news of Jackson's death, he said "the weather immediately changed drastically. It suddenly rained so hard. Wind blew like crazy. Clouds did something different."[45] In spite of his uncannily shifting shape, the universe has deeply registered Jackson's presence. At the same time, like Peter Pan, the light of the world that Jackson made audible and visible can never be fully grasped. His rhinestone-studded, shimmering white glove sold for $420,000. Only through artifacts like music, art, video, film—those very dreamscapes where the tangible body is not—will Michael Jackson continue to come back to us.

---

[43]   Author emphasis.

[44]   Jackson, *Moonwalk*, 96.

[45]   *Michael by the Editors of Rolling Stone*, 155.

Chapter 4
Michael Jackson and the Quandary of Black Identity

Sherrow O. Pinder

The life of Michel Jackson is the perfect illustration of what colloquial conversation has termed the "identity crisis." In this Chapter, Sherrow Pinder focuses on the peculiarity of Jackson's racial identification by drawing on, among other ideas, W.E.B. Du Bois' "double consciousness" which leads to the existential question: "In reality, who am I?" Working through issues of White privilege and systematic violence towards deviant bodies, the chapter below posits that Jackson transcends dialectical relationship of self and other. Caught somewhere in between these categories, Jackson becomes an example of one possible outcome of postmodern otherness.

> The Negro is a sort of seventh son, born with a veil and gifted with second-sight in this American world—a world which yields him no true self consciousness, but only lets him sees himself through the revelation of the other world. It is a peculiar sensation, this double-consciousness, this sense of always looking at one's self through the eyes of others, of measuring one's soul by the tape of a world that looks on in amused contempt and pity.
>
> W.E.B. Du Bois, *The Souls of Black Folk*

> There is a fact: White men consider themselves superior to black men. There is another fact: Black men want to prove to white men, at all costs, the richness of their thought, the equal value of their intellect.
>
> Frantz Fanon, *Black Skin, White Masks*

In this chapter I focus on the peculiarity of Michael Jackson's racial identification by drawing from W.E.B. Du Bois' "double consciousness," and what the post-colonial scholar Frantz Fanon reveals as the doubling of identity, functioning as a narcissistic manifestation of the self in the "other," which represents a form of racial liminality. This alignment of a constructed and constructing self, or the "twoness" as Du Bois calls it, leads to the following question: What does it mean to be black in America?[1] In this discussion, this question is answered through

---

[1]   W.E.B. Du Bois, *The Souls of Black Folk* (New York: Modern Library, 2003), 5.

the theoretical lens of Frantz Fanon's *Black Skin, White Masks*. Like all blacks in America, Michael Jackson had difficulties in developing his sense of "self" in a culture that normalizes whiteness as an ontologically neutral category and upholds the subject as raceless and unmarked. Normalized whiteness created an identity "crisis" for Jackson that invites a negative reading, and also fuels famous comments such as "weird" or, as the tabloids nicknamed the singer, "Wacko Jacko." In fact, "weirdness" in the face of blackness should be subjected to the most excessive form of derision because blackness constructs a body that is already defiant of social norms. Given that the construction of blackness relies on an absolute contempt for the lived complexities of blackness and is always reduced to an authentic otherness, Jackson's identification process, as "a variation, a deviation, and a spacing" in relation to racial classification is far from simple.[2]

Jackson's desire to anchor himself in racial particularity, neither black nor white, is not dominated by a longing to undo blackness and retrieve towards whiteness but towards a form of racial ambiguity. Jackson's simultaneous performance and resistance to impose racial definitions, discussed by several authors in this collection, serve as an impasse between blackness and whiteness, which is locked in a symbiotic relationship of subordination (blackness) and domination (whiteness). Yet Jackson's racial in-betweenness still signals blackness and he continued to be seen through what Fanon calls the "corporeal malediction" of his unavoidable blackness.[3] Hence, like every black person in America, Jackson must live the color line, the racial divide, which bears witness to the existential dilemma that inhabits the very core of his sense of "self."

Identity is associated with norms of identification including blacks, women, and homosexuals, which assimilate individuals into social groups. An identity determines how a person belonging to an ascribed group should be treated. In this respect, the remorseless attempt to construct the category "black" has certain implications for racial identification. Because blackness is measured against whiteness and is reduced to otherness, it is, theoretically speaking, difficult for a black person to develop a solid sense of "self." As we will see with Jackson, racial identification becomes a deeply ambivalent and fragmented process, which for the most part leads to "the fragmentation of identity into infinitesimal plural identities,"[4] to use Diana Fuss's phrase, or what Homi Bhabha refers to a "third space," a liminal space of ambivalence in which I see Jackson as a racialized subject being discursively confined.[5]

---

[2]   Judith Revel, "Identity, Nature, Life: Three Biopolitical Deconstructions," *Theory, Culture & Society* 26, no. 6 (2009): 46.

[3]   Frantz Fanon, *Black Skin, White Masks*, trans. Charles Lam Markmann (New York: Grove Press, 1967), 111.

[4]   Diana Fuss, *Essentially Speaking: Feminism, Nature and Difference* (New York: Routledge, 1989), 104.

[5]   See Homi Bhabha, *The Location of Culture* (Oxford: Routledge, 1994), 53–6. Also see Marjorie Garber, *Vested Interests: Cross Dressing and Cultural Anxiety* (New York:

Blackness and Black Identity

Though blackness is surrounded by mythical and stereotypic expectations that preoccupy the collective imagination, what it means to be black in America has specific implications. In fact, the essentialization of blackness, which is fundamental for the representation of identity and the politics of difference,[6] is a fixated projection of a distinctly white intervention, where blackness, as a "device, can purify the impure … straying brothers and sisters," as Stuart Hall puts it.[7] However, as Jackson has shown, blacks' racial identity can never be fixed. If black identity is thought to be fully determined, we treat it as if it was genetics and, as such, it is constantly policed. Indeed, the aura of an authentic blackness feeds a special kind of comfort in America, because it conversely guarantees the status of whiteness.

Notwithstanding some common cultural particularities that make blacks "authentically" black (for example, there is a "black way," or tradition, of singing and dancing), as Anthony Appiah points out, "this putative authenticity screams out for recognition."[8] For Cornel West, this explicitly "rest[s] on a homogenizing impulse that assumed that all black people are really alike—hence obliterating differences (class, gender, sexual orientation) between black people."[9] Drawing on West's observation, bell hooks asserts that there is "the assumption that there is a black essence shaping all African American experience."[10] And if this is the case, then the fundamental complicatedness is that those elements that remain unique and particular to blacks as individuals have to be concealed or denied.

While blackness for the most part is wrought by the preeminence of whiteness and is constantly shaped and reshaped by a dominant white identity, blacks are trapped within the dialectics of performing whiteness on the one hand and resisting whiteness on the other. Consequently, racial self-identification develops

---

Routledge, 1997), 15. Here, Garber focuses on a "third" space created by transvestite activity. For her, this third space is "a mode of articulation, a way of describing a space of possibility," which for her, because of it binary logics of male/female, it provides little room for creative, counterhegemonic self-expression. On the other, I think it challenges normative gender performativity and creates Judith Butler's gender troubles.

[6]   The differences amongst blacks, women, and homosexuals, for example, have to be disregarded in the name of the politics of difference.

[7]   Stuart Hall, "What is this 'Black' in Black Popular Culture?," in *Black Studies Reader*, ed. Jacqueline Bobo et al. (New York: Routledge, 2004), 261.

[8]   Anthony Appiah, "Identity, Authenticity, Survival: Multiculturalism Societies and Social Reproduction," in *Multiculturalism: Examining the Politics of Recognition*, ed. Amy Gutmann (Princeton: Princeton University Press, 1994), 153.

[9]   Cornel West, *Keeping Faith: Philosophy and Race in America* (New York: Routledge, 1993), 17.

[10]   bell hooks, *Yearning: Race, Gender, and Cultural Politics* (New York: South End Press, 1990), 37.

into a pathological condition in which blacks' subjectivity becomes subjugated by a gaze that is directed through the episteme of whiteness. This experience of subjugation leads to an identity "crisis" and a mis-identification where the "self" and "other" have become implicated. The subject, hence, becomes an unsettled agent, in-between sameness (whiteness) and otherness (blackness). This in-betweeness is experienced first as corporeal, the material foundation of one's social and subjective continuation.[11] The experience of Jackson is the perfect illustration of this condition where his image starts and ends viciously disjointed. In this disjointedness, according to African American philosopher George Yancy, "one ceases to experience one's identity from a locus of self-definition and begins to experience one's identity from a locus of externally imposed meaning."[12] In other words, one is "forever in combat with [one's] own image" as the essential "other" of whiteness.[13] This is aptly analogous to Jean-Paul Sartre's articulation that it was the anti-Semite that fashioned the Jews and Simone de Beauvoir's understanding of white women as the indispensable "other" of white men. This is what is referred to as, "the order of otherness," to use Homi Bhabha's phrase.[14]

Given that whiteness can exist only as the immanent possibility of blackness as its assumed opposite (inferior, unnatural, and impure), "whiteness alone," as Toni Morrison cautions, "is mute, meaningless, unfathomable, pointless, frozen, veiled, curtained, dreaded, senseless, and implacable."[15] Blacks are held imprisoned by the overall power of whiteness, manifesting itself in two opposite directions, either outdoing or undoing blackness that is performatively acted out. Jackson and his quandary of identity, besides demonstrating the problematics of self-identification for blacks in America, provides a useful starting point to analyze the preeminence of whiteness and how it has constructed blackness.

While the black "self" is an infraction of a constructed "other," it is constantly interrogated, policed, and subverted. A black person is persistently, to use the title of one of the tracks from Jackson's album *Bad*, "A Man in the Mirror," haunted by a "self" that is persistently constituted and reconstituted by the tenacity of a white gaze that does not see blacks as equal to themselves. Hence, it is important for whites to position themselves as "different" from blacks. Whites project what Diana Fuss explains as identification's "alienation effect" onto blacks, who are "enjoined to identify and to dis-identify simultaneously with whites, to assimilate

---

[11]   Teresa de Lauretis, "Difference Embodied: Reflections on Black Skin, White Masks," *Parallax* 8 (2002): 56.

[12]   George Yancy, "Whiteness and the Return of the Black Body," *Journal of Speculative Philosophy* 19, no. 4 (2005): 235.

[13]   Fanon, *Black Skin, White Masks*, 194.

[14]   Bhabha, *The Location of Culture*, 61.

[15]   Toni Morrison, *Playing in the Dark: Whiteness and the Literary Imagination* (Cambridge: Harvard University Press, 1993), 59.

but not to incorporate, to approximate but not to displace."[16] Racial identification, in this respect, "carries an ontological and epistemological valence, such that the question, Who or What am I? becomes a question of being and knowing, a question of desire."[17]

The black self is made foreign and subsequently reconstituted within the discourse of race, which draws our attention to an identifiable source of power, safeguarding and replicating racial distinctions. The question, then, of what it means to invoke race as a social concept organizing blacks' identification is fundamental because blackness subjects individuals to an identification that is marked on the body. Consequently, a black person in North America has difficulties in developing his/her sense of self because the body is surrounded by an atmosphere of antagonism, which comes with an "implicit knowledge" about the black body that has a non-liberating effect. One of the repercussions of this is an ambivalent self-identification, a denial of the self. With remarkable insistence, this knowledge is insightfully described by Jackson in his song "I Can't Help It," in which he has this to say: "I look in my mirror and it took me by surprise … I can't help it if I wanted to." This identification provides for a radical reading of identity formation, which reflects Jackson's identity as solely representational, consequently alienating him from the self. With Jackson, what we see is a kind of self-othering in relations to the dominant norms of race constructions, another form of otherness within the "other," a sort of racial ambiguity, neither black nor white, a kind of postmodern racial subject as the only possible self. In fact, as Judith Butler recognizes, "the disruption of the Other at the heart of the self is the very condition of the self's possibility."[18]

The "possible self" symbolizes one's thought of what one ought to be and what one is fearful of becoming. Jackson's life is a good demonstration of this possible self, which is revealed on his body, not black or white, woman or man, heterosexual or homosexual. This conclusion is consistent with his claim, "I wouldn't help it even if I could," pointing to the fact that Jackson does not see his representation "as an awkward or deliberate failure."[19] According to Cynthia J. Fuchs, "whenever he appears in public—say on stage for '*Motown* 25,' on television with Oprah Winfrey for their momentous interview, in Monte Carlo at the 1993 World Music Awards—his history is recounted through video imagery, reconfirming that his body is the site of a visibly identity, an effect of erasure,

---

16   Diana Fuss, "Interior Colonies: Frantz Fanon and the Politics of Identification," *Diacritics* 21, no. 2/3 (1994): 24.

17   de Lauretis, "Difference Embodied," 54.

18   Judith Butler, "Imitation and Gender Insubordination," in *Inside/Out: Lesbian Theories, Gay Theories*, ed. Diana Fuss (New York: Routledge, 1991), 27.

19   Seth Silberman, "Presenting Michael Jackson," *Social Semiotics* 17, no. 4 (2007): 423.

repetition, and resurrection."[20] It is indeed a body that is discursively constructed and deconstructed, culturally imposed and refuted, and undoubtedly bound by the "corporeal malediction," as Fanon calls it, of his inescapable "otherness" buried deep within his blackness.[21]

Jackson and Racial Identification

Jackson is positioned on the borderline between the self and the "other." This ambivalent self-identification or, in this case, dis-identification of the subject from himself is the consequence of a perverse uncertainty many of my fellow authors in this collection are examining: the unnatural/ natural, black/white, woman/ man, mother/father, homosexual/heterosexual, disabled/non-disabled matrix. Is Michael Jackson an other *other*? Diana Fuss defines other "others" as "subjects who do not quite fit into the rigid boundary definitions of (dis)similitude, or who indeed may be left out of the Self/Other binary altogether."[22] Because of Jackson's severe redundancy of artifactual otherness made possible through skin bleaching, hair straightening, and countless plastic surgeries, I want to suggest that he is "an other other." Drawing from Butler's notion of gender performativity to a non-normative construction of sexuality as "queer performativity," the non-normative construction of Jackson's raced identity can be seen as race performativity, which become reified and realized through repetitive performativity and daily acts.

Jackson's disquieting racial ambiguity has significantly been marked as postmodern and posthuman.[23] There is no "real" Jackson. Elizabeth Taylor once compared him to E.T. because of "their mutual alien-ness, their distance from the planet earth, their ambiguous sex."[24] As many of my colleagues in this book point out, Jackson's art provides him a space wherein he is able to perform multiple identities: in his video for *Thriller*, Jackson is a werewolf and zombie; in the *Smooth Criminal* video, he is a Robocop-like metallic figure and 1920s gangster icon; Jackson appears as a 30-foot tall statue in his 1995 promotional video for *HIStory*; and so on. Gilles Deleuze and Félix Guatteri call Jackson a "body without organs," a declaration that is discussed and debated with a postmodernist flair, which as a result reads non-being, non-human. Similarly, blacks can often be positioned in such a way that they are constantly dehumanized. In fact, if blacks

---

[20]   Cynthia J. Fuchs, "Michael Jackson's Penis," in *Cruising the Performative: Interventions into the Representation of Ethnicity, Nationality, and Sexuality*, ed. Sue-Ellen Case et al. (Bloomington, IN: Indiana University Press, 1995), 17.

[21]   Fanon, *Black Skin, White Masks*, 111.

[22]   Fuss, "Interior Colonies," 22.

[23]   Greg Graham-Smith, "Habeas Corpus: Bodies of Evidence and Performed Litigiousness: The Spectacle of Michael Jackson's Trial," *Communication: South African Journal for Communication Theory and Research* 34, no. 2 (2008): 279.

[24]   Fuchs, "Michael Jackson's Penis," 19.

are seen as being equally human as whites are, they can go beyond the boundary of race and, like whites, can be viewed as raceless. Sadly, in the end, blacks are not, in Morrison's words, seen as being "worthy to be treated as whites."[25] It makes sense, then, that specific epistemology, ideologies, and practices are in place to systematically sanction and protect white privilege.

Jackson is determined to break away from the construction of blackness as a sign of deficiency, disapproval, and lack. Instead, he forges a form of identity that goes against constructed blackness. In so doing, he displays a fragmented self-representation, a sort of non-self-representation. However, blacks cannot escape America's practice of "physical identity formation"[26] and are forever confronted by what W.E.B. Du Bois describes as a "peculiar sensation," this "double consciousness ... this sense of always looking at one's self through the eyes of others," shaping blacks' subjectivity as "mixed up" and fragmented.[27] And as a result of this fragmentation, inner/outer, self/other, Jackson seemingly appears for the masses as not "normal." In fact, that which is "normal" is inevitably natural and it becomes the source of "truth." This emphasis on the natural is another way to transform the subject or social being into, what Judith Revel observes, "a new instrument of control."[28]

Jackson's appearance deconstructs and challenges the corporeal notions of natural bodies and fixed identities as prearranged and controlled; in Chapters 10 and 11, Raphael Raphael and Julie-Ann Scott respectively discuss this in the context of disability and normative physicality. It is exactly for this reason that Jackson must be politically and culturally resisted, restricted, or worse, punished and humiliated in order for society to safeguard the realm of normality. Indeed, Jackson must be "normalized." In an effort to "normalize" Jackson, the police brazenly photographed and displayed his penis as a part of the evidence in the alleged child molestation charges against Jackson. Jackson's penis, as Erni explains, "stands for the 'alleged crime' scene ... unlike hair samples, fingerprints, or human tissues that can serve to mark a crime and the crime scene."[29] And even though child molestation is a serious issue in the United States, it cannot be treated as something separate and apart from the laws and institutes that construct and define race, gender, and sexuality norms. For instance, in his work "A Foucauldian (Genealogical) Reading of Whiteness," George Yancy explores:

---

[25]   Toni Morrison, "Unspeakable Things Unspoken: The Afro-American Presence in Literature" (presentation, Tanner Lecturers on Human Value, University of Michigan, October, 1988), 144.

[26]   Fuss, "Interior Colonies," 22.

[27]   Du Bois, *The Souls of Black Folk*, 5.

[28]   Revel, "Identity, Nature, Life," 51.

[29]   John Enri, "Queer Figurations in the Media: Critical Reflections on the Michael Jackson Sex Scandal," *Critical Studies in Mass Communication* 15 (1998): 169.

> how members of a society are trained to perceive themselves as having a certain sexual nature through the deployment of theories and practices that define that nature and so determine the realms of the normal and the abnormal.[30]

Yet we must be cautious of the operation of "truths" about sexuality that control and stigmatize the racialized body as a sexed being. With the media coverage of Jackson's child molestation charges, where his penis is treated as evidence, morality and ethics are transformed into a provocative forum of a familiar black racial aesthetic.

Displaying Jackson's penis in the evidence files in order to humiliate him recasts the focus on child molestation to black masculinity within the framework of heteronormativity and the larger racial discourse concerning the sexuality of black men as a threat to the white social body. The mythical norm of the black penis plays into whites' fears, vulnerabilities, and hypersensitivities of the imaginary dangers of black masculinity. In Michel Cournot's *Martinique*, Cournot gets to the heart of the issue. Quoting Cournot, Lewis R. Gordon writes:

> The black man's sword is a sword. When he has thrust it into your wife, she has really felt something. It is a revelation. In the chasm that it has left, your little toy is lost ... Four *nègres* with their penises exposed would fill a cathedral. They would be unable to leave the building until their erections had subsided; and in such close quarters that would not be a simple matter.[31]

The penis is a metaphorical substitute for the black man. As Gordon explains, "one is no longer aware of the *nègre* but only of a penis. He is a penis" and consequently in constant danger of literal and symbolic castration.[32]

In America, to use Fanon's title of chapter 5 in *Black Skin, White Mask*, "*L'expérience vécue du Noir*" (the lived experience of the black), is one of dislocation from the self, split by black skin and white masks. For this reason, a black man "suffers in his body quite differently from the white man."[33] The harrowing inscription of race on the body makes it difficult for a black person to construct a solid and secure sense of "self." For this reason, the development of a sense of "self" for the black subject is never physiological but always cultural-

---

[30]   George Yancy, "A Foucauldian (Genealogical) Reading of Whiteness: The Production of the Black Body/Self and the Racial Deformation of Pecola Breedlove in Toni Morrison's *The Bluest Eye*," in *What White Looks Like: African-American Philosophers on the Whiteness Question*, ed. George Yancy (New York: Routledge, 2004), 111.

[31]   Lewis R. Gordon, "A Questioning Body of Laughter and Tears: Reading Black Skin, White masks Through the Cat and Mouse of Reason and a Misguided Theodicy," *Parallax* 8, no. 2 (2002): 21.

[32]   Ibid.

[33]   Fanon, *Black Skin, White Masks*, 138.

physical because black identity is culturally inscribed on his/her body. Stuart Hall writes:

> It is one thing to position a subject or a set of people as the other of a dominant discourse. It is quite another thing to subject them to that kind of 'knowledge' not only as a matter of imposed knowledge and domination, by the power of inner compulsion and subject confirmation to the norm."[34]

In the end, for the marginalized like Jackson, coming to terms with the existential dilemma of self-definition becomes problematical.

The outcome is always looking at oneself through the eyes of the culturally constituted white gaze. This gaze forces upon a black person an unusual weight, which can lead to pathological behavior, as the multiple plastic surgeries that Jackson underwent attest. What he can hope for, at best, is pseudo-recognition, a white mask. In fact, this is the trick of whiteness as structured in everyday life. As Yancy has shown, "it is to give the appearance of fixity, where the look of the white subject interpolates the black subject as inferior, which in turn, bars the black subject from seeing him/herself without the internalization of the white gaze."[35] Hence, the black body has to police and regulate itself because it has internalized the white gaze.

A black person who entertains the very possibility of crossing over racial boundaries must be policed at whatever cost. Fanon's analysis in *The Wretched of the Earth* and Michel Foucault's in *Discipline and Punish*, on how the body, the state, and violence are linked, corresponds with America's history of institutionalized violence, which counted on "men to kill some white people to keep them white and to kill many blacks to keep them black."[36] At the moment when the biology of race as a foundation for racial knowledge has been attacked from the left through the discourse of race as a social construction and the right through the discourse of colorblindness, fixing the truth of race on the body is fundamental.[37]

Even though Jackson's skin became "whiter" —"less ebony, more ivory"— as Michael Awkward puts it,[38] it is too simplistic to argue that he was unfixing "race

---

[34]   Stuart Hall, "Cultural Identity and Diaspora," in *Colonial Discourse and Postcolonial Theory: A Reader*, ed. Patricia Williams and Laura Chrisman (New York: Columbia University Press, 1994), 395.

[35]   Yancy, "Return of the Black Body," 217.

[36]   Lerone Bennett, Jr., *The Shaping of Black American Thought: The Struggles and Triumphs of African-Americans, 1619–1990s* (Chicago: Johnson Publishing Company, 1975), 73.

[37]   Macarena Gómez-Barris and Herman Gray, "Michael Jackson, Television, and Post-op Disaster," *Television & News Media* 7, no. 1 (2006): 44.

[38]   Michael Awkward, *Negotiating Difference: Race, Gender, and the Politics of Positionality* (Chicago: University of Chicago Press, 1996), 179.

on the body."[39] In fact, there are many blacks that pass for white. However, while hooks has rightfully located blacks' desire for lighter skin as a result of a "racist imagination" and "a colonized black mindset," today, passing is no longer about looking white; it is about getting a license for entry into "honorary whiteness."[40] Yet, it does, unfortunately, require freeing oneself from the labels associated with blackness and adopting a way of life that permits for the association of white images, presenting oneself, or being presented to a white society in a way that make whites feel protected and unsusceptible. It is like joining a private club. Once you have become a member you must put up with the rules. Consequently, even if Jackson passed for "white," he needed to adhere to a specific form of whiteness, which unremittingly accompanied the interior "whitening" process. Whiteness, in this sense, does not stand apart from the exterior inscription of whiteness upon the body. For this reason, a poor white person learns the attitudes and behaviors that are tied to whiteness as a fundamental defining signifier of white superiority. In the end, even if Jackson is savaging his African physiognomy, as Greg Tate's "'I'm White!' What's Wrong with Michael Jackson" notes, Jackson's skin becoming "whiter" cannot be considered transformative of an unavoidable script of a particular morphological body that is considered as black.[41] Hank Steuever, a journalist for the *Washington Post*, says it best: "a black man is still a black man, underneath it all, no matter where life takes him even if that man is Michael Jackson."[42]

For Jackson, having a black American identity was important. We use identities to construct our lives. Identities provide a nexus for membership into groups based on race, gender, sexuality, ethnicity, nationality, disability, and religious prescriptions. Jackson, in an interview with Oprah Winfrey on February 10, 1993, stated: "I'm a black American ... I'm proud to be a black American. I'm proud of my race." Interestingly, the emphasis here on black American suggests a split subjectivity, black and American, "two souls ... in one dark body," as W.E.B. Du Bois explains it.[43]

For Jackson, even though he acknowledges his pride in being black, in songs like "Black and White," it is not about him confirming his racial identity, but, as Julian Vigo has argued in Chapter 2, about refusing the constraint of identification in racial terms. "I am tired of this stuff ... I am not going to spend my life being a color," he acknowledges. In the end, he merely begs society not to "black or white [him]." These words read as Jackson's intimation to move beyond race because

---

[39]   Gómez-Barria and Gary, "Michael Jackson, Television, and Post-op Disaster," 44.

[40]   bell hooks, *Outlaw Culture Resisting Representation* (New York: Routledge, 1994), 179.

[41]   Greg Tate, "'I'm White!' What's Wrong with Michael Jackson," *The Village Voice*, September 22, 1987, 15–17.

[42]   Hank Steuever, "Moonwalker in Neverland," *The Washington Post*, December 11, 2000, C1.

[43]   Du Bois, *The Souls of Black Folk*, 5.

race is, as Jackson claims, "where your blood comes from." In this sense, he is "a slave" not to racial normalcy and cultural inscriptions, but to his own sense of his racial identity as "different, non-identical, and non-identitary."[44] Even though what constitutes a black identity is never fixed, he is considered a traitor to his race, as is expressed by several tabloids. Indeed, in Jackson's quest to transcend racial boundaries, he is the precise embodiment of James Weldon Johnson's "ex-colored man," a liminal figure, living on the margins of racial normalcy, neither black nor white, the embodiment of a fragmented self, fractured, and dislocated repeatedly.

Jackson and His Fragmented "Self"

According to Seth Clarke Silberman:

> Despite his showy style, Michael Jackson remains something of an enigma. On stage with one of his sequined jump suits, he's a flamboyant picture of grace, a sleek jaguar ready to pounce. In photographs, he's a creature of sweet sexuality, beguiling, angelic, androgynous. In person, though, he's quiet and reserved, a gangling young man of cagey reticence, with a childlike aura of wonder."[45]

The "polymorphous ambiguities of Jackson,"[46] as Erni puts it, demonstrate "a maze of narrative all running in complex and different directions,"[47] which is often simplified by popular media as "weird." How does Jackson's "weirdness" challenge identification as well as mis-identification, the doubling of "otherness"—informing his race and gender self-alienation? Does his "weirdness," anchored in being not black or white, man or woman, create anxiety because it can be positioned in a framework of meaning and subjectivity as sites for interrogation and subversion? It is to Jackson's "weirdness" that I will like to redirect our attention. In what follows, I want to locate his "weirdness" within a larger framework of identification. Identification, as a desired accomplishment, is never achieved. What it does is unnerve the "self."

Jackson's numerous plastic surgeries can be interpreted as a denial of his black identity. They are a way to reconfigure, what Everett V. Stonequist, borrowing Robert E. Park's phrase, calls, "the marginal man," caught up in the meta-language of race.[48] The marginal man is "living and sharing intimately in the cultural life and

---

[44]   Revel, "Identity, Nature, Life," 46.

[45]   Silberman, "Presenting Michael Jackson," 421.

[46]   Enri, "Queer Figurations in the Media: Critical Reflections on the Michael Jackson Sex Scandal," 158.

[47]   Graham-Smith, "Habeas Corpus," 279.

[48]   For others responses to Jackson's plastic surgeries, see Kathy Davis, "Surgical Passing: Or Why Jackson Nose Makes 'Us' Uneasy," *Feminist Theory* 4, no. 1 (2003):

traditions of two distinct people," one is black and the other is white.[49] Blacks in America live with this contradiction. Jackson, for one, is incapable of convincing himself that he is not white, unwilling to accept the harsh consequences of being black in a racist society. Instead he relegates himself to moving between racial spaces. In a white world, the black man is *bad* and *dangerous*. Fanon explains that "in the unconscious, black equals ugliness, sin, darkness, immorality."[50] Paradoxically, Ruth Frankenberg argues that whites see themselves as unraced, as just "human."[51] Hence, whites have the misanthropic audacity to bolster the meaning of the "human." In the white imaginary, to be black and human is impossible; black and human are paradoxical terms.

There is a particular racial etiquette, a particular performance of blackness that has to measure up to whiteness and thus is reduced to otherness. A black person is made aware of his or her condition as a second-class status through what Fanon labels an "implicit knowledge" of systemic racial inequality such as racial profiling. In this regard, we can follow Fanon's logic that for blacks, the unconscious is nonexistent "since the racial drama is played out in the open, the black man has no time to make it unconscious."[52] His feelings of inferiority are always "conscious"[53] and not repressed in the Freudian sense.[54] However, how this consciousness (implicit knowledge) is played out becomes important. For one, blacks are not free from the trauma that accompanied such knowledge.

"What is often called the black soul is a white man's artifact," Fanon concludes.[55] Living in a society marked by whiteness, Jackson, like all blacks in America, is split into this "twoness," an inner and an outer being, the black skin and the white mask. To use the words of Gordon, "he is 'out there' without an inside";[56] or as Fanon suggests, as "an object in the midst of other objects, [experiencing] his being through others," caged in by this overpowering objectivity.[57] This location Jackson finds himself in consequently begs the question that Du Bois asks in *The Souls of Black Folk*: "How does it feel to be a problem?" To contemplate this issue, I must return to Yancy:

73–92; Awkward, 176–7.

[49]   Everett V. Stonequist, "The Problem of the Marginal Man," *American Journal of Sociology* 41: 1 (1935, 1–12): 3.

[50]   Fanon, *Black Skin, White Masks*, 192.

[51]   See Ruth Frankenberg, ed., *Displacing Whiteness: Essays in Social and Cultural Criticism* (Durham: Duke University Press, 1997).

[52]   Fanon, *Black Skin, White Masks*, 111.

[53]   Ibid., 150.

[54]   Fanon is indeed aware that the fragmented or disjointed identification of the subject from himself/herself is in dire need of psychoanalysis. Also, see de Lauretis 2002, 59–61.

[55]   Fanon, *Black Skin, White Masks*, 16.

[56]   Gordon, "A Questioning Body," 15.

[57]   Fanon, *Black Skin, White Masks*, 109.

When black people are asked the same question by white Americans, the relations of being black and being a problem is non-contingent. It is a necessary relation. Outgrowing this ontological state of being a problem is believed impossible. Hence, when regarding one's existence as problematic, temporality is frozen. One is a problem forever. However, it is important to note that it is from the white imaginary that the question 'How does it feel to be a problem?' is given birth.[58]

In other words, blacks are not the "problem"; the "problem" is the propensity to construct blacks as the source of conflict. Blacks cannot break away from the objective frame of power and its authoritarian dimensions, which is exercised on the lived reality of their daily life. Jackson, for one, wants to rid himself of the stigma of color, to become what dialecticians terms an "absolute being; a being that stands in the way of human being or a human way of being."[59]

Conclusion

In this chapter, I draw on the problematics of an essentialized blackness and the specific implications that are associated with blackness, in an attempt to provide particular insights into racial identification. Given that blacks experience their being through a normalized whiteness, "identification becomes a pathological condition,"a melancholia and a perversion, which inadvertently takes on an unusual form of racial identification.[60] Jackson's racial identification is related to the other cultural representation of alterity that implicates him as being "weird." His preoccupation with racial and gender in-betweenness, not black or white, man or woman, an otherness within the "other," a body that is unrepresentative but yet signals blackness has promoted anxiety among the masses. As Butler reminds us, some modes of appearance for category such as race "are marked and some are unmarked, which means that some stand out, such as blackness, as visible social signs, whereas whiteness, which is no less social is nevertheless part of the taken-for-granted visual field, a sign of its presumptive hegemony."[61]

---

[58]   Yancy, "Return of the Black Body," 237.

[59]   Gordon, "A Questioning Body," 10.

[60]   Fanon, *Black Skin, White Masks*, 109.

[61]   Judith Butler, "Appearances Aside," in *Prejudicial Appearances: The Logic of American Antidiscrimination Law*, ed. Robert C. Post et al. (Durham, NC: Duke University Press, 2001), 79.

PART II
Music and Image

Chapter 5

The "Split" Biography: *Man in the Mirror*: *The Michael Jackson Story*

Jesse Schlotterbeck

This chapter centers on the made-for-TV biopic Man in the Mirror: The Michael Jackson Story *(VH1, 2004). However, as many of the artifacts made by or about Jackson exhibit, this highly un-theorized film proves to be much more than simple entertainment. Jesse Schlotterbeck uses key ideas from media studies and psychoanalytic theory to help readers see how the film becomes a salient metaphor by which to understand split subjectivity, divided reception, and conflicted star image. Moving beyond the film itself and into discussions of our consumption of celebrity, this chapter works to expose the vivid details of "ambivalent fandom," a process by which we both desire benefit for and destruction of those we deem stars.*

A scene near the end of VH1's *Man in the Mirror: The Michael Jackson Story* shows Jackson overworking himself to the point of utter exhaustion in a dance space before a studio mirror. His manager, concerned for the star's health, tries unsuccessfully to restrain Jackson's preparation. A series of jump cuts (portraying the obsessive practice of the same act) and a rhythmic, foreboding score mark Jackson's preparation as repetition-compulsion. Finally, as Jackson collapses, the film's optical point-of-view moves from unstable to intentionally incoherent. While the jump cuts which conveyed his excessive rehearsal were difficult to view, his fall is accompanied with rapid panning shots and such decentered, mobile short takes that the scene is nausea-inducing, even on television. Jackson is completely decentered and unstable. Then, the scene's tone shifts entirely. A series of close-ups appear surrounded by the glare of spotlights (of Liz Taylor, Jackson's father, Diana Ross, and his manager) accompanied with a mild, lullaby-like score. Diana Ross tells him "We love you Michael," while his father insists, "I made you what you are." Thus, the scene divides Jackson into two self-perceptions: one of a dissolving, failing self and another of a great, incredibly accomplished self. Just after Jackson collapses, he is visited by voices telling him he is entitled and obligated to greatness. What is it that attracts the mass audience to such a split presentation of the star subject—the celebrity that appears to be so much more and so much less than we are?

It should not be surprising that cultural texts play out this drama of overvaluation and devaluation if we consider the centrality of splitting to ego formation. In Lacan's well-cited account of the mirror stage, the infant's recognition of his own reflection reveals a mode of understanding the self that is central to psychic life. At this moment, the infant has a dual sense of both power and powerlessness, as he is both aware of his own neediness and lack of mobility, while, at the same time, he aggrandizes the image he sees before him, as more than it actually is, as a self whose importance, attractiveness, and so on, is greatly exaggerated.[1] This sense of a split self will continue to define the subject's experience of his relationship to the social world. To know both an insufficient self from within while also imagining and performing a fully sufficient self from without "gives rise to an inexhaustible squaring of the ego's audits" whose perpetual conflict will continue to define the subject's negotiation of self-image and satisfaction.[2] Where the ego's negotiation of these identifications is largely an unconscious process, a film like *Man in the Mirror* makes this movement visible and accessible—but in a way that is located comfortably outside of the self. Here, the valuation of a subject is the central question at stake in the drama. The film pitches two opposite conclusions and moves dizzyingly between the possibilities that Jackson may be a misunderstood, childlike star who we ought to celebrate, or that he may be a monstrous predator. In short, he is either the best sort of person or the worst. The fact that this split-identification is carried out via this bizarre star (such an other) frees spectators from supposing that this representation might have anything to do with them—an ideal condition for a powerful unconscious identification.

My analysis of *Man in the Mirror* positions this television biopic as a symptomatic cultural text which has much to teach us about popular investment in scandalous celebrity. While some of this analysis is specific to Jackson (the magnitude of his stardom is matched by appropriately greater degrees of overvaluation and undervaluation), split consumption is broadly characteristic of media coverage and fan reception of stars. Discussions of celebrities provide a social sphere in which ruthless evaluations of worthiness are permitted and safe. By comparison, everyday gossip requires much more careful and cautious negotiation.

---

[1]   "[T]he mirror stage is a drama whose internal pressure pushes precipitously from insufficiency to anticipation—and, for the subject caught up in the lure of spatial identification, turns out fantasies that proceed from a fragmented image of the body to what I will call an "orthopedic" form of its totality—and to the finally donned armor of an alienating identity that will mark his entire mental development with its rigid structure. Thus, the shattering of the *Innenwelt* to *Umwelt* gives rise to an inexhaustible squaring of the ego's audits." Jacques Lacan, "The Mirror Stage as Formative of the *I* Function as Revealed in Psychoanalytic Experience," in *Ecrits: A Selection*, trans. Bruce Finkin (London: Norton, 2002), 97.

[2]   The private self and the self seen in the mirror coordinate with the other dichotomies that define psychoanalysis: Superego and Id, Object and Lack, and Fantasy and the Real.

In her study of diva narratives, Melissa Bradshaw considers this apparently contradictory kind of fandom. Looking at the rise-and-fall stories of female pop singers (such as Britney Spears), Bradshaw finds fans equally invested in the star figure's success *and* failure. Bradshaw's description of the fan's ambivalent investment in the star bears close resemblance to the double-sidedness of Jackson's reception:

> Even as we cheer her on, buy her records, and stare at the pictures of her we have taped to our walls, our adoration is equivocal: we are resentful of her successes and secretly hope for her failures. We want her to give and give until she cracks, and when she cracks we want to be in the front row, ready to witness every moment of her abjection and shame.[3]

In explaining the appeal of this ambivalent figure, Bradshaw reads the diva "as a stand-in for the fetishized mother—and a properly feminine self—that we ambivalently adore, mourn, and hate."[4] This reading of the diva's social/ psychological function helps explain the attraction of Jackson's narrative to a mass audience as well. Although Bradshaw correlates this kind of ambivalent consumption with the "diva" and the "mother," this analysis of Jackson illustrates that ambivalent fandom (equally invested in celebrating and denigrating) is not restricted to the female star. Bradshaw outlines the "straightforward narrative trajectory" of divadom as follows:

> [U]nderdog with big talent and/or hunger for fame overcomes hardships of impoverished beginnings to make it big; along the way makes choice to sacrifice normative womanhood for artistic and/or commercial success; with stardom comes the crisis of maintaining stardom; star inevitably dims, either through tragedy or aging; diva dies alone.[5]

This plotline bears very close resemblance to the musical biopic narrative— whether the protagonist is male or female. Bradshaw's gender specific approach elides the fact that identity formation (as elaborated in Lacan's "mirror stage") for both men *and* women is characterized by this dual process of aggrandizement and doubt. This ambivalence is expressed often in the biopic. By Robert Rosenstone's broad account, this genre positions lead subjects "as exemplars of lives, actions, and individual value systems we either admire or dislike or admire and dislike."[6]

---

[3]   Melissa Bradshaw, "Devouring the Diva: Martyrdom as Feminist Backlash in *The Rose*," *Camera Obscura* 21 (2008): 71.

[4]   Ibid.

[5]   Ibid.

[6]   Robert Rosenstone, "In Praise of the Biopic," in *Lights, Camera, History: Portraying the Past in Film*, ed. Richard Francaviglia and Jerry Rodnitsky (College Station: Texas A&M University Press, 2007), 12.

In Jackson's case, the presentation of the celebrity as *more than* and *less than* is consistent across both his own work and cultural productions about him. In addition to a close analysis of the VH1 film, I will analyze how Jackson's own work contributes to his split presentation and reception. In the latter half of his career, Jackson increasingly made his life story and reputation the subject of his songs. The commercial, pop style of Jackson's songs pairs oddly with the personal appeals of his lyrics. In a broad-ranging analysis of his work since the late 1980s, I analyze Jackson's performance of his star image in songs ("Man in the Mirror," "Leave Me Alone," "Black or White," "Scream," and "Childhood"), videos, and cover art. While Jackson denounced *Man in the Mirror* as an inaccurate representation of his life, I show how the unauthorized film and Jackson's own material display a similar investment in splitting. This tendency, to divide understandings of the self and others into categories of absolute sufficiency or lack, is a textual commonality of both the entertainer's material and the biopic.

Man in the Mirror bears out the kind of double-sided presentation—with both an aggrandized and devalued representation of Jackson. VH1 produced this biopic at a time when Jackson was more defined by scandal and infamy than celebration. After Jackson was first accused of child abuse in 1993, his musical production was sporadic. He released just two albums in the final 16 years of his life: *HIStory: Past, Present, and Future, Book I* (1995) and *Invincible* (2001). A 2002 decision by Jackson's camp to authorize a tell-all television special in which the star would openly discuss his now-scandalous reputation ended up backfiring. This 2003 documentary *Living with Michael Jackson*, discussed in more detail by Amy Billone and others in this collection, appeared as a feature special on British television and ABC. In part of the interview, Jackson holds the hand of an adolescent and discusses the fact that they sometimes share a bed. Just after the special aired, the boy who appeared in the film alleged abuse and "Jackson was charged with seven counts of child molestation and two counts of administering an intoxicating agent in relation to the boy."[7]

Ironically, Jackson's effort to be better understood and more widely accepted via participation in this project resulted in the opposite effect: not only increasing the scandal of his star image but leading to criminal charges. These charges and the British-produced television special are the key antecedents to the VH1 film. Both events are prominently featured in *Man in the Mirror* which, remarkably, was conceived, created, and aired within a year of their occurrence. Much like Jackson's own songs, this tele-film works via the presentation of a split self. Jackson is portrayed as scandalously out of control and as a great talent who was also a victim. Before turning to a close analysis of the film and its reception, it is worth considering the biographical film (or biopic) as a genre.

---

[7]   John Randall Taraborrelli, *Michael Jackson: The Magic, The Madness, The Whole Story, 1958–2009* (London: Sidgwick & Jackson, 2009), 640.

Legitimating the Biopic

The biopic stands as one of the most popular but least analyzed Hollywood genres. George Custen, one of the few film scholars to devote significant attention to the biopic, writes that "a biographical film is one that depicts the life of a historical person, past or present ... whose real name is used."[8] While this is a broad definition, he clarifies that this is a product of the variation that the genre has accommodated: "Other than this trait [of treating a true life story] the definition of what constitutes a biopic—and with it, what counts as fame—shifts anew with each generation."[9] Custen notes the wide variation of biographical subjects and the tenor of their treatment, from the biopic as "hagiography," to "headliners (good or bad)," to the increased treatment "entertainers themselves."[10]

The emergence of television shifts the balance in the biopic's typical treatment of their star subjects. Mary Desjardins notes that "Contemporary biopics associate authenticity with knowledge of scandal."[11] Custen correlates this shift of emphasis with television's increased use of biographical programming: "TV biopics would, for the most part, focus on the seedy or pathological angle of fame, leaving Hollywood with its increasingly outdated and unhip 'great man' approach."[12] While I agree with Custen's claims that the biopic increasingly became a television genre characterized by "pathography," I disagree with his conclusion that its movement toward scandal and television makes the genre less important or less worthy of critical attention.[13]

Instead of dismissing the biopic's turn against the "great man" film, the increasing presentation of the split subject offers a way of understanding our investment in consuming stars and celebrities. Jackson's story, which features even more exaggerated contrast between dysfunction and massive popularity, is a case-in-point film for the genre as a whole—as every biopic (to a certain extent) relies upon a selectively presented, split subject whose goodness, badness, or potential for both is exaggerated for dramatic effect.

If critics of the biopic have noted how part of the genre's appeal lies in the spectator's identification with the lead's desires and anxieties, this has been explained at an undertheorized, everyday level. Dennis Bingham offers the following conclusion:

---

[8]   George F. Custen, *Bio/Pics: How Hollywood Constructed Public History* (New Brunswick: Rutgers University Press, 1992), 5–6.

[9]   Ibid.

[10]   Ibid., 6.

[11]   Mary Desjardins, "The Incredible Shrinking Star: Todd Haynes and the Case History of Karen Carpenter," *Camera Obscura* 19 (2004): 34.

[12]   George F. Custen, "The Mechanical Life in the Age of Human Reproduction: American Biopics, 1961–1980," *Biography* 23, no. 1 (2000): 148.

[13]   Ibid., 134.

> We would love to imagine our own lives in story form, wouldn't we, ourselves as the subjects of our own biopics? Perhaps in cultures that most celebrate a myth of the individual, biopics are devoutly to be desired, for the same reasons that any hint of conventional generic form is deplored.[14]

As Bingham indicates, the biopic's contradictory valuation is matched by the social anxiety that attends the "myth of the individual." Richard Dyer has also addressed the maintenance of an ideology of the "individual" through star studies. He writes that stars:

> articulate both the promise and the difficulty that the notion of individuality presents for all of us who live by it. "The individual" is a way of thinking and feeling about the discrete human person, including oneself, as a separate and coherent entity.[15]

While ideas of freedom and meritocracy remain dominant values in capitalist societies, "a necessary fiction for the reproduction of the kind of society we live in," Dyer emphasizes that maintenance of this discourse is always incomplete and emotionally fraught: "Stars articulate these ideas of personhood, in large measure shoring up the notion of the individual but also at times registering doubts and anxieties attendant on it."[16] In this study, I combine both approaches, studying both the construction of celebrity, and the biographical film genre as primary sites where we work out the problems of the individual.

Representing the Split Subject

The presentation of a split subject, such as Jackson, both threatens and appeals to the spectator due to unconscious identification. We are compelled by such a vision of the outermost possibilities of our being—someone both much greater and more able than ourselves, and someone much more shameful and abject, as well. How is this duality expressed, more specifically, by the film? Few viewers, save the most invested Jackson fans or followers, would describe *Man in the Mirror* as a good film. It is a bewildering, restless depiction that moves rapidly among many of the high and low points of Jackson's career. The production values of the film are middling, the script is merely sufficient, and the acting is fair. In nearly every textual dimension, *Man in the Mirror* resembles a film that was rushed through production in order to capitalize on the timeliness of its subject. Yet, curiously,

---

[14]   Dennis Bingham, *Whose Lives Are They Anyway?: The Biopic as Contemporary Film Genre* (New Brunswick: Rutgers University Press, 2010), 403.

[15]   Richard Dyer, *Heavenly Bodies: Film Stars and Society* (New York: Routledge, 2004), 7.

[16]   Ibid., 9.

the same features that make it flimsy and inconsistent are the same aspects that also make the film especially open—to a diversity of interpretations and audience interests.

Jackson stands out as a divisive public figure—adored and worshipped by some, lampooned and reviled by others, with an added vigor on both sides proportionate to his status as a superstar. Thus, the existence of a split spectatorship, which producers could anticipate and cater to, is fully plausible here. Splitting in this tele-film finds expression in both the style and content. First, the visual style displays a restlessness that underscores the instability of meaning in, or reading of, the story. Second, the most controversial aspects of the musician's life story (his relationships with young children and his use of plastic surgery to alter his skin tone) are included in the narrative. Yet, the restless perspective of *Man in the Mirror* can be understood as working for its audience at a deeper level than pleasing both those who wish to see Jackson celebrated and those who wish to see him shamed. Similar to the diva narrative, Jackson's story appeals to the consumer equally and unconsciously invested in the star figure's success *and* failure.

The film's opening scene frames the narrative in terms of the victimist discourse that increasingly defined Jackson's musical output and public appearances in the latter half of his career. Following a montage of Jackson memorabilia, we see a young Jackson sitting forlornly on a stoop, watching children play baseball. An eerie instrumental track accompanies the scene, as Michael (Flex Alexander) reports in the voiceover: "By the age of 13, I had four number one hits with my brothers, the Jackson Five." This apparent triumph, fitting the melancholy music, is read with a sense of resignation and defeat. His father suddenly appears in the doorway and berates him for taking this short break. He continues, "I was already one of the most famous people in the world, but my father and Motown had even bigger plans." We see the young Michael trying to sleep but disturbed by a nightmare. The pops and flashes of press cameras disturb him, followed by a vision of Diana Ross as a kind of fairy godmother. She gives him a bizarre and incoherent message: "Michael, it's me, Diana. You are going to be a big star. But there will be hurt and pain. Always. Follow your heart. Follow your heart." This contradictory and anxious message is, paradoxically, accompanied by propulsive, synthetic drums, which lend a sense of purpose and certainty. The tone of the scene shifts towards a more definite resolution when Jackson wakes up from this vision to shadows on his wall: profiles of himself as a confident adult entertainer, striking a number of his signature poses. Thus, we have another compressed version of the movement between the split versions of Jacksons—from the abject, abused-abuser who seeks our pity (as encouraged by tearful appearances on Oprah or his appeal in the song "Childhood") to the defiant entertainer who fully believes in his greatness and his right to follow his creative fantasies.

Quickly, though, the film turns dark again. An abrupt edit carries us to a contemporary Jackson concert. A series of rapid jump cuts within the same concert is overlaid by the roar of an airplane engine. After just a few seconds of his on-stage performance, we rapidly transition to Jackson off-stage—to his "life," which, more than his music or his performance style, is the true subject of most biopics. A hysterical mob of fans rush Jackson, who can barely make it to his limousine. The scene not only features screaming, hysterical fans, but is closely framed and rapidly edited. While the effect of the scene is threatening and claustrophobic, Jackson is blasé and unaffected by the crushing crowd. After escaping to the privacy of his car, the singer muses dreamily about his commitment to his craft and the connection he has with his fans:

> Jackson: I need a smoother transition for the last number.
>
> Ziggy: What, are you nuts? You see what's happening out there? It was an amazing show, they love you! As long as they keep buying the albums, we love them!
>
> Jackson: It's not about the money, Ziggy.
>
> Ziggy: Everything's about the money, Mike.
>
> Jackson: Not for me, or for them. I sing for them and they cheer for me. It's about love.
>
> [A blonde woman slams herself against the car]
>
> Ziggy: [laughs] I guess sometimes love hurts.

This conversation between Jackson and his manager concisely expresses the star's pathological commitment to stardom, and his mis-recognition of the nature of this connection. The "love" between fan and star is, really, the desire for consumption (as Ziggy tries to remind Jackson), and one that will never find satisfaction (as illustrated by the masochistic fan). Where this phenomenon succeeds as commerce, it fails to satisfy. In an elaboration of the "superego paradox," Slavoj Žižek usefully differentiates the relationship between desire as it is expressed in consumerism as opposed to love. The consumer economy propels desire by sustaining the idea that:

> the more you buy, the more you have to spend: that is to say, of the paradox which is the very opposite of the paradox of love where, as Juliet put it ... "the more I give, the more I have." The key to this disturbance, of course, is the surplus-enjoyment, the *object petit a*, which exists (or, rather, persists) in a kind of curved space—the nearer you get to it, the more it eludes your grasp (or the more you possess it, the greater the lack).[17]

---

[17]   Slavoj Žižek, *The Fragile Absolute: or, Why is the Christian Legacy Worth Fighting For?* (London: Verso, 2000), 23–4.

This is precisely the slippage that Jackson fails to recognize by mistaking his production of the self-as-consumer-product for a self that will deliver love or resolution.

Man in the Mirror continues with this insistence of having it both ways. Consider the scene in which investigators follow up on a search warrant of Jackson's Neverland Ranch: the arrival of police cars at the Jackson property accompanied by a danceable rap song about being "busted." A quick series of jump cuts hurries the progress of the police. This rhythmic sequence positions the viewer to read the sequence lightly, as an outsider bemused by Jackson's deepening problems. At the same time, small details also encourage us to sympathize with him more. The introduction of this scene also includes two rapid panning shots from within the Jackson residence. These shots both position us, implicitly, in the Jackson camp, looking outside at the police invading his home, while also using a style of MTV editing that has a markedly different effect. While the unnecessary jump cuts suggest lightness and excitement, rapid pans are simply dizzying and disorienting. Thus, in just these few seconds of the sequence we can tease out aspects of *Man in the Mirror* visual design that caters to a diversity of perspectives regarding Jackson. As the scene continues, this portrayal continues to broadly target the mass audience through diverse, contradictory readings of the star subject.

As the investigative team makes their way through Neverland, they voice opposing readings of the location and Jackson's culpability. After a handheld camera shakily takes in the first room in Jackson's mansion, littered with glitzy, entertaining objects, one cop comments in awe, "Wow," while another says skeptically, with a furrowed brow, "A grown man lives here?" The "wow" cop continues to admire Jackson's collection of toys and souvenirs. Smiling while he holds up a glittered glove, he comments, nostalgically, "Look at this! I had one of these when I was little." The credulous cop tries to dissuade the skeptical one when he reads off a series of children's movies as questions: "*Cinderella? Snow White? Peter Pan*?" Though the credulous cop tries to say, "That's nothing, that's just kid's stuff," a superior officer is also skeptical. He concludes, "There could be child porn on these tapes, let's check 'em out." Another cop also muses over a toy he enjoyed as a child, then another comments on "a complete wet bar with no alcohol." In this way, the scene moves, comment by comment, between skepticism to credulity. Quickly, the scene moves forward to the cops meeting Manny, the boy whose allegations sparked the investigation. The most skeptical cop carries the conversation, asking, "Are you scared of us?" Manny says no, and the cop replies, "Well that's good because we're on your side." The boy responds, "I didn't realize we were taking sides."

Manny's reply aptly describes the film's dominant approach to Jackson and the scandal of child abuse. The ideal spectator to *Man in the Mirror* does not simply withhold judgment on the star subject, but both actively believes and does not believe in him. Jackson is at once the innocent, childlike, misunderstood subject (worthy of sympathy and understanding) while also the monster worthy of rejection and shame. The chaotic, contradictory organization of *Man in the Mirror*—which aims more to simply participate in generate profit from the Jackson scandal than to deliver any kind of truth or meaning from it—also underscores this function of the film to provide for both readings of the star subject. The film is never interested in providing answers, but, merely, playing and evoking this state of in-between-ness.

Celebrity Management in Jackson's Songs

Man in the Mirror is unusually illustrative in this respect, presenting a star subject that is both elevated and denigrated. The film's skittish treatment of Jackson manages two opposed audience segments for the film: a fan audience which rejects the dominant criticisms of Jackson and a tabloid/celebrity culture audience who relishes in the faults and failings of star figures. These segments of the viewing audience represent the outermost spectrum of the potential consumers—those most invested in witnessing a romanticized, aggrandized portrayal of the star figure, and those who want to see him embarrassed, mocked, and exposed.

Jackson, undoubtedly noticing *Man in the Mirror*'s investment in the darker side of his celebrity image, issued a public statement disparaging the film. Shortly after the film aired, Jackson countered that:

> [*Man in the Mirror*] in no way, shape, or form, represents who we are as a family. It is unfortunate that for years, we have been targets of completely inaccurate and false portrayals. We have watched as we have been vilified and humiliated. I, personally, have suffered through many hurtful lies and references to me as "Wacko Jacko" as well as the latest untruth about me fathering quadruplets. This is intolerable and must stop.[18]

Jackson misses how cooperative this film is with the contradictory personality defined by his own work. Much of *Man in the Mirror*, after all, relies on rather bare-bones dramatizations of media episodes which Jackson actively orchestrated: for instance, the baby incident from Germany and his participation in the *Living with Michael Jackson* documentary. Far from operating as an antagonist to Jackson, the VH1 film works within the same discourses that Jackson employs in his songs, videos, and cover art. *Man in the Mirror* negotiates a divided audience, interested in both celebrating and denigrating this star figure, just as Jackson generates a split reception by arguing with critics in song lyrics and presenting increasingly fantastical, aggrandized versions of himself. To conclude, I shift my focus from the VH1 biopic to a reading of Jackson's songs, seeking similarities that continue our understanding of the split nature.

In "Man in the Mirror," a pop ballad and #1 single from the 1988 album *Bad*, Jackson narrates a moment of self-recognition. After seeing "kids in the

---

[18]   "Jackson Smashes 'Mirror'," last modified August 20, 2004. [Online]. Available at: www.imdb.com/title/tt0411377/news#ni0088219.

street," the singer vows to improve himself and the world. The chorus repeats the following resolution: "I'm starting with the man in the mirror / I'm asking him to change his ways." While the song, lyrically, promises self-reflection, renewal, and a dedication to social service, Jackson's singing style belies the claims stated in the lyrics. Backed with a synthetic, propulsive sound design, Jackson's delivery of the song lines remain more pop than reflective. His staccato singing style gives the performance a driving appeal, but one that places it firmly in an exterior, entertaining, pop aesthetic. The singer eventually moves from lyrics with content, to a series of emphatic, trademark series of "Hoo! Hoo! Hoo!" drawing out us an image of a reflective and private realization, and towards Jackson's specific performance style.

Simon Frith provides a useful framework for understanding the relationship between the star singer and particular songs in his repertoire. He writes that the star's song performance is "involved in a process of *double enactment*: they enact both a star personality (their image) and a song personality, the role that each lyric requires, and the pop star's art is to keep both acts in play at once."[19] In this case, the character invoked in "Man in the Mirror" stands more in conflict with Jackson's star image in the late 1980s than in support of it. A critic in the commemorative edition of *Time Magazine*, published just after the singer's death, contrasts the self implied by the song with the troubled star's public image: "[the song] contains a fleeting glimpse of autobiography ("I'm starting with the man in the mirror/ I'm asking him to change his ways."). But by then, we knew better than to confuse the singer with the song."[20] While this song tries to articulate a fresh start (Gotta make a change for once in my life / It's gonna feel real good / Gonna make a difference / Gonna make it right), the breezy, naïve hopefulness of Jackson's claim stands out much more clearly than its plausibility.

Starting with *Bad*, this sort of song, in which Jackson and his own reputation is the primary point of reference, would increasingly characterize the singer's sporadic output in the latter half of his career. In "Leave Me Alone," Jackson rebukes his critics for manufacturing his scandalous star image. ("I don't care what you talkin' 'bout baby / I don't care what you say … Leave me alone / Stop it / Just stop doggin' me around.") The lyrics of the song work both as a telling off of a former partner and as a representation of Jackson's tumultuous relationship with the press. A lavish music video, further discussed by Raphael Raphael in Chapter 10 below, clarifies this ambiguity, emphasizing Jackson's life and management of his image (in opposition to the press) as the preferred meaning of the song.

In the surreal music video, Jackson moves through a stop-motion animated landscape. This universe is populated by carnival rides, humans with dog-heads, and mock-tabloid newspapers with headlines screaming about the latest Jackson

[19]   Simon Frith, *Performing Rites: On the Value of Popular Music* (Cambridge, MA: Harvard University Press, 1996), 212.

[20]   Richard Corliss, "Superstar: 1978–1989," *Time Magazine Special Commemorative Edition: Michael Jackson 1958–2009*, July 7, 2009, 34.

scandal. Jackson rides merrily through this world in a miniature rocket ship wearing historical, aviator goggles. In one particularly bizarre juxtaposition, an oversized torso of Jackson lies corpse-like in the background while a second version of the singer flies along in the foreground. The smaller, rocket-bound singer turns around to see the larger version of himself in the background and, facing us again, smiles more broadly while swaying happily back and forth, all the time claiming that he wants to be "left alone."

A differently imagined music video could have emphasized the more generic, end-of-a-love-affair meaning of the song. What if the video had a parallel narrative played by actors or featured a more direct display of singing and dancing skills? Either of these choices would have pitched Jackson's work as a performance rather than an explicit revelation of personality. Instead, "Leave Me Alone" works in the very register it also rejects. He protests the tabloid's coverage of him while, at the same time, continues to relish the attention and produce another narrative that encourages consumption and investigation of his "true" self. Thus, Jackson effectively performs and contributes to exactly the sort of the celebrity image that he claims to be working against.

After *Bad*, Jackson would continue to work in this vein, producing songs which increasingly drew on his attempts to respond to and recalibrate public perceptions of himself. His single/video *Black or White* from 1991, discussed by many of my colleagues in this book, makes a plea for a trans-racial future. The video features a broad range of ordinary people of multiple races who are "morphed" from one to another, while Jackson makes a bid for the race as an outmoded social category. Though phrased at a social level, this song is clearly intended to address criticism toward Jackson for lightening his skin via plastic surgery. Where Jackson is castigated for being racially in-between, "Black or White" envisions a future in which these distinctions are no longer so salient and wherein Jackson's in-between racial identity would be just as accepted as someone with a more normative racial appearance. As with "Leave Me Alone," though, Jackson actively contributes to the very scandal that he later counter argues: how can he claim to believe in a trans-racial future when he is actively investing thousands of dollars and much of his valuable time into appearing more white?

The 1995 single "Scream," again, addresses his frustration with the tabloid press. The presence of Janet Jackson in this duet (a more forceful, even masculine performer than her brother) gives Jackson the necessary chutzpa to act more angrily in both the video and song. At this point in his career, Jackson is frustrated that his attempts to tell his own story have not been adequately understood—"Tired of you tellin' the story your way / It's causin' confusion / You think it's okay"—and, again, expresses frustration at this "injustice": "The lies are disgusting / So what does it mean / Kicking me down / I got to get up."

His next single, "Childhood," would continue his management and presentation of his personal story and image. This was the first song of Jackson's which openly asked for the public's sympathy on the grounds that he was a wounded and troubled performer. In this ballad, Jackson asks for the adoration of fame as compensation for past abuse: "Before you judge me, try hard to love me, / The painful youth I've had / Have you seen my Childhood?" In exchange for this compensatory love, Jackson offers escapist entertainment of "fantastical stories to share / The dreams I would dare, watch me fly." By this time, Jackson had publicly acknowledged his abusive childhood, most notably on an appearance on *Oprah Winfrey* in which he described his adult relationship with his father: "There were times when he'd come to see me, I'd get sick ... I'd start to regurgitate. I'm sorry ... Please don't be mad at me ... But I do love him."[21] Jackson's description of his relationship with his father, here, is torn between opposing feelings: of sickness and of love, of anger and of fear. The lyrics of "Childhood" reflect a similar split feeling: of inadequacy and shame, on the one hand, but also entitlement and aggrandizement.

Conclusion

Of the songs I discuss, "Childhood" features the most frank admission of Jackson's feelings of inadequacy and his "unintentional" contribution to his tabloid image. He admits that his persona is an attempt "to compensate" and "keep kidding around like a child." While this opposition may be expected at the level of consumption, it is surprising to see how fully Jackson's material is already invested in this split discourse. His songs effectively break down the distinction between textual and extra-textual materials. While it would be more common to preserve a stronger degree of contrast between a star's original materials and discussions of their persona and textual output in secondary forums (such as television appearances, magazine articles, or Internet pages), in this case, Jackson is already so engaged in the kinds of discourse that so often define these secondary forums that this distinction does not hold. In the very songs and videos he produces, Jackson's desire to be loved and understood as a good person is set against the fear that he may be misunderstood as exactly the opposite: a freak, an outcast, someone unloved, who is covered by the press only for shame and mockery.[22]

Instead of accepting the inevitability of overvaluation and undervaluation that comes with celebrity status, Jackson tries in vain to manage the presentation of a split self so that he appears (and, by extension, understands and identifies himself) only in the most positive terms. His unusual biography brings into focus the ambivalence of the identifications he solicits. On the one hand, one can feel sympathy for the star and accept his desire for understanding as genuine and deserved: he was abused in his youth, he never had a chance for a normal childhood,

---

[21]   Taraborrelli, *Michael Jackson*, 620.

[22]   See Brook for a fuller account of splitting's place in psychology. He writes that splitting was first theorized by Freud in terms of Id, Ego, and Superego, but is more commonly applied in contemporary psychology as "the splitting of objects and affects into good objects (or part objects) of affection and bad objects of hostility." J.A. Brook, "Freud and Splitting," *The International Review of Psycho-Analysis* 19 (1992): 335.

and so on. On the other hand, the ways he wishes to atone or compensate for this lack stand out as misguided and self-punishing. While Jackson wishes to be loved and accepted, wholly and unequivocally, by his fans, the kind of admiration that the mass audience can give a star is, by definition, an investment that can only be made in selective terms. Since the fan is consuming what is only, after all, a carefully managed and packaged version (or image) of a self, this relationship is destined to be very partial.

Jackson mis-recognizes the fact that the pursuit of this distanced, mediated adoration necessarily entails the production of the other half of the story that he wishes to prevent, manage, or disavow. This very desire (to be so fully "loved" and accepted by millions of fans) ensures the perpetuation of the split sense of the self that Jackson seeks to reconcile by producing more and more mass mediated versions of himself and his story. Thus, Jackson condemns himself to reenact this very tension rather than resolve it. Judging by Jackson's persistent and increasing solicitations of pity, all the admiration and attention that the star attracted could not compensate for his sense of lack. The inability of fan-love to compensate for the star's inadequacies reveals the perverted nature of the symbolic exchange that Jackson promises himself and his fans. This exchange is stated in the starkest terms in "Childhood," where Jackson correlates his lack with his ability to create "fantastical stories to share" for his audience. Jackson's assumption of this sacrificial role is consistent with the pervert's resolution of desire. As Renata Salecl explains, "In contrast to the hysteric, the pervert readily assumes this role of sacrificing himself, that is, of serving as the object-instrument that fills in the Other's lack."[23] The problem with this exchange is that the object that Jackson presents to his mass audience is predicated on a fictive construction: an illusion of wholeness that is (as the song lyrics attest) borne of instability and inadequacy.

Ironically, the false hope that Jackson sustains (to be fully accepted or understood) would short-circuit the consumer cycle. While the singer's videos and songs evince a desire to be understood and accepted, they, instead, perpetuate a ritualistic enactment of misunderstanding and mis-recognition. By providing numerous versions of a "split" self, Jackson encourages the audience to read him ambivalently. Thus, Jackson's own material works more in cooperation with both the biopic and the tabloid, scandal-based media than in opposition to it. Like the extra-textual materials, Jackson profits from and encourages a divided reading of himself and his life story.

---

[23]   Renata Salecl, *Sexuation* (Durham, NC: Duke University Press, 2000), 247.

Chapter 6

From Pop Icon to Postmodern Kitsch: Images of Michael Jackson in Contemporary Art

Brett M. Van Hoesen

While many of the authors writing for this collection focus on Michael Jackson's life and art vis-à-vis a wide variety of analytic agendas, none approach the artist like Brett M. Van Hoesen. As an art historian she chooses to look at Michael himself as a piece of artwork, as evidence of a complicated visual culture. More specifically, she looks at Jackson as the constructed work of many contemporary artists, including Andy Warhol, Jeff Koons, and Yasumasa Morimura. Van Hoesen helps the reader make this phenomenological shift by contextualizing Jackson as iconography, postmodern kitsch, and as the subject of experimental photography.

Michael Jackson's complicated public persona, in life and death, has predictably influenced the way in which he has been represented visually. For some, he has symbolized the prerequisite innocence of a pop vernacular. For others, he has embodied the grotesque nature of mega celebrity and robust consumerism. A musician whose success exploded during the MTV generation, Jackson's fame is based as much on his music as on his image. Indeed, the visual culture of Michael Jackson is a rich, seemingly endless stream of promotional photographs, advertisements, record and CD covers, videos, posters, and a plethora of other collectable memorabilia. In response to the ubiquity of Jackson imagery, visual artists have employed the musician as an emblem of the times and a vehicle through which to read the consumptive character of popular culture. Andy Warhol's silk screen portrait of the musician, featured on the cover of Time magazine on March 19th, 1984, and Jeff Koons' large-scale ceramic sculpture entitled, Michael Jackson and Bubbles from 1988, were memorable, early, contemporary art world representations of Jackson. While the playful tone of these two works point to Jackson's legendary status as a popular icon, both artists used the musician as a means to reinforce more complex, often disquieting discourses concerning international fame, identity politics, and postmodernism.

Starting in the mid 1990s, Jackson emerged as a popular figure in the increasingly globalized contemporary art scene. As Jackson's own physical appearance morphed with greater intensity and his personal life became more controversial, contemporary artists produced works that mimicked the enduring power of Jackson's persona. Yasumasa Morimura, a contemporary Japanese artist renowned for his vivant-styled appropriations of famous paintings and social figures from Western culture, parodied Jackson and Madonna in his 1994 double portrait entitled *Psychoborg 22*. Staged in exaggerated metallic outfits reminiscent of signature performance attire worn by both megastars, Morimura's unflattering portrayal openly criticizes Japanese willingness to adopt Western pop icons.

More recently, Candice Breitz, a South African-born artist based in Berlin, chronicles the cult of global fandom surrounding Jackson in her video installation *King (Portrait of Michael Jackson)* from 2005. For this work, Breitz recruited 16 German-speaking fans to sing, karaoke-style, Jackson's 1982 album *Thriller*. In her installation the 16 separate audio-visual recordings of tracks such as "Wanna be Startin' Somethin'" are joined in quirky choral unison, simultaneously capturing the individual and communal appeal of Jackson's music despite his visual absence. Contributing to this trend of representing Jackson as a global icon, the Korean artist, Donghyun Son's series of over 20 large-scale ink paintings titled *Portraits of the King* from 2008, chronicle signature stages of Jackson's career from his role in The Jackson Five until the year before his death. Modeled in style and appearance after royal portraits from the Chosun dynasty in Korea and inspired by pop imagery of Jackson taken from a range of media, Son's series seems to purposefully strike a confusing balance between nostalgia and indifference.

Soon after Jackson's death in June 2009, a whole new range of art works emerged, many of which expectedly sought to honor in some fashion Jackson's life and musical career. While some functioned as art world sanctioned *high art*, many took the form of artistic intervention, either on the street or in cyberspace. Other works set out to pointedly rectify the controversies surrounding the latter years of Jackson's life. The most notable example is *Martyred Jackson*, a series of large-scale photographs created by the videographer and celebrity photographer David LaChapelle. The work debuted in December of 2009 at the hip contemporary art fair Art Basel held annually in Miami Beach and was later featured in the 2010 exhibit, *American Jesus* at the Paul Kasmin Gallery in New York City. LaChapelle's contrived impersonations of the pop star consider the musician's lasting power and seem to imply that his passing marks yet another chapter in the spectacle of a redemptive Jackson. Contemporary artists such as the Czech Republic-based painter, Helena Kadlicikova, markets glorified images of Jackson to his worldwide fandom through her online gallery. Despite its apparent sincerity, the overtly commercial appeal of her work confirms the unstoppable consumptive character of Jackson culture. New media artists, such as the Australian Georgie Roxby Smith have recently resurrected Jackson in yet another way; he serves as the dance companion to her avatar in the digital other world of Second Life. Under these auspices, Jackson continues to perform, his mass appeal undeterred by his death. Collectively, all of these projects produced from the eighties until today testify to Jackson's immortality and to larger culture's seemingly insatiable fascination for his epic persona. This chapter examines the ways in which contemporary artists have portrayed Jackson as a pop icon, emblem of postmodern kitsch, and larger-than-life persona of increasingly globalized proportions.

Consumptive Culture and the Visual Turn—Post-Michael Jackson

The interdisciplinary field of Visual Culture Studies began in the late 1980s. A fusion of disciplinary methodologies from fields including film studies, art history, anthropology, and cultural studies, this field of inquiry is closely linked to the expanding visual nature of popular culture, what some scholars have referred to as the "visual turn."[1] For better or for worse, privileging the visual over other sensory experiences has prompted a new awareness of the role that visual cultures play in articulating the striations of majority culture. While the time period since Michael Jackson's death has confirmed if not heightened our understanding of his impact and legacy, for me, the most memorable acknowledgment of his dual presence and absence occurred during a trip to Paris and Berlin in the summer of 2009, roughly one month after the musician's death. In Paris you heard "Thriller," "Billy Jean," and "Beat It" playing in clothing stores and supermarkets. Jackson soundtracks blared from the boom boxes of teenagers communing outside of the shopping center Les Halles and buzzed lightly from the headphones of those waiting to ride the Metro. While this remembrance and revival was certainly an auditory experience, you also saw Michael Jackson everywhere. There was an impersonator break-dancing in front of the Centre Pompidou, young adults in Michael Jackson T-shirts, and Jackson's CDs for sale in outdoor markets. At the Palais de Tokyo, a large contemporary art exhibition hall located next to the Musée d'Art moderne de la Ville, a tapeography of Jackson commemorated his golden years of the 1980s (Figure 6.1). This tribute piece signed by Lagoutte, otherwise known as Thibaut Vankemmel, a renowned street artist, was the product of a casual partnership with the Palais de Tokyo.[2] Lagoutte has been an established part of skater culture in Europe over the last decade and has worked with a variety of graffiti techniques including his now refined use of duct tape to create large-scale urban portraits. The locale for the Jackson image was a section of metal lattice surrounding a storage unit connected to the exhibition halls' outdoor cafe. To reinforce the subculture appeal of this work and its unique venue, the skater friendly blog *Frenchyfries* notes that the Palais de Tokyo is not only "a world renowned skate spot, but also a museum of contemporary art."[3] This union between the established art world and the subversive culture of tapeography and graffiti reinforces that Lagoutte's

---

[1]   Margaret Dikovitskaya, *Visual Culture and the Study of the Visual after the Cultural Turn* (Cambridge, MA: MIT Press, 2005), 47.

[2]   For a videography of Lagoutte's tapeography see: http://vimeo.com/5777250.

[3]   Freddy White, "Kulture: Lagoutte's Tapeography," *Frenchyfries* blog (September 2009): www.frenchyfries.fr/index.php?2009/09/28/119-kulture-lagoutte-s-tapeography.

memorial connects with a wide spectrum of visitors to this site. Indeed, the work, which is not located within the walls of the exhibition hall and bears no official museum label, feels impromptu in nature. Its ambiguous status perhaps intentionally connects it to the happenstance run-ins with Jackson one encounters throughout the city.

Figure 6.1   Lagoutte, tapeography of Michael Jackson, 2009

In Berlin there were equally intriguing tributes to the musician. While you heard his music and observed T-shirts bearing his likeness, you ran into odd collectibles like sets of Russian nesting dolls at the popular Mauerpark flea market. The family of figurines charted the evolution of Jackson's physical appearance over the course of his career. On par with other collectable novelties such as the presidents of the United States and Russia as well as The Beatles, the Jackson nesting dolls reinforce a well-acknowledged trope of the musician's persona; the novelty and intrinsic humor of these objects lies in their ability to affirm Jackson's chameleon character as the essence of his popular identity.

Berlin hosted a number of more dramatic tributes to Jackson as well. At the Hallen at Borgsisturm, a shopping mall on the U6 subway line, a giant sand sculpture was erected to honor the King of Pop. Located in the central corridor of the shopping center and commissioned by a consortium of merchants, this grand gesture was created with 200 tons of sand. Historiographic in nature, it charted the visual history of Jackson from his early years in The Jackson Five to his success with *Thriller* to the *HIStory* era.[4] Members of the public left candles, letters, and other mementos in honor of the deceased star. The now non-extant sculpture lives on in featured articles and footage available through the MTV Newsroom, YouTube, and a variety of fan blogs.[5] Lastly, the online consortium "Michael Jackson Dance Tribute Flashmob" gathered at a number of public locales in Berlin in late August including the new main train station (Hauptbahnhof), the Brandenburg Gate, and at the Marlene Dietrich Square at Potsdamer Platz.[6] Swarms of youths dressed in Michael Jackson inspired attire broke into choreographed unison to songs like "Beat It." Warranting crowds of cheering onlookers, these dancers inspired a newfound, multigenerational enthusiasm for Jackson's legacy. This event, similar to others that occurred in Paris, Amsterdam, and Stockholm confirmed not only a German fascination for the deceased pop star but, solidified the significant geographic breadth of his fandom that continues to draw upon the acoustic as well as the visual culture of Michael Jackson.

Pop Art and its Star Power

> Pop Art is: Popular (designed for a mass audience), Transient (short-term resolution), Expendable (easily forgotten), Low cost, Mass produced, Young (aimed at youth), Witty, Sexy, Gimmicky, Glamorous, Big business … This is just the beginning.[7]

Writing in a letter to fellow members of the Independent Group, the British Pop artist, Richard Hamilton, defined this concept of Pop Art well before it had become a household name in the United States. Indeed, Andy Warhol, Roy Lichtenstein, James Rosenquist, Jim Dine and other artists we now associate with the term were not discovered until nearly a half a decade later. Hamilton's definition of Pop Art importantly identified a number of traits that would make the genre appeal to a popular taste—particularly the connection between the gimmick factor, the prerequisite interest in glamour, and ultimately, the notion that Pop Art would be big business. When Andy Warhol's first major public recognition took place in 1962 with the debut of his series of paintings of Campbell's soup cans at the Ferus Gallery in Los Angeles, the public ceased to comprehend the relationship between

---

[4]   For the details of this sand monument see article provided by the MTV Newsroom: http://newsroom.mtv.com/2009/07/27/michael-jackson-sand-sculpture/.

[5]   For video footage of the sand sculpture see: www.youtube.com/watch?v=VyUozDEY28A.

[6]   For a video clip of the Michael Jackson Dance Tribute Flashmob' at Hauptbahnhof see: www.youtube.com/watch?v=o9X-Yj_NkBg.

[7]   Richard Hamilton, "Letter to Peter and Alison Smithson, 1957," in *Theories and Document s of Contemporary Art: A Sourcebook of Artist's Writings*, ed. Kristine Stiles and Peter Selz (Berkeley and Los Angeles: University of California Press, 1996), 296–7.

popular culture and Pop Art. The British art critic Lawrence Alloway explained that, "Pop art is not the same as popular culture, though it draws from it."[8] This seemingly obvious point took a long time to be understood by the general public. It also eventually became a hyperbole as Pop Art did become synonymous with popular culture.

A good example of this conflation was the signature portrait style of Andy Warhol. Starting in the 1960s with the subject of Marilyn Monroe, Warhol used his bright palette and silk screen technique to mass-produce images of the recently deceased starlet. By the 1970s and 1980s, his portrait aesthetic was highly sought after and was used to depict a wide range of celebrities including the actors Liza Minnelli and Dennis Hopper, the gallerist Leo Castelli, the artist Jean-Michel Basquiat, and the pop music phenomenon Mick Jagger. In the 1980s, *Time* magazine commissioned portraits from Warhol for their cover illustrations. While Warhol's rendition of Michael Jackson might seem like a perfect aesthetic union of the Pop artist and the King of Pop, Warhol also completed a Pop Art style portrait of John Gotti, the head of the Gambino crime family in New York, for the September 29, 1986, issue of *Time*. The odd juxtaposition between Jackson and Gotti reinforces the fact that Warhol was not selective in using this particular style; for Warhol, Gotti as well as Jackson embodied the culture of the times.

By the middle of the 1980s, Warhol's signature portrait style had become a trope of popular culture, perhaps even passé. At the very least it was a recognizable brand. While this might dovetail with the fact that Jackson had become a household name in his own right with the meteoric success of *Thriller*, unlike Warhol's aesthetic, Jackson's fame was fresh. The key to the original avant-garde edge of Pop Art as it emerged in the early 1960s was its ability to jolt audiences into questioning whether the image in front of them was indeed *Art*. According to Roland Barthes, "Pop art reverses values. 'What characterizes pop is mainly its use of what is despised' (Lichtenstein). Images from mass culture, regarded as vulgar, unworthy of an aesthetic consecration, return virtually unaltered as materials of the artist's activity."[9] Other critics such as Max Kozloff saw Pop Art as a subversive means of "transforming taste" by reveling in subjects that were perceived to be vulgar.[10] By the time Warhol completed his portrait of Jackson, the avant-garde edge of the Pop Art *look* was long gone. There was no reversal of values or transformation of taste. There was simply the acceptance that Pop Art was an apt aesthetic to capture the wide market appeal of the proclaimed King of Pop. When the *Time* magazine issue appeared, *Thriller* had been the number one album for 33 weeks, the bestselling album of its kind. The album and Jackson's mass appeal were undeniable.

---

[8]   Lawrence Alloway, *Topics in American Art since 1945* (New York: Norton, 1975), 18.

[9]   Roland Barthes, "That Old Thing, Art ... ," in *Pop Art: The Critical Dialogue*, ed. Carol Anne Mahsun (Ann Arbor: UMI Research Press, 1989), 234.

[10]   Sara Doris, *Pop Art and the Contest Over American Culture* (Cambridge: Cambridge University Press, 2007), 107.

If Warhol's style was predictable, it did still behold a seedier twist that would have gone undetected by most observers. While Warhol applied his silk screen style to a wide range of sitters, he did have the propensity to use it in conjunction with subjects who were perceived to be emotionally delicate, in a state of flux, or on the brink of destruction. His portraits of Marilyn Monroe were begun immediately following her death in 1962. Warhol seemed to recognize that the complicated details of her life and death would soon challenge the public's previously unconditional adoration. His series of portraits immortalize Monroe, placing her into an untouchable realm. Similarly, his 1963 works of Elizabeth Taylor were executed at a time when her career was at a crossroads. Her recent film, *Cleopatra* (1963), was a financial nightmare and was panned by the critics for its unforgivable overacting and historical inaccuracies. Warhol captured Taylor at a transitory point in her life; as with Marilyn, he seemed intrigued by the tension between success and scandal. Portraits of Jackie Kennedy from 1964 also fit into this reading. Works like *16 Jackies* present the First Lady in a range of vignettes that reveal a wide spectrum of emotions preceding and following the death of her husband. All of these expressions are documented in press photographs; Warhol exploits the fact that her joys and sorrows are made available for immediate public consumption.

Warhol's portrait of Jackson, completed nearly 20 years later, seems to identify some of the same haunting traits associated with the onset of worldwide fame. While the brightly colored, lighthearted quality of the image speaks to Jackson's innocence, Warhol was well aware of the inevitable, mounting pressures of celebrity. The glamour of Pop Art, and Pop music for that matter, is based upon a certain culture of naiveté. Maintaining this freshness is part of the trick. Like his images of Monroe, Warhol preserved the moment, divorcing it from the inevitable ebb and flow of successes and failures that were to come in Jackson's career. Indeed, Warhol's portrait captures a version of Michael Jackson that many have longed for in recent years. Depicted in his signature red jacket from his *Thriller* video, his youth is intact, his face bears little if any evidence of cosmetic altering, and his aura emits an ease and lightness. Warhol's simplified Pop Art image remains innocent despite the bevy of observations and expectations that linger in the phrases of the garrulous author of *Time*'s feature article, "Why He's a Thriller":

> His highflying tenor makes him sound like the lead in some funked-up boys choir, even as the sexual dynamism irradiating from the arch of his dancing body challenges Government standards for a nuclear meltdown. His lithe frame, five-fathom eyes, long lashes might be threatening if Jackson gave, even for a second, the impression that he is obtainable. But the audience's sense of his sensuality becomes quite deliberately tangled with the mirror image of his life: the good boy, the God-fearing Jehovah's Witness, the adamant vegetarian, the resolute non-indulger in smoke, strong drink or dope of any land, the impossibly

insulated innocent. Undeniably sexy. Absolutely safe. Eroticism at arm's length.[11]

If Warhol intimated the darker side of fame by preserving a more innocent version of Jackson, the fate of Warhol's own work was to undergo the rude commercial realities of the contemporary art world. While the painting used as a model for the *Time* magazine cover is part of the permanent collection at the Smithsonian's National Portrait Gallery, a second version of the work (with a green background) has been in hands of a private collector.[12] This work, a 30″ × 26″ synthetic polymer painting on canvas went up for auction less than three weeks after the Jackson's death. While certainly an opportune time to sell a painting depicting the recently deceased pop star, the calculated timeliness was a blunt reminder of the greed that underlies commercial success. The Vered Gallery in East Hampton received the work for auction from an anonymous seller. The gallery estimated a sale of $1 million to $10 million for the work; the final price was undisclosed. The gallery modestly revealed that the portrait fetched more than $1 million. The hesitancy to share more details was apparently linked to the fact that the media buzz around the sale prompted an overflow of interest in the work causing the gallery to delay the auction by over a month.[13] Given that today the average price of works by Andy Warhol sell in the ballpark of $17 million, the final price of the Jackson portrait was likely well beyond the low-end estimate. The urge to profit and the clamor to collect underscore the original sentiment of Warhol's innocent Jackson; these actions also confirm Richard Hamilton's prophetic assessment that Pop Art is "big business."

The King of Postmodern Kitsch

Jeff Koons is a victim, and I hope that everyone is a victim. One must be victimized in order to absorb one's culture and to participate. If people can accept that position they will be able to listen closely to life. Life will be a close-up.[14]

---

[11]   "Why He's a Thriller," *Time*, March 19, 1984. [Online]. Available at: www.time.com/time/magazine/article/0,9171,950053,00.html.

[12]   Warhol's painting for *Time* magazine is featured on the frontispiece of a recent catalogue on portraits from the Smithsonian. See Carolyn Kinder Carr, *Americans: Paintings and Photographs from the National Portrait Gallery* (Washington, D.C. New York: Watson-Guptill, 2003), 2; 164–5.

[13]   For further details on this transaction see the feature story provided by the MTV Newsroom: http://newsroom.mtv.com/2009/08/19/michael-jackson-andy-warhol-painting/.

[14]   Jeff Koons, *The Jeff Koons Handbook*, (London: Thames and Hudson in association with the Anthony d'Offay Gallery, 1992), 31.

Beginning in the early 1980s, Jeff Koons emerged as one of the bad boys of the contemporary art world. His seemingly flippant tone as espoused by his sculptures made out of plastic inflatable bunnies or Plexiglas cases filled with new Hoover vacuums belied his core intention of mining the cultural values attached to "Art":

> *Aesthetics* on its own: I see that as a great discriminator amongst people, that it makes people feel unworthy to experience art. They think that art is above them. But there are basic aesthetics that I use to communicate.[15]

While Koons exploited the elitist hierarchy of high art, he also compounded the notion that postmodernism requires translation. The purposefully grotesque, trashy, and banal aspects of his projects prompt many viewers to self-consciously ponder Koons' true intentions. Part of this questioning lies within the fact that the artist's work often invokes the concept of kitsch. Theorists such as Matei Calinescu note the difficulty in pinning down a precise definition of the term; kitsch most certainly relates to postmodernity, it also has a reciprocal relationship to the tactics of the avant-garde.[16] Calinescu further notes that kitsch "suggests repetition, banality, triteness"; its language also depends upon fads, imitation, and rapid obsolescence.[17] The challenge is that what constitutes kitsch functions on an ever shifting playground between universally recognizable traits and subjective judgment. For instance, while many might agree that garden gnomes are kitsch, a certain percentage of people will discount this appellation, claiming that they appreciate these objects. The question is not whether or not it is acceptable to like or dislike kitsch, the issue lies in how one defines the visual codes that designate something as kitsch.

Koons' sculptures, particularly those from the mid-to-late 1980s, masterfully explore these complexities. His *Banality* series, which include his large-scale ceramic sculpture, *Michael Jackson and Bubbles* from 1988 (Figure 6.2), wittingly employs markers and mechanisms of a decisively postmodern strategy. One important ingredient to making kitsch work is humor or, at the very least, "amused astonishment." This is certainly achieved with Koons' rendition of Jackson and his pet chimpanzee. The work is based off of actual promotional photographs of the musician and Bubbles from the mid 1980s. Given this visual history, Koons' work appropriates popular imagery already recognizable to his audience. In fact, he purposefully selected a subject matter that was beyond the stage of the "popular." By 1988, the imagery of Jackson and Bubbles was at risk of becoming an uncomfortable joke. Indeed, pop culture commodities like Bubbles plush toys or a Lego set of the duo commemorated a shift from what

---

[15]   Jeff Koons, *Jeff Koons: Easyfun–Ethereal* (Berlin and New York: Deutsche Guggenheim and the Solomon R. Guggenheim Foundation, 2000), 36.

[16]   Matei Calinescu, *Five Faces of Modernity: Modernism, Avant-Garde, Decadence, Kitsch, Postmodernism* (Durham, NC: Duke University Press, 1987), 225–32.

[17]   Ibid., 226.

had once been considered the familiar to what had become the strange. Koons exaggerated this reading by presenting the owner and his pet in tonal unison. As noted by Janet Bishop, Curator of Painting and Sculpture at the San Francisco Museum of Modern Art, one of the institutions that owns this piece, their limbs are confusingly intertwined.[18] An increased uneasiness comes from the fact that the replica of Jackson never makes eye contact with the viewer; his mannequin-like stare is juxtaposed with Bubble's direct gaze.

Figure 6.2   Jeff Koons, *Michael Jackson and Bubbles*, 1988

In just the short time period since Warhol's *TIME* magazine cover, at the creative hands of Koons, Jackson had gone from mega pop star to *king of postmodern kitsch*. The scale and materials used for this piece were integral to this shift. The aesthetics purposefully mimic the appearance of a regal Rococo collectable. Indeed, eighteenth century figurines made out of fine porcelain and gold leaf would have been produced exclusively for royal consumption. Koons'

---

[18]   Listen to Bishop's short audio description of the sculpture in *Making Sense of Modern Art*, an online program that provides interpretations of the works in the SFMOMA's permanent collection. [Online]. Available at: www.sfmoma.org/multimedia/interactive_ features/74#.

grossly enlarged postmodern version still references the social hierarchy associated with the material. According to Koons:

> … [p]orcelain is a material that was created in the service of the monarch and made in the King's oven. Of course, over the centuries it has become totally democratized but still the material always wants to return to the service of the monarch. There is this uplifting quality about it, this feeling of one's social standing being increased just by being around the material.[19]

At the root of this choice in material also lies an overtly symbolic reference to the whitening of Jackson's skin. Indeed, the spectacle of race is literally embedded in the work. By this time, Jackson's appearance was undergoing noticeable change. According to Jackson and his spokespeople this was due to a dermatological disorder, however, the public remained skeptical. As curator Thelma Golden, Director and Chief Curator of the Studio Museum in Harlem explains, "to many, particularly in the African American community, this ever lightening skin was something that he did by choice to appeal to a larger audience."[20] Regardless of what caused or prompted Jackson's skin changes, the public perception was that he was "becoming white." Golden stresses that in the midst of Jackson's increasing fakeness, Koons' sculpture appears "real." This mentality was part of the artist's aim. While his target might seem to be Jackson, the true focus lies within exploring the spectacle of fixed racial identities in America and questioning what it means to embody icon status in American consumer culture. To be certain, by the early 1990s, nearly every aspect of Jackson's behavior was under scrutiny. Koons' knee-jerk humor that quickly diffuses to unease when today's public views this piece reflects less upon Jackson and more upon the disquieting nature of celebrity consumption.

Koons' postmodern ploys were recently put to the test by a 2008 exhibition of his work at the Palace of Versailles located just outside of Paris. The famed home of King Louis XIV, considered a site of great national pride, was invaded by Koons' culture of kitsch. Most notably, Koons' *Michael Jackson and Bubbles* was installed in the same room as an opulent statue of Louis XIV posed as Hercules. While other signature Koons' works such as a 38-foot-tall topiary sculpture entitled *Split-Rocker* from 2000 reigned over the intricately groomed gardens of the palace, the pairing of the Sun King and the King of Pop garnered significant attention. Co-curated by Laurent Le Bon, curator at the Centre Pompidou, the show was criticized for being a calculated marketing event geared to enhancing international exposure to Koons' work. Indeed, roughly five million visitors view

---

[19]   Koons, *Jeff Koons Handbook*, 100.
[20]   Golden in a review of the piece, courtesy of SFMOMA's *Making Sense of Modern Art*. [Online]. Available at: www.sfmoma.org/multimedia/interactive_features/74#.

the Versailles Palace each year, while an estimated 8–10 million tour the gardens.[21] Koons and others associated with organizing the show vehemently denied claims that this was simply a means to drive up the market for his sculpture. Instead, Koons insisted that great care and time was given to the installation. "Exhibiting my works at Versailles has the most profound meaning to me. It gives them the chance to engage in historical dialogue with works from the seventeenth and eighteenth centuries."[22] While the aesthetics of Koons' *Michael Jackson and Bubbles* indeed fit the visual richness of Versailles, staging Jackson's image in this setting was certainly a strategic move exemplary not only of the Koons' cachet, but the enduring aura of Jackson. Nonetheless, a number of lingering questions remain as to why the exhibition engendered such extreme responses of contempt and enthusiasm. Were reactions to the show simply linked to the fact that contemporary art was exhibited in this unlikely context? Or was it that Koons' work was perceived to openly mock the culture of preserving such opulence? Was the gimmick that the King of Pop shared top billing with the Sun King enough to drive the naysayers and the supporters? Could the very intrusion of "American Pop culture" have ignited French protectiveness? What role, if any, did race play in this equation of disapproval and acceptance?

Globalism and Impersonation

Since the mid-to-late-1990s, scholars of all fields have noted the impact of globalization on local and global economic and cultural structures. Of particular note is the way in which certain brands and products have become global entities. While this does not necessarily discount cultural specificity and unique adaptations of "global phenomena"—such as McDonald's, Starbucks, and pop icons like Michael Jackson or Madonna—it does mean that there is a level of connectedness and shared recognition, the extent to which has not been experienced before.[23] While globalization has been credited with positive changes, for some it has also been an unwelcomed development due partly to its imperialistic nature. This aspect of globalism is explored in the work of Japanese artist Yasumasa Morimura. Since the 1980s, his photographic projects have embraced the signature tactic of restaging famous paintings from Western culture. In all of them, Morimura serves as the protagonist or, in some cases, multiple characters of interest. In each appropriated image he dons the proper attire and make-up necessary to complete the transformation, yet in each work his physiognomy or body type remains recognizable. Pastiches of the work of modern European masters such as

---

[21]   Richard Covington, "Where Michael Jackson Meets Louis XIV," *Art News* (November 2008): 102.

[22]   Koons cited in Covington, 104.

[23]   For further information on this topic see: Frederic Jameson and Masao Miyoshi, eds., *The Cultures of Globalization* (Durham and London: Duke University Press, 1998).

Da Vinci, Velazquez, Vermeer, Goya, Manet, Van Gogh, Frida Kahlo, and others diffuse the power dynamic that allows a Western canon to consistently trump cultural production from the East. Additional so-called *portraits* from his oeuvre stage Morimura as pop culture icons from the West including Marilyn Monroe, Audrey Hepburn, Che Guevara, Hitler, and Marlene Dietrich, to name a few. Morimura's computer-manipulated double-portrait of himself as Michael Jackson and Madonna falls in line with this genre of role-playing. Entitled *Psychoborg 22* from 1994, the image depicts robotic, futuristic versions of both mega stars, their gold metallic outfits contrast starkly with the diffused blue screen backdrop. Neither subject makes eye contact; they are emotionally distanced stand-ins for the normally animated performers. Morimura's impersonation of the American icons presents a critique of the Japanese obsession with Jackson and Madonna, a palpable sign of growing global celebrity and the "Westernization" of East Asian culture.[24] The flat tone of the work seems to suggest that globalized culture, no matter how seemingly mundane and innocent, comes at a cost.

The South African-born, Berlin-based artist Candice Breitz further explores the tension between the local and the global in her series of works devoted to popular music figures including Bob Marley, Michael Jackson, Madonna, and John Lennon. These multimedia installations explore the "ongoing anthropology of the fan."[25] Indeed, the fan-star relationship is closely examined in this series from 2005. Breitz identifies specific geographic contexts for each project—*Legend (A Portrait of Bob Marley)* was filmed in Jamaica, *King (A Portrait of Michael Jackson)* was shot in Berlin, *Queen (A Portrait of Madonna)* was set up in Milan, and *Working Class Hero (A Portrait of John Lennon)* took place in Newcastle. Each locale provides a core group of subjects namely devoted enthusiasts who are given the opportunity to record an entire album in a professional recording studio. While the specific album is selected by Breitz fans maintain a certain level of autonomy and authenticity in their appearance and style of singing. While each recording session is done individually, the final work unifies the subjects in a multiscreen layout; collectively, they sing one song from the hit album. Breitz's work *King (Portrait of Michael Jackson)* is appealing on many levels (Figures 6.3 and 6.4). On one hand, it captures the objectified oddity of 16 devoted Jackson followers, some of whom take very seriously the role of personifying the King of Pop in both vocal and choreographic forms. In another sense her work explores the inherent democracy and individuality of mass culture. For some, Jackson is a prideful model of queer identity, for others he is a reminder of one's youth, and still for others his music magically engenders uninhibited creative freedom. The interplay between the individual and the collective connects with the larger concept of globalization.

---

[24]   Penelope Mason, *History of Japanese Art* (Upper Saddle River, New Jersey: Prentice Hall, 2005), 389.

[25]   Jessica Morgan and Octavio Zaya, "Essays on Candice Breitz," in *Multiple Exposure*, exhibition catalogue (Léon: Museo de Arte Contemporáneo de Castilla, 2007), 159.

Mass, monolithic interpretations of Jackson are purposefully challenged by the potential role that national, regional, and social specificities play in determining the 'meaning' of Jackson, his image and his music.

Figure 6.3   Candice Breitz, *King (A Portrait of Michael Jackson)*, 2005

Figure 6.4   Candice Breitz, still from *King (A Portrait of Michael Jackson)*, 2005

If Breitz's work presents a rare opportunity for viewers to assess the myriad cultural components of fandom, the Korean artist Donghyun Son strikes a more ambiguous tone with his series of masterfully rendered large-scale ink paintings entitled *Portrait of a King* from 2008. A group of 24 works, the portraits each measuring just over six feet high, chronicle multiple stages of Jackson's career from his early days as a youth performer until roughly a year before his death (Figures 6.5 and 6.6). The detailed imagery of Jackson is based upon a range of popular media sources dating from the past to the present. The format of the paintings is modeled upon regal portraits from the Chosun dynasty—the longest dynastic period in Korea dating from 1392 until 1910.[26] The era, comprising roughly 25 monarchs, makes an interesting analogy to the dramatic phases and shifts in appearance characteristic of Jackson's long reign. The straightforward reportage character of Son's paintings discount pangs of nostalgia yet one is struck by the awe-inspiring comparative quality of the series. If Morimura chides Japanese audiences for their blind appropriation of Western pop stars, Son situates Jackson in a decidedly Korean historical context. Here, the ever evolving culture of globalization is alive and well.

Figure 6.5   Donghyun Son, *Portrait of the King*, 2008

---

[26]   Joan Kee, "The Curious Case of Contemporary Ink Painting," *Art Journal* (Fall 2010): 104.

Figure 6.6   Donghyun Son, *Portrait of the King*, 2008 (2)

Michael Jackson and Art Now

> I believe Michael in a sense is an American martyr. Martyrs are persecuted and
> Michael was persecuted. Michael was innocent and martyrs are innocent. If
> you go on YouTube and watch interviews with Michael, you don't see a crack
> in the facade. There's this purity and innocence that continued [throughout his
> life] … you'll see such uplifting beauty and a message that you won't see in any
> other artist of our time.
>
> —David LaChapelle

If Warhol and Koons attempted to engage with the looming complexities of
Jackson's public persona during the 1980s and more recent artists have examined
him as a global phenomenon, since Jackson's passing artists have engaged with
lingering questions concerning his identity and legacy. David LaChapelle, the
celebrity photographer and videographer as well as a close friend of Jackson's set
out to posthumously refurbish the perception of the King of Pop with his photo
series, *American Jesus*. The Paul Kasmin Gallery in New York City, the host for
the exhibition, noted that this group of three large-scale photographs was begun
a decade prior to the musician's death. That said, the completed work clearly

attempts to canonize Jackson as a contemporary martyr. LaChapelle, who has photographed an endless array of stars including Lady Gaga, Gene Simmons, Mariah Carey, Whitney Houston, David Bowie, Courtney Love, Tom Jones, and Pamela Anderson, intentionally exploits the vulgarity of mainstream consumer culture. His images are notoriously garish in color and culture. The saturated tones and surrealistic style of the *American Jesus* series doesn't overpower, however, the serious tone of the work, which seeks to redeem Jackson and demonize past public scorn.[27] The first large-scale photograph in the group depicts Jackson in the arms of Christ—a powerful manipulation of the Pieta. Set in a mystical forest environment, Christ cradles the limp body of Jackson, who dons performance attire; an abandoned glove rests at Christ's feet. In the second work, LaChapelle represents Jackson as the Archangel Michael trampling Satan, a conical image of Christianity. Absolved of any insinuations of moral misconduct during his lifetime, Jackson's innocence and heroism prevail. In the final photograph Jackson notably wears the Sacred Heart of Christ—a symbol of purity, innocence, and unwavering devotion. He is paired with a golden haired virgin—together they hold hands. Clutched in his other hand is a timepiece; a white dove rests upon this hand as well. Despite the overt reference to Jackson's peaceable, saintly status, the exact intentions for LaChapelle's symbolism remain somewhat ambiguous. In short, the artist attempts to counter previous troubled readings of the pop star; seen through LaChapelle's eyes, and perhaps in death, the *true* Jackson has been resurrected.

Additional contemporary artists have embraced the King of Pop as a viable subject matter for their work. Helena Kadlicikova, based in the Czech Republic, renders idealized portraits of Jackson, presumably geared toward members of his loyal fandom. Her online gallery presents a vivid array of marketable oil paintings of the musician as well as her *Michael Jackson Art Book*.[28] A dreamy rendition of the pop star in the work, *After the Storm (Back in Peace)* dated to 2002, overshadow Jackson's court battles and public relations troubles. He exudes a sexuality that might hearken back to the assessment of *Time* magazine's feature article in 1984. The scope of Kadlicikova's work speaks to the ever-growing, consumptive character of *Jackson culture*. In a similar vein of examining just what it is about Jackson that makes him so popular, especially in death, the Australian new media installation artist Georgie Roxby Smith works on projects involving the King of Pop in the virtual other world of Second Life. In pieces like *Michael and Me* from 2009, her avatar dances to the 1979 hit, "Rock with You" with a pair

---

[27]   For images of David LaChapelle's photographic trilogy, *American Jesus*, see his website: www.lachapellestudio.com/. It is important to stress that LaChapelle's images are not actual photographs of Michael Jackson, but rather, according to his staff, are stand-ins dressed to look like Jackson.

[28]   For Kadlicikova's online gallery see her website: www.helenakadlcikova.com/michael_jackson_art/michael_jackson_paintings.html.

of computer generated, historical versions of Jackson[29] Her Second Life stage set-up also features actual video feed of Jackson in concert. Visitors to Roxby Smith's Jackson tribute events reinforce the ubiquity of the Jackson revival—whether in the streets of Paris, Berlin, New York City or Second Life.

Conclusion

Part of the visual revival that has occurred following Jackson's death is due to the musician's own aggressive marketing campaign during his lifetime. The multiple alterations to his physical appearance, his signature fashion aesthetic, and his masterful dance moves contributed to a visual culture that was integral, if not essential, to his musical success. Part of this phenomenon is owed to the culture of the MTV generation. Another component, however, is intrinsic to Jackson and his keen understanding of the power of the visual. While contemporary artists over the past four decades have portrayed Jackson for their respective agendas, Jackson has also helped to build his own visual legacy in the form of portraiture. For nearly the last 25 years, Jackson commissioned portraits from the artist Nate Giorgio. At the pop artist's request, many of Giorgio's renditions were based upon historical promotional photographs of Jackson, rendered in a style of photographic realism. This taste for realism was paired with Jackson's admiration for the classics; he allegedly studied and loved the art of Michelangelo and Leonardo da Vinci.[30] In early December of 2009, Giorgio released the *The Official Michael Jackson Opus*, a mega-sized book of photographs and artworks devoted to the musician. The 404-page book sells for $249 and weighs in at an impressive 38 pounds. According to the publicist, 80 percent of the images in the book have never been seen before. There is an ironic twist to this project in that many of the featured painted portraits of Jackson could be read as kitsch. Indeed, they exude such pomp and artificial grandeur that one wonders if they are intended to be taken seriously. Many of these works pose Jackson as a figure of modern-day royalty, adorned in opulent garb and paired with backdrops that befit the aesthetic environment of French monarchs from centuries ago. In light of these images Koons' controversial gesture of staging Jackson at Versailles is reduced to a self-serving act given that Jackson long-before imagined himself in such a context. The further irony here is that while Jackson's choice of self-depiction, particularly paintings dating from 20 years ago, might seem out of style and out of touch, they predate the hugely popular work of the contemporary painter Kehinde Wiley, one of the ultra successful darlings of Jeffrey Deitch, the infamous New York gallerist and promoter of Deitch Projects. Wiley paints large-scale portraits of everyday

---

[29]   For video footage of Georgie Roxby Smith's Second Life project, *Michael and Me*, see: www.youtube.com/user/georgieroxbysmith#p/a/f/2/tsC5SWbVmGo.

[30]   Interview by Korina Lopez with Deborah Wald, photo editor for *The Official Michael Jackson Opus* in *USA Today* (November 27, 2009): 5D.

African American male youth, aggrandized to the scale of kings.[31] These young men espouse the culture of hip-hop and street culture in general; they are majestic and self-possessed. Wiley's canvases carefully delineate a well-studied coterie of Art Historical references that hearken to the Dutch and Italian Renaissance.[32] In short, as with many of his aesthetic decisions, Jackson was ahead of the game. His commissioned portraits, you might say, were prophetically *proto-Wiley*; they imagined a world of opulence and historical pride that seemed grotesque or exaggerated at the time, but in light of today's resurgent interest in the deceased pop star might be all too accurate. The question as to why so many contemporary artists have taken Jackson's image and interpreted it for their own purposes speaks to a conundrum solved only in acknowledging that Jackson is a moveable target. For better or for worse, we continue to chase the spectacle.

---

[31] For representative, selected works by Kehinde Wiley see the artist's page on the Deitch Project site: www.deitch.com/artists/sub.php?artistId=11.

[32] Krista Thompson, "The Sound of Light: Reflections on Art History in the Visual Culture of Hip-Hop," *The Art Bulletin* (December 2009): 490.

Chapter 7

Putting the Music Back into Michael Jackson Studies

Christopher Wiley

This chapter seeks to recenter Michael Jackson's music within the context of his videos, and provide particular attention to their cultural value. Focusing on Jackson's collaborations with director John Landis, Thriller *(1983) and* Black or White *(1991), Christopher Wiley redirects existing interpretations of the videos by instead placing music at the nexus of the analysis. Following these musically oriented revisionist readings, the chapter proposes that popular music scholars have a responsibility to make the music itself as important as the cultural spectacles in which they sometimes become entrenched.*

While news of Michael Jackson's death sent shockwaves around the world, it was keenly felt in London, the city that was to have been the site of his much-hyped, and rapidly sold-out, *This Is It* comeback concert series.[1] For that reason, Jackson had been locally topical for some months, making London possibly the only place in the world where record stores were prepared (albeit for entirely the wrong reasons) for a sudden resurgence in sales of his music. Amongst the many tributes paid to the departed megastar in the days that followed, notably at the Glastonbury Festival and the Black Entertainment Television Awards, the reference hastily included within popular London-based soap *East Enders* provided one of the most artful commemorations.[2] London was also no exception in witnessing the scenes of mass mourning and impromptu pilgrimages seen across the world in response to the news (stirring up memories, at least in Britain, of similar occurrences following the premature death of Princess Diana

---

[1] The "This Is It" concerts were due to have taken place on 50 dates between July 2009 and March 2010. The opening nights of the series had previously been postponed, and its scope significantly expanded from the 10 dates originally planned. Footage of rehearsals for the concerts was posthumously included in the documentary film *Michael Jackson's This Is It* (dir. Kenny Ortega), released across the world for a limited period in October 2009 and subsequently on DVD.

[2] In a specially written scene, the June 26 2009 installment of the show saw Denise Wicks (Diane Parish) discuss the news of Jackson's demise with her surrogate father Patrick Trueman (Rudolph Walker).

12 years earlier). It also saw renewed interest in *Thriller–Live*, the stage show celebrating Jackson's music established in the UK three years earlier, which, in addition to various international tours, had found its present home at the West End's Lyric Theatre that January. Other local concerns included the question of whether refunds would be issued for the *This Is It* bookings—assurances from the major ticket-selling companies that the money would be returned in full being complemented by the offer from concert promoters AEG Live for customers to receive the specially issued souvenir tickets as originally planned in order that they might keep them as collectors' items.

Reflection on my own participation in UK-based press coverage of the tragic events of Thursday, June 25, 2009 reveals that disproportionate attention continues to be paid, even after his passing, to aspects of Jackson's life and career rather than his music. My intentions in this chapter are to rehabilitate Jackson's music within the context of his videos and their sociocultural (particularly racial) backgrounds, thereby situating him within wider disciplinary debates concerning academic engagement with music in popular culture. By way of introduction, I briefly attempt diagnosis of the perceived problem with reference to the discourses that emerged in the wake of Jackson's death as well as broader tendencies in scholarship on musical multimedia. The following sections are dedicated to examination of themes emerging from two thought-provoking studies of Jackson's music videos, Kobena Mercer's "Monster Metaphors: Notes on Michael Jackson's *Thriller* and Robert Burnett and Bert Deivert's *Black or White: Michael Jackson's Video as a Mirror of Popular Culture*.[3] In the course of these discussions, I seek to reorient the authors' readings by placing the music (and its relationship with lyrics and images) closer to the center of analysis, exposing certain biases towards the images with reference to more musicologically oriented writings on music video by Andrew Goodwin, Alf Björnberg, and Nicholas Cook. In a concluding section, I explore the danger of over-interpreting music videos through the lens of the artist's own biography, and propose that academia has a duty to recontextualize popular music for non-specialist communities as a means of refocusing public opinion to the art rather than the controversy.

Informed by Jackson's wider *œuvre*, this study crystallizes around two of his most famous songs and music videos, *Thriller* (music 1982; video 1983) and *Black or White* (1991),[4] which form an apposite pair in that they are the products

---

[3]   Another stimulating article on Michael Jackson, by Susan Fast, appeared too late for inclusion within my chapter. In brief, Fast's study discusses both Jackson's music and the controversies with which he was famously associated, exploring manifestations of difference in his artistic output and his biography and proposing counter-narratives by which he might be posthumously reconceptualized. See Susan Fast, "Difference that Exceeded Understanding: Remembering Michael Jackson (1958–2009)," *Popular Music and Society* 33, no. 2 (2010): 259–66.

[4]   Amongst various other sources, both the "Thriller" music video and the full-length version of *Black or White* appear on Jackson's DVD *Video Greatest Hits – HIStory* (2000).

of Jackson's two collaborations with Hollywood A-list director John Landis.[5] They also represent, respectively, the iconic title track of the album *Thriller* and the first single released to promote *Dangerous*, two of the best-selling albums of Jackson's career, and they are the two of Jackson's songs with notable spoken voice sections (only one of which can correctly be termed "rap"). Intertextuality and image-manipulation effects are important features of both music videos, and, at 14 minutes for *Thriller* and 11 (in its uncensored form) for *Black or White*, each exemplifies Jackson's expansion of the genre in the direction of the short film. Ultimately, my choice of case studies has been governed by the availability of suitable academic literature with which to engage. Yet this chapter should not be considered in any way an attempt to devalue previous research or to reclaim Jackson for musicology, more a demonstration of the additional knowledge contributed by reconfiguring discourse on music video such that the music is accorded more of a central position. Given the obvious value of cross-disciplinary enquiry, I have resisted specialist or exhaustive methods of musical analysis in order to highlight the more immediately comprehensible insights that may be garnered through non-discipline-specific means of examining music, images, lyrics, and sociocultural contexts in tandem. But before we reinterpret past scholarship on Jackson in light of more recent developments, we must first return to the events that prematurely ushered in a new era of contemplation of his career.

The King of Pop is Dead

Since the news of Jackson's passing first appeared on the celebrity website TMZ. com shortly after 2:30 p. m. Pacific time on June 25 (10:30 p. m. British Summer Time), the story essentially broke overnight in the UK, such that the press was fully mobilized the following day to enable major coverage of what looked set to become one of the most important music-related news items of the decade. It was certainly difficult not to come to the conclusion that one news story eclipsed all others that weekend—so much so that the British Broadcasting Corporation received a significant number of Jackson-related complaints remarking that, in the words of the Head of BBC Newsroom, Mary Hockaday, "his death didn't justify the prominence and scale of our reporting through Friday [June 26] and into the weekend."[6] By way of keeping the story running as long as possible, the press were understandably anxious to interview as many spokespeople as they could, from all walks of life. Fans were approached on the streets to share their

---

[5] Landis's other directorial credits include such blockbuster films as *The Blues Brothers* (1980), *An American Werewolf in London* (1981), *Trading Places* (1983), *Coming to America* (1988), and *Beverley Hills Cop III* (1994).

[6] Mary Hockaday, "Michael Jackson coverage," *BBC News – The Editors* (blog), June 29, 2009 (6:30 p.m.). [Online]. Available at: www.bbc.co.uk/blogs/theeditors/2009/06/michael_jackson_coverage.html.

feelings as to what the star had meant to them and how they had reacted to the news of his passing; a plethora of high-profile popular musicians offered personal stories of their memories of Jackson and his music; medical doctors shed light on the circumstances of his death, at the time still very much shrouded in mystery. Predictably, tabloid journalism quickly ensured that the controversies, many of which are analyzed by my colleagues in this book, that had afflicted Jackson's career for the past two decades or more—the cosmetic surgeries, the fading skin pigmentation, the dependency on drugs, and of course the serious allegations of child sex crimes—were also revisited at some length.

My own contribution to the UK-based news coverage, much of it for the BBC, was made in my capacity as an academic teaching and researching on the phenomenon that was (and is) Michael Jackson.[7] I adopted the line that the focus of posthumous discussion should fall on Jackson's contribution to music and the entertainment industry, rather than allowing the controversies to predominate—in short, that he should be remembered as the King of Pop and not as Wacko Jacko.[8] In the course of the many interviews I gave in the days and weeks following Jackson's death, two themes emerged strongly, both of which are to be extended and developed in the course of this chapter. The first I was expecting: while various questions were put to me about my teaching on Jackson and whether I might go about it differently in future given the news, inevitably more controversial ground was also thoroughly ploughed. The second, however, I was not. In my newfound role as "music expert" to the British media, I envisaged being asked about Jackson's songs and his place within the history of popular music, yet much of the questioning on Jackson's videos and musical performance did not extend very far into the realm of the music per se.

I am by no means suggesting that we should retrospectively endeavor to gloss over the unavoidable fact that certain areas of Jackson's life story represent extremely sensitive terrain; I was doubtless not the only viewer uncomfortable with some of the revelations of, for instance, Martin Bashir's documentary interview *Living with Michael Jackson* (2003), previously discussed by Amy Billone in Chapter 3 as well as others in the collection.[9] My contention is simply that these controversies should not allow us to lose sight of his historical import

---

[7]   These activities included several live televised appearances on BBC One and the BBC News Channel on June 26 and 27, 2009, as well as a number of subsequent interviews on regional BBC radio stations.

[8]   See, for example, "Lecturer says Michael Jackson should not be remembered as Wacko Jacko," *The Daily Record*, June 26, 2009. [Online]. Available at: www.dailyrecord. co.uk/entertainment/showbiz-news/showbiz-news/2009/06/26/lecturer-says-michael-jackson-should-not-be-remembered-as-wacko-jacko-86908-21473728/.

[9]   First broadcast on ITV1 in the UK on February 3, 2003 and subsequently in the US and elsewhere, *Living with Michael Jackson* quickly led to official complaints made to the Independent Television Commission and the Broadcasting Standards Commission by lawyers acting for Jackson, as well as to the rebuttal program *The Michael Jackson*

as an artist. After all, his international renown derived almost exclusively from his contributions to music—his childhood career with (and without) The Jackson Five, and the monumental success of the solo albums *Off the Wall* (1979), *Thriller* (1982), *Bad* (1987), *Dangerous* (1991), and *HIStory* (1995)—though it was the controversies that kept him in the media spotlight during the later decline of his professional activity exemplified by the comparatively lukewarm (though nonetheless impressive) reception of *Invincible* (2001). Often, as we shall see in this chapter, the two are inextricably linked in that our engagement with the art becomes informed by our knowledge of the artist, especially since listeners unfamiliar with Jackson's basic biographical details are very few and far between.

The second of the aforementioned themes is illustrative of a general lack of focus on Jackson's music;[10] yet it seems utterly superfluous to state the case for the global importance of the best-selling artist of all time, whose songs numbered among the top downloaded tracks in virtually every major country in the days following his death (the UK being particularly enamored of "Man in the Mirror"). In addition, as I demonstrate below, the contextual issues that have pervaded discussions of Jackson can be seen reflected not just in the images of the videos, but also in the music itself. More widely, such practices of privileging images at the expense of the associated music are firmly embedded within discourses on multimedia art forms; in a landmark study that aimed to redress the balance, Nicholas Cook even complained that despite the substantial attention paid to Madonna's "Material Girl" music video, there had yet to appear "a single sentence specifically about the music."[11] Nonetheless, Alf Björnberg has proposed that "the distinctive features of music video may arguably be better explained on the basis of an understanding of the syntactical characteristics of popular music than by prevalent theories of postmodernism," and Andrew Goodwin has advanced a compelling case for what he termed "A Musicology of the Image."[12] The height of the careers of artists such as Jackson (and Madonna) may have been coincident with the mainstream ascendancy of music videos and MTV, but the fact that he is well known for the precision of the execution of his trademark choreography alone testifies to the importance to his work of the coordination of images and music, as well as to the suitability of that music (in terms of mood, rhythm, and "groove")

Interview: The Footage You Were Never Meant To See, which featured material shot by Jackson's own videographer.

[10]   One important exception is provided by Björnberg, whose work includes a brief analysis of Jackson's music video for the lesser-known "Remember the Time" from *Dangerous*. See Alf Björnberg, "Structural Relationships of Music and Images in Music Video," *Popular Music* 13, no. 1 (1994): 64–6.

[11]   Nicholas Cook, "Credit Where It's Due: Madonna's 'Material Girl'," in *Analysing Musical Multimedia* (Oxford: Clarendon Press, 1998), 150.

[12]   Björnberg, 51. Also see Andrew Goodwin, *Dancing in the Distraction Factory: Music Television and Popular Culture* (Minneapolis: University of Minnesota Press, 1992), 49–71.

in motivating the body to the visual spectacle of dance.[13] Clearly, then, the time is ripe for the music to be reintegrated within Michael Jackson studies.

Mercer, "*Monster Metaphors*," and the Music Video of a Megastar

Thriller has set records that are unlikely ever to be broken: becoming the best-selling album within 15 months of its release in November 1982, it has sold tens of millions of units to date. By the time that the music video to its title track appeared in December 1983, Mercer argued, there was no need for it to fulfill the usual function of public promotion, leading him to suggest that it instead "celebrates the success the LP has brought Michael Jackson."[14] But the mammoth success of the album has nonetheless since been eclipsed by the video, which reinvented the genre to the extent that it reportedly cost around half a million dollars (10 times the industry average at the time) to produce. So thoroughly intertwined are the histories of the song and video that it is easy, three decades later, to forget that one preceded the other by such a long period. For example, the commemorative album *Thriller 25*—which sold several million copies independently of the original—was actually released in the anniversary year of the video (2008), and features a publicity shot from the video on the cover. BBC news coverage commemorating twenty-five years since the release of the album placed a notable focus on the video.[15]

The length of time between the appearance of the "Thriller" song and that of the video provides an apposite point of comparison with Cook's essay on "Material Girl," in which he remarked that the song's music and lyrics together yielded such a tightly ordered structure that little space remained for new meaning to be created by its postmodern video, which similarly followed the year after the song's original release on *Like a Virgin* (1984).[16] However, even Cook's acclaimed case study led him to contend that "The pictures ... are ultimately there to foreground and sell the music," which, while it may have been true of "Material Girl," would seem rather unnecessary as a primary aim of the *Thriller* video given the album's prior sales figures.[17] *Thriller* therefore raises a number of distinctive questions. How was the song used in the music video in the absence of its conventional

---

[13]   Of course, following the star's demise, music videos represent one of the few remaining means of accessing the visual experience of Jackson in performance.

[14]   Kobena Mercer, "*Monster Metaphors*: Notes on Michael Jackson's Thriller," in *Sound and Vision: The Music Video Reader*, ed. Simon Frith, Andrew Goodwin, and Lawrence Grossberg (New York: Routledge, 1993), 83.

[15]   See Denise Winterman, "Thrills and spills and record breaks," *BBC News Magazine*, November 30, 2007. [Online]. Available at: http://news.bbc.co.uk/1/hi/magazine/7117000.stm.

[16]   Cook, 151, 158.

[17]   Ibid., 167.

commercial function, and given its elevation to the genre of short film? And how might that video have subverted the music and lyrics in order to open up new space (as "Material Girl" did) for the resulting multi-parametric narrative, an original story combining 1950s B-movie pastiche with the more contemporary setting in which this "film within a film" is supposedly screened?

Mercer's reading of *Thriller* considers the music insofar as it informs discussion of visual phenomena, including Jackson's own image (as evidenced by album covers and publicity shots) as well as the video itself. While he identifies at the outset of his study that "it is the voice which lies at the heart of [Jackson's] appeal," his endeavors to locate Jackson within the African American soul tradition are exclusively concerned with the extent to which his image fits the mold of female antecedents (notably Diana Ross, his onetime mentor and lifelong friend) rather than male counterparts such as James Brown (to whom his style of dance is indebted) and Al Green.[18] Likewise, in investigating the mythology that has emerged around Jackson, Mercer located the site of what he terms the "definite sense of racial ambiguity … and sexual ambiguity" in his image, specifically, the cosmetic surgeries that he held to have lessened his visual appearance as an African American male and given him more of an androgynous, white European look instead.[19] Yet the indeterminacy that Mercer identified in Jackson's image may equally be located in his voice. His description of him as "Neither child nor man, not clearly either black or white and with an androgynous image that is neither masculine nor feminine" is surely as applicable to his sound as to his look: his vocally high tessitura and quasi-falsetto whooping perfectly exemplify the gendered contradiction he embodies.[20] Even Mercer subsequently conceded, with reference to the work of Iain Chambers, that "the power of soul as a cultural form to express sexuality does not so much lie in the literal meanings of the words but in the passion of the singer's voice and vocal performance."[21] Jackson's voice, however, functions as an implicit indication not merely of the sexual boundaries he has navigated, but those of age and race as well. Its idiosyncratic pitch calls to mind his formative career as a lead singer of The Jackson Five and as the teenage solo artist whose chart hits included "Rockin' Robin" and "Ben" (both in 1972). Similarly, as I discuss further below, his music inherently embraces racial plurality given its distinctive fusing of the predominantly non-white traditions of soul, disco, and funk with more mainstream pop and rock.

One of the principal ways in which *Thriller* itself is revealed to be extraordinary stems from the fact that the music of the original song by Rod Templeton is completely restructured for the purposes of the video. As Table 7.1(a) demonstrates, the track that appears on the *Thriller* album proceeds via alternating verses and choruses, with a bridge section included between the second chorus and the final

---

[18]   Mercer, "*Monster* Metaphors," 93.

[19]   Ibid., 94.

[20]   Ibid., 95.

[21]   Ibid., 97.

verse, and culminating with the celebrated voiceover by veteran horror-genre actor Vincent Price. However, the video, which is charted in Table 7.1(b), places all three verses first, followed by Price's voiceover, before the song is interrupted for dramatic effect for nearly half a minute, during which we hear one of the non-diegetic cues of "scary music" by renowned film composer Elmer Bernstein;[22] the groove is then retrieved, yielding an instrumental section during which the zombies' famous dance routine is executed, and only at the end do the three choruses appear in succession (plus a reprise for the end credits).[23] Consequently, while the original song adopted the verse-chorus structure paradigmatic of pop, the music video rejects this normative sequence in its coherent pursuit of a fresh narrative. Indeed, the delay between the end of the final verse and the choruses, with the spoken voice section in between, makes nonsense of the lyrics: the closing words of verse 3 ("I'll make you see") are clearly intended to lead into the first line of the ensuing chorus ("That this is thriller, thriller night"). This is all, of course, completely irregular for the genre of music video; though traditions have emerged (as seen elsewhere in Jackson's *œuvre*) of extending the time frame on either side of the music and even of repeating the groove to lengthen instrumental passages, the song itself is sacrosanct.

Table 7.1(a)   *Thriller* (album version, 1982)

Counter	Section
0	Introduction
0.21	(groove starts)
0.59	Verse 1
1.29	Chorus 1
1.55	Verse 2
2.26	Chorus 2
2.45	Bridge
3.06	Verse 3
3.37	Chorus 3
3.57	(repeats)
4.24	Spoken voice section
5.14	(second stanza)
5.57	End

[22]   Bernstein, whose major credits as film composer include *To Kill a Mockingbird* (1962), *Thoroughly Modern Millie* (1967), and *Ghostbusters* (1984), had contributed the scores to both Landis's *An American Werewolf in London* and *Trading Places* in the years immediately prior to *Thriller*.

[23]   The counter markings supplied in the tables that appear within this chapter are taken from the PAL-format DVD available in the UK; timings for NTSC-format DVDs may differ.

Table 7.1(b)   *Thriller* (music video version, 1983)

Counter (from DVD)	Section
52.43	Introduction (groove under dialogue)
53.13	Verse 1
53.46	Verse 2
54.19	Verse 3
55.02	Spoken voice section
56.02	(second stanza)
56.32	Music stops ("scary music" by Elmer Bernstein takes over)
56.58	Music restarts (extended instrumental section)
58.11	Chorus
58.28	(repeats)
58.47	(repeats)
59.22	Groove fades out (Bernstein's "scary music" again takes over)

Mercer's aforementioned proposition that the video commemorated *Thriller*'s success is therefore exemplified by the music's being reordered to culminate with the choruses—typically the defining section of any pop song, and *Thriller* is no exception—rather than with Vincent Price's contribution, which functions in the video to bring the first half of the song to a close rather than as the natural conclusion of the whole. Particularly remarkable is the interruption of the song, the very aesthetic product that music videos would normally function to sell, partway through in order to advance the video's narrative at its expense. Likewise, once the music is recovered, an instrumental section absent from the original track serves to showcase Jackson's characteristic dance moves.[24] Conversely, the song's bridge is omitted in its entirety, hence the line of lyrics that Mercer specifically highlighted as informing the visual content, "Night creatures call and the dead start to walk … ," does not actually appear in the video itself—instead, the instrumental is substituted in its place.[25] *Thriller* is thereby revealed as the generic exception that proves the rule: a music video of filmic proportions, commercially superfluous in a very real sense, whose late appearance relative to the song necessitated the development of alternative strategies (the dismantling of the original) in order to cultivate new layers of meaning.

---

[24]   Such extended repetitions of the groove were, however, a feature of Jackson's stage shows (for example, during performances of "Billie Jean") precisely in order to enable the execution of choreographed routines.

[25]   Ibid., 99, 103–4.

Burnett and Deivert, *Black or White*, and Intertextuality

Burnett and Deivert persuasively argued that the *Black or White* music video may be understood as a polysemous nexus of intertextual references, whether intentionally constructed or not, which they unraveled through systematic analysis of its scenes informed by ethnographic research conducted with Swedish and Norwegian undergraduates. Reading their study (which, like Mercer's, made some consideration of the music in examining its associated images) alongside the video itself reveals that its constituent scenes fall fairly neatly into a total of seven larger sequences: the opening father–son dialogue; the sequence in which five different global cultures are presented; the scene in which Jackson sings against a background of flames; the section featuring the kids' street gang; the scene where Jackson dances in the Statue of Liberty's torch; the sequence of morphing heads; and the so-called "panther" ending, discussed in detail below in Chapter 10. For clarity, this information is summarized in Table 7.2, together with further description as to the contents of individual sequences; also indicated is the striking level of correspondence between the overall structure of the video and that of the song. Notably, the song's bridge is coincident with the "background of flames" sequence, while the rap section corresponds to the scene with the kids' street gang. The start of the song proper also matches perfectly the switch from the opening father–son segment (an audio version of which similarly introduced the song on the album) to the sequence depicting different ethnicities, which marks Jackson's first appearance in the video as well as the commencement of the choreography. Other sections, conversely, are characterized by the absence of music: in the "panther" ending, in which Jackson executes dance moves in the street, unaccompanied and in free time, the aural backdrop instead comprises Jackson's feet-tapping, vocalizations, and the exaggerated "swooping" sound design accompanying his body movements.

Table 7.2   *Black or White* (structure of the video as articulated by the music)

Counter (from DVD)	Sequence	Description	Corresponding music
17.50	The opening father–son dialogue	The camera descends from the sky through the clouds to reach a house; inside, a child (Macaulay Culkin) is listening to heavy metal music and his father (George Wendt) tells him to turn it off; as payback, the child blasts his father through the roof with his over-amplified guitar	Generic heavy metal music (also heard as the introduction to the song on the album), ending at 18.44 to enable the dialogue to take place

19.38	The sequence presenting different global cultures	Depicts people from five different global cultures (with whom Jackson dances in turn): Africa (19.38), south-east Asia (20.28), Native America (20.53), India (with a Westernized urban backdrop) (21.16), and Russia (21.38); ends (22.02) with a shot of two babies sitting astride the world	Introduction (African scene); verse 1 (south-east Asian scene); instrumental (Native American scene); verse 2 (Indian scene); second instrumental (Russian scene)
22.11	The "background of flames" scene	Jackson performs in front of backdrops depicting violence and race hate (flames predominant in backdrops)	Bridge
22.27	The kids' street gang	Macaulay Culkin (as the leader of the gang) lip-synchs the rap performed by guest artist L.B.T.	Rap section
22.46	Jackson dancing in the Statue of Liberty's torch	Jackson sings and dances inside the Statue's torch, ending with the camera panning out to reveal other global landmarks too	Verse 3
23.18	The sequence of morphing heads	Different models lip-synch the song's refrain in turn, their heads morphing into one another; ends with a cameo by director John Landis as he calls out "cut"	Coda
*c.*24.12	The so-called "panther" ending (frequently cut for its controversial content)	The camera follows the panther outside (24.25) and it morphs into Jackson; Jackson dances solo in the deserted street before starting to smash some windows (c.26.30), interspersed with his dancing, transforming back into the panther to end; a clip of The Simpsons follows (28.39)	None (groove of "Black or White" music restarts at 28.39)
28.50	End		

The video juxtaposes the "Black or White" track, written by Jackson himself, with multiple visual intertexts explicitly referencing different films, cultures, and landmarks as revealed by Burnett and Deivert's reading; the images and choreography accompanying the song's opening verses alone lead the viewer from Africa to South-East Asia, Native America, India (within a Westernized urban setting), and finally Russia.[26] That the same song appears throughout this pluralistic

---

[26]   This sequence therefore provides a precursor to the renowned video for Jackson's "Earth Song" (1995), which was filmed on four different continents.

visual *bricolage* (albeit one constructed from a North American perspective) provides a continuity that binds the various scenes and sequences together. Thus it is the music in collaboration with the images, rather than the images alone, that explicates the overall messages of worldwide unity and multicultural acceptance (where the lyrics to some extent refer instead to a more personal, romantic narrative concerning an interracial relationship). It is the music that ultimately clarifies the video's meaning of bringing different countries and demographics together, where the images might (for their fragmentariness) have been taken to emphasize their separation. Finally, the music provides the "constant" that aesthetically connects the complex mesh of what Burnett and Deivert termed "recurring motifs"—felines, broken glass, father–son relationships, and so forth—that occur in different segments of the video that at first glance are seemingly unrelated.[27]

However, while the identity of the musical text of "Black or White" may be a unified one, it does not merely speak with a single cultural "voice." Much modern popular music is ultimately traceable to two very different roots, African American blues and European classical music. However, Jackson's idiom is more racially complex, for although he inherited the artistic mantle of the Motown label with which he was associated during his childhood career, his mature sound (as noted) combined soul, disco, and funk with commercial pop and rock, creating an aural product whose congruity implicitly embodies the messages of "Black or White" itself. Its video also offers various allusions to the far-reaching extent of the influences that informed Jackson's music. The featuring of an Eddie Van Halen model guitar in the opening sequence calls to mind that artist's contribution to *Thriller*, notably the virtuosic solo of "Beat It"; and it is undoubtedly not by accident that the start of the "Black or White" song proper (and Jackson's initial appearance within the video) occurs in the setting of Africa, which, as Burnett and Deivert noted, reflects another facet of Jackson's musical heritage.[28]

One of the most distinctive of the various musical elements incorporated within *Black or White* is the central rap section, with lyrics by Bill Bottrell (who co-produced the *Dangerous* album) and performed by guest artist L.T.B. Rap is otherwise relatively uncommon in Jackson's best known output, one obvious comparator being the spoken voice section of "Thriller," whose delivery by a Caucasian horror actor matched well the video's 1950s B-movie intertext (which, as previously observed, it antedated by over a year) but not the music's own intertextual allusion to this stereotypically African American artform, in which context it was clearly intended ironically.[29] In *Black or White*, however, the opposite is the case: the rap is executed by a perceptibly African American voice

---

[27]   Robert Burnett and Burt Deivert, "*Black or White*: Michael Jackson's Video as a Mirror of Popular Culture," *Popular Music and Society* 19, no. 3 (1995), 24.

[28]   Ibid., 26.

[29]   Cf. Mercer's discussion of elements of parody and ironic humor inherent in Price's voiceover (1993, p. 98).

but lip-synched onscreen by child actor Macaulay Culkin.[30] Surely it cannot be coincidence that this scene is immediately followed by one in which Jackson is seen singing and dancing in the torch of the Statue of Liberty, referencing the city in which rap and hip-hop emerged in the later 1970s. It also has its parallels in the images that soon thereafter accompany the song's closing section, which demonstrates the racial plurality of what has hitherto been constructed as a black-white dichotomy through its series of 13 morphing heads—recognizably of different ethnic origins, and including a mix of males and females—all lip-synching the same refrain to Jackson's voice on the soundtrack and, by extension, sharing in his message. Both instances exemplify the music's unification of a blend of races and cultures: it doesn't matter that an African American voice apparently emanates from Culkin's Caucasian lips because it doesn't matter if you're black or white; in keeping with the messages of the lyrics, the music and images also refuse to be defined by color. Earlier I discussed how Jackson's crossing of boundaries of gender, age, and race is embodied by his voice, and its literal transference to onscreen characters of different sexes and cultures—and, correspondingly, that of L.T.B.'s voice to a white child—provides visual reflection of the point.

Consideration should also be made of one final intertext not explored in Burnett and Deivert's study: the prominence of the image of the burning cross in both the "background of flames" scene that immediately precedes the rap section, and the music video to Madonna's *Like a Prayer*. Not only did Madonna's celebrated video appear in 1989, just two years before *Black or White*, but it was notoriously linked to an advertising campaign for Pepsi, with which product Jackson was likewise associated during the 1980s; and both videos courted controversy at least in part for their openly anti-racist content.[31] Granted, the burning cross seen behind Jackson (together with other images of violence), like its intertextual counterpart in *Like a Prayer*, makes explicit reference to the Ku Klux Klan and the history of racism in the United States, amplifying the subtler allusion embedded in the lyric "I ain't scared of no sheets." The pacing of the music accompanying this scene, the song's bridge, similarly suggests a stark contrast from the verses given the tighter phrase structure, shorter lines, and fiercer tone of Jackson's voice; and it is through contemplating musical factors in addition to visual ones that the intertext's ultimate significance is revealed. The characteristic mix of far-flung elements of popular music in *Black or White*, discussed above, is also a feature of *Like a Prayer*, which notably combined Madonna's commercial pop idiom with gospel courtesy of the Andraé Crouch choir. Moreover, as Susan McClary has

---

[30]   Born in 1980, Culkin had been catapulted to fame one year prior to *Black or White* by the first *Home Alone* movie (which thereby provides another of Burnett and Deivert's intertexts).

[31]   For an effective critique of the controversy elicited by *Like a Prayer* in relation to the Pepsi advertising campaign, see Leslie Savan, "Commercials Go Rock," in *Sound and Vision: The Music Video Reader*, ed. Simon Frith, Andrew Goodwin, and Lawrence Grossberg (New York: Routledge, 1993), 85–90.

demonstrated in her provocative analysis of the song and images in tandem, the music of *Like a Prayer* for its blend of stereotypically white and black traditions, is complicit in the construction of the racial and religious messages that prompted the video to be received so controversially.[32] The meanings of *Black or White* are thereby strengthened by an intertextual connection with a well-known musical precursor in recent American pop-culture with whom its conceptual themes are shared.

Long Live the King of Pop

If the scope of this chapter has precluded comprehensive examination of the detailed relationships between music, images, and lyrics in the videos *Thriller* and *Black or White*, it has at least provided various indications as to how music might be positioned closer to the center of a revised reading of the narratives of these songs and their videos. I now propose to bring my enquiry full circle by considering the perils of the general tendency towards interpreting such art in accordance with aspects of the biography of its originating artist, seemingly inevitable though it may be; Andrew Goodwin, indeed, has written of the "centrality of understanding the star's persona(s) as an element in reading video clips."[33] Jackson again provides an ideal case study given the extent of his association with serious controversy coupled to the contradictory stance he has adopted with respect to publicly aired speculation about him, as reflected in his musical output: on *Thriller*, he commemorated a fan's paternity claim in "Billie Jean" and responded to the spreading of rumors in "Wanna Be Startin' Somethin'"; later in his career, however, "Leave Me Alone" (from *Bad*) and several songs on *HIStory* condemned media intrusion into his private life. With this fresh objective in mind, I shall briefly revisit one final time the two articles that have formed the backbone of my discussion.

Mercer's reading of *Thriller* is clearly indebted to its two metamorphosis sections as exemplifying the elements that separate it from other music videos, responding to the intertextual connotations of the song's title and disrupting the narrative—the "thrill" being revealed as one of horror rather than romance.[34] His conclusion, however, leads us away from the art and towards the realms of biography and controversy: in foregrounding the constructedness of Jackson's own image, he views the metamorphoses (the first in particular) as "a metaphor for the aesthetic reconstruction of Michael Jackson's face" through making explicit the use of make-up, emphasizing the facial features, and implicitly drawing

---

[32]   Susan McClary, "Living to Tell: Madonna's Resurrection of the Fleshly," in *Feminine Endings: Music, Gender, and Sexuality* (Minneapolis: University of Minnesota Press, 1991), 163–5.

[33]   Goodwin, 98.

[34]   See especially Mercer, "*Monster Metaphors*," 85–7.

attention to his cosmetic surgery.[35] Yet if early evidence of Jackson's reconstructive treatment was visually discernible when the video was released in 1983, then the rather more extreme changes to his appearance that have since been witnessed only serve to augment the perceived relationship between the image of the actor, prosthetically enhanced and made up as a werewolf, and the real-life Jackson as a product of extensive cosmetic treatment. From the present vantage point, the danger of retrospective reading based on our knowledge of Jackson's subsequent biography threatens to color the reader's view of what essentially then becomes a revisionist interpretation of his video.

Likewise, as Burnett and Deivert discovered, it seems difficult not to draw connections between the connotations of the song "Black or White" and Jackson's fading skin pigmentation which was very apparent by 1991, two years before the public explanation (vitiligo) was given in Jackson's interview with Oprah Winfrey.[36] The dissolving of racial boundaries is critical to the messages imparted by "Black or White," and more widely recalls Jackson's success as a path-breaking African American artist at a time when black music was still notably under-represented within the mainstream entertainment industry. But there is also another motif prominent in the video with deeply problematic biographical associations, namely the prevalence of children: Jackson dances with a Native American child in the sequence presenting global cultures; two babies sit astride the world in the shot just prior to the song's bridge; the street gang scene includes seven children led by Macaulay Culkin, together with Jackson dressed in a juvenile manner; and the video is bookended by father–child relationships, opening with Culkin in the role of son to George Wendt's character and closing with a brief animation featuring Bart and Homer from *The Simpsons*. In retrospect, this whole line of enquiry calls to mind the serious accusations of child sexual abuse and molestation made against Jackson in his later life as well as such controversies as the dangling of his nine-month-old son from the third-floor balcony of a Berlin hotel in 2002 and the media speculation as to the identity of the child's surrogate mother.[37] Yet the extent to which any of this can be held to apply to *Black or White* is somewhat limited. If the 1993 allegations (settled out of court) were temporally proximate, those of 2003 (for which Jackson was acquitted two years later) are not, while the other episodes cited are similarly located in the last decade of Jackson's life; possibly the only direct link with *Black or White* is that Culkin's testimony reluctantly contributed to Jackson's trial in 2005 was consequential to

---

[35]   Ibid., 91.

[36]   Burnett and Deivert, "*Black or White*," 34–5.

[37]   Having delivered versions of this chapter in the form of a research-led seminar on many different occasions, I find it particularly revealing that whenever discussion turns to issues related to children, controversies such as the above are quickly cited, whereas not a single student has ever mentioned (for instance) Jackson's extensive charitable and humanitarian work through the Heal the World Foundation he founded in 1992 to benefit disadvantaged children worldwide.

his defense.[38] From today's standpoint it seems almost unavoidable to think about these more recent controversies in connection with the motifs featured in *Black or White*; but whether we should do so is another question entirely.

By way of conclusion, I should like to propose that in cases such as Jackson's, academia has a social responsibility to reorient the public focus to the artistic output rather than the controversies. I am not for one moment suggesting that we dismiss or deny the seriousness of episodes such as those to which I have alluded above; rather, I am merely seeking reassessment of the publicly articulated balance between the two. One of the most significant debates to have emerged in modern popular music studies has concerned the extent to which discourse should focus analytically on the aesthetic texts themselves, rather than on their sociocultural contexts; John Covach, for instance, has advanced the view that "popular music can ... be considered as inherently *musical*, and only secondarily social."[39] Yet my own experiences of participating in the media coverage of Jackson's death have suggested that in non-specialist arenas, it is the contextual (and controversial) issues that are foregrounded, and that even endeavors to engage with the art itself tend to crystallize around visual rather than musical elements. So, while it would obviously be undesirable to present the music as being devoid of its cultural contexts, we may at least seek to reposition it nearer to the heart of discussion, for just as reflection on Jackson's *œuvre* seems invariably to lead us to aspects of his biography, so it should be important to contemplate the artistic fruits borne of his exceptional career and not merely the controversies that tainted it. We should not be allowed to not lose sight of the fact that Jackson met with extraordinary success in the late twentieth-century entertainment industry, that he made a major contribution to contemporary popular music, and, as the public reaction to news of his death abundantly testifies, that he continues to be held dear to millions of fans worldwide. The day following Jackson's passing, I was repeatedly quoted in the British press as having described him as one of those "rare geniuses" capable of transcending boundaries (of race, age, and gender) through his art; and as we have seen above, the music is absolutely central in this respect.

If this closing note is felt to be controversial, then it is surely testament to the life of a controversial figure. But Jackson's influence, impact, and legacy remain so phenomenally important to global culture that I am confident he will still be acclaimed as a great artist long after the tabloid frenzy has abated, and that his music will continue to be discovered, and enjoyed, by generations of listeners yet to come.

---

[38]   In addition, around one month after Jackson's death, unconfirmed claims emerged that Culkin may have been the biological father of his third child, the result of Culkin's having donated sperm at Jackson's request.

[39]   John Covach, "Popular Music, Unpopular Musicology," in *Rethinking Music*, ed. Nick Cook and Mark Everist (Oxford: Oxford University Press, 1999), 466. Emphasis in original.

Chapter 8

"We Are Here to Change the World": *Captain EO* and the Future of Utopia

Carl Miller

Captain EO is a work that has traditionally been characterized as technologically advanced and intellectually devoid. However, recent decisions to bring it back to Disneyland rekindled interest from critics and fans alike. First appearing in 1986, at the height of Michael Jackson's popular appeal, the work has also been complicated in the years since as Jackson's public perception underwent several radical changes. However, as Carl Miller points out in this chapter, Captain EO *showcased a new focus for Jackson's music, which would turn increasingly utopian the decade to follow. By applying utopian theory, concepts of postmodernity, and keen insights from film studies, Miller offers a detailed analysis of this often bypassed artifact in Jackson's catalogue.*

> Where does this difference between the past and the future come from? Why do we remember the past but not the future?
>
> Stephen Hawking, *A Brief History of Time*

The announcement on December 18, 2009 that *Captain EO* would return to Disneyland in February 2010 represents a significant milestone in Michael Jackson's critical history. It is a decision that would have seemed unlikely if not unthinkable—only a decade earlier, when, for reasons clearly outlined in the chapters of this collection, Jackson had fallen out of critical favor with the family entertainment mainstream. By the time *Captain EO* was initially dropped by Disneyland in 1997, it appeared that Jackson's commercial appeal and critical reputation had been irreparably damaged, a public notion challenged only recently by his death at the age of 50. As Richard Corliss wrote shortly before Disney's announcement:

> Jackson's bizarre resculpturing of his features; his litigious shenanigans with young boys; his obsession with being an external preadolescent, a petrified Peter Pan; all these eccentricities gave him an otherworldly cast. It took death to restore his standing as a one-of-a-kind entertainer—to bring him back to life.[1]

---

[1]   Richard Corliss, "He's Still a Thriller," *Time*, November 9, 2009, 57.

This popular reversal was most immediately evident in the astounding success of *Michael Jackson's This Is It*, the film documenting the making of Jackson's would-be final concert, which in three months grossed over $250 million worldwide. That film was significant not only for the financial success it generated, but just as surely for the public stage it again granted Jackson, to an audience now willing to look beyond the biographical hearsay and physical alterations that had long overshadowed Jackson's art. As Corliss emphasized, "Full redemption, not to mention true resurrection, requires a personal appearance."[2]

The Return of the King

While lacking the intense global publicity surrounding *This Is It*, the re-release of *Captain EO* represents perhaps an even more significant event-offering the resurrection of not only Jackson himself but also one of his most overlooked cultural achievements. A quarter-century after its production, it is easy to forget the spectacle that greeted *Captain EO*'s initial release at the height of Jackson's popularity. The film opened at Disneyworld's EPCOT on September 12, 1986, building anticipation for its release at Disneyland's Tomorrowland six days later, where the park remained open for 60 hours straight to accommodate the masses lined up to view the film. The throng of celebrities that attended the film's latter opening was rivaled only by that at Disneyland's grand opening in 1955, and the star power involved in the work itself-including executive producer George Lucas and director Francis Ford Coppola—was virtually unprecedented for a film of that length: 17 minutes long, about $1/_7$ the length of the average feature film. *Captain EO* would run continually until being discontinued at EPCOT in July 1994 and at Disneyland in April 1997–in each case being replaced by another sci-fi attraction, *Honey, I Shrunk the Audience*, which was by that time judged less controversial (and, consequently, more family friendly) than its predecessor.

Despite the intense anticipation surrounding the film's development and its long run in each of Disney's parks, it bears reminding that, even at the time of its release, the critical reception was underwhelming, with very few established critics offering any assessment of the picture at all. The overall plot of *Captain EO* is relatively simple, borrowing heavily from Lucas' previous work in character and setting, and reminiscent of the music video for Jackson's "Beat It" in terms of narrative resolution. Writing at the time of its release in 1986, Corliss accurately described the first half of *Captain EO* as "an energetic rehash of the *Star Wars* space battle," and the second half as "an elaborate Michael Jackson video."[3] Corliss further critiqued the film as being "sugar but no spice, coating an audio-animatronic gridwork. What can be exhilarating and depressing about

---

[2]   Ibid.

[3]   Richard Corliss, "Let's Go to the Feelies; Michael Jackson and George Lucas give Disney a 3-D Dream," *Time*, September 22, 1986, 80.

Walt Disney World is true of *Captain EO*: it is a triumph of the artificial, of high-tech wizardry and secondhand emotions."[4] The technical wizardry could not, it seemed, compensate for the apparent lack of character development and emotional depth. In turn, Corliss proclaimed the movie to be "only the fourth-best film at EPCOT"—behind travelogues on China and France and a documentary about energy—on the grounds that in the latter instances "the imagination is served, not dominated, by special effects."[5]

Furthermore, despite the innate star power of the three primary figures in the making of *Captain EO*, each was at a seeming crossroads of their respective careers: Lucas released the disappointing *Howard the Duck* just prior to *Captain EO*; Coppola was coming off a pair of financial flops in *Rumble Fish* and *The Cotton Club*; and Jackson had not released a new album in almost four years. Retrospectively, Lucas, Coppola, and Jackson had already done their best career work by the time of *Captain EO*, and this film would not come to stand as a true turning point for any of them. Jackson's 1988 autobiography, *Moonwalk*, contains only three paragraphs on *Captain EO*, and Jackson's own children had never seen the film until a special test screening in anticipation of Disney's re-release.

In spite of this, the very decision by Disney to re-release *Captain EO* points to a deeper cultural connection with the film than might have first been perceived, and raises the film's continued relevance as a work of the future—rather than simply the past.[6] To begin with, *Captain EO* was never designed to be a film so much as a 17-minute amusement park ride; to judge it against the more notable work of Lucas and Coppola is unfair, as is Corliss' critique of Jackson as an "improbable Han Solo." (Was Jackson any more convincing as a gang peacemaker in his *Beat It* video?) Whatever failures *Captain EO* might demonstrate as a feature film are presumably offset by its contribution as a successful Disney attraction.

Just as surely and significantly, *Captain EO*'s critical assessment suffers from the film's sci-fi utopian narrative and resolution; as Fredric Jameson contends, "the more surely a Utopia asserts its radical difference from what currently is, to that very degree it becomes, not merely unrealizable but, what is worse, unimaginable."[7] Viewed from this angle, however, the film presents a fascinating study in heteroglossia between traditional Disney narratives and the postmodern

---

[4]   Ibid.

[5]   Ibid.

[6]   *Captain EO* was eventually reopened at all of Walt Disney's major parks. The initial reopening at Disneyland on February 23, 2010, was quickly followed by second premieres at Disneyland Park in Paris (June 12, 2010), Tokyo Disneyland (July 1, 2010), and EPCOT Center (July 2, 2010). The timing of these re-openings in proximity to Jackson's death can hardly be considered coincidental. Even more than *This Is It*, *Captain EO* allows the audience to nostalgically re-establish the image of Jackson as the "King of Pop" in his mid 1980s prime and to behold the potential that his artistic vision offered at that time.

[7]   Fredric Jameson, *Archaeologies of the Future: The Desire Called Utopia and Other Science Fictions* (New York: Verso, 2005), xv.

science fiction epics it is often compared with. The viewing audience engages with *Captain EO* in a way that it does not with any number of other amusement rides. The film offers a contemporary-specific message taken to abstract dimensions, and in this regard Jackson's utopian performance stands in complex opposition to *It's a Small World* or the *Haunted Mansion*. As Sergei Eisenstein originally said of film's form, it is only when cinema establishes itself as a socially relevant text that it rises "above the level of the music-hall, the amusement park, the zoo, and the chamber of horrors, to take its place within the great family of arts."[8]

Back to the Future

Of course, much of the work's artistry has traditionally been located in its cutting-edge technical achievements, made possible by its unprecedented budget. Although *Captain EO* is only 17 minutes long, it cost an estimated $30 million to produce, rendering it the most expensive film per minute ever made (costing approximately $1.76 million per minute). The decision to do the film in 3-D would have a lasting impact on Jackson and his visual legacy: in the concert preparations for *This Is It*, *Thriller* was to have featured 3-D effects, and there was a 3-D tribute paid to Jackson at the 2010 Grammys Awards. But *Captain EO* was not innovative simply because it employed 3-D effects; the film it replaced at both Disneyworld and Disneyland—the *Magic Journeys* attraction—was itself a 3-D film.[9] *Captain EO* would move beyond its predecessor by becoming the first mainstream "4-D" film, with in-theatre special effects such as fog and laser lighting designed to augment the audience's live viewing experience (and leading to technical producer Randy Lemorande becoming known as the "Father of 4-D"). Another sizable component of the film's cost was the sheer collection of name talent involved in its production. In addition to the aforementioned Jackson/Lucas/Coppola trio, Jeffrey Katzenberg, Michael Eisner, John Napier (the set designer for *Cats*), Jeff Hornaday (the choreographer for *Flashdance*), and James Horner (who would go on to write the score for *Titanic*) all had a hand in the making of *Captain EO*.[10]

---

[8]   Sergei Eisenstein, *Film Form: Essays in Film Theory*, ed. and trans. Jay Leyda (San Diego: Harcourt, 1949), 181.

[9]   Not surprisingly, a number of the most striking technical features of *Captain EO* were borrowed from elsewhere, such as the shot of Jackson floating above the audience, which was filmed on the same blue screen used for Disney's 1979 sci-fi thriller, *The Black Hole*. The "innovation" of *Captain EO* is instead its amalgamation of existent talent and technology into a single seventeen-minute text.

[10]   The cost could easily have run even higher: Jackson originally wanted Stephen Spielberg to team with Lucas on *Captain EO*. Spielberg declined, as he was in the midst of directing *The Color Purple* and had just finished producing *Back to the Future* (which would itself be adapted into an amusement park ride in 1991 at Universal Studios Florida).

An exclusive focus on the film's technical wizardry and budget, however, misses the fact that the film operates on an artistic level that goes beyond mere special effects. As a cultural document *Captain EO* offers a compelling commentary on mid 1980s America, and as a creative text the film reflects an interesting historical intersection of critical theory. For example, the question of whether *Captain EO* functions as a "postmodern" text (along with the artistically progressive implications that such a term accords) becomes relevant in light of the emerging theories of both Jean-François Lyotard and Fredric Jameson. Lyotard's *The Postmodern Condition*, which first appeared in English translation in 1984, argues that there is "a musical property of narrative" that is most commonly evident in "nursery rhymes ... and repetitive forms of contemporary music."[11] Such forms, Lyotard continues, "are like little splinters of potential narratives, or molds of old ones, which have continued to circulate on certain levels of the contemporary social edifice."[12] In this instance, Jackson's pop cultural influence is crucial in considering the role of *Captain EO* as both a conception of the future *and* a tool of nostalgia for the past. Jackson's musical contributions to the film showcase a new utopian direction for his art (a point to which this chapter will return), while his participation in the film provides a familiar face that many audience members had grown up watching (or watched grow up) in the 1970s. In short, he provides a bridge to the future through the comfort of a familiar past.

Jameson's "Postmodernism and Consumer Society," first published in 1983 and republished in several forms before emerging as his iconic *Postmodernism* (1990), provides an even more compelling commentary on this sort of nostalgia. In the article, Jameson identifies *American Graffiti*—one of only two previous collaborations between Lucas and Coppola[13]—as "one of the inaugural films in this new 'genre'" known as the "nostalgia film."[14] More interestingly still, Jameson suggests that Lucas' *Star Wars* is just as surely a nostalgia film, at least in an associative (*metonymical*) sense. "Unlike *American Graffiti*," Jameson says, *Star Wars* "does not reinvent a picture of the past in its lived totality; rather by reinventing the feel and shape of characteristic art objects of an older period [in this case, Buck Rogers] ... it seeks to reawaken a sense of the past associated with those objects."[15]

---

[11]   Jean-François Lyotard, *The Postmodern Condition: A Report on Knowledge*, trans. Geoff Bennington and Brian Massumi (Minneapolis: University of Minnesota Press, 1984), 21–2.

[12]   Ibid., 22.

[13]   Coppola produced each of Lucas' first two directorial efforts: *THX 1138* (1971) and *American Graffiti* (1973).

[14]   Fredric Jameson, "Postmodernism and Consumer Society," *The Norton Anthology of Theory and Criticism*, ed. Vincent Leitch (New York: W.W. Norton & Company, 2001), 1965.

[15]   Ibid., 1966.

With this in mind, *Captain EO* takes Jameson's concept of the nostalgia film one step further: it is a rather immediate work of nostalgia *for* a work of nostalgia (Lucas' *Star Wars* trilogy). Beyond the films' similar sci-fi themes, the parallels between *Captain EO*'s cast and that of *Star Wars* are readily apparent:[16] a wookie-like character named Geex (made up of conjoined twins Idee and Odee); a C-3PO figure named Major Domo (with a smaller robot named Minor Domo strapped to his back); and a small, flying creature named Fuzzball that resembles an Ewok in both sound and appearance. The battle scene in the first half of *Captain EO* is undeniably reminiscent of the climatic Death Star battle scenes in both *Star Wars* and *Return of the Jedi*. And the dark, evil villain—the Supreme Leader (played by Anjelica Huston)—is revealed to be, not unlike Darth Vader/Anakin Skywalker, wholesome inside, thanks to the cosmically attuned powers of the protagonist.[17] To call the *Star Wars* trilogy a bygone era might seem a stretch, but it is crucial to recognize that *Captain EO* was also designed to appeal to very young children, who would not have seen Lucas' previous work in the theatre. Viewed independent of its predecessor, *Captain EO* is in essence like *Star Wars* itself: a work of the future that is a nostalgic pastiche of a work of the past.

Nineteen Eighty-Six

It is also instructive to remember that, by the unveiling of *Captain EO*, "Star Wars" had come to refer to the Reagan administration's proposed Strategic Defense Initiative every bit as much as (if not more than) Lucas' film trilogy. The Cold War offered a very real nuclear threat and the Chernobyl nuclear accident had occurred only a few months prior, in April 1986. *Captain EO* is reflective of this apocalyptic specter, being set on an industrial planet that has been laid to waste.[18] This doomsday scenario seems much less threatening in retrospect; we know that the 1980s did not give way to nuclear apocalypse, and that the United

---

[16]   Beyond *Star Wars*, there are a number of clear associations with other productions and franchises throughout *Captain EO*. For example, the Supreme Leader (played by Angelica Huston) is highly reminiscent of the characters in the musical *Cats*, from her feline facial features to the fact that she has claws instead of fingers. Even Major/Minor Domo's transformation from a robot into a guitar and drum set at the outset of "We Are Here to Change the World" is an obvious nod to Hasbro's Transformers, which had reached staggering popularity in just two years after their initial release in 1984.

[17]   Contrary to Corliss's prior assessment, Jackson's character bears more resemblance to Luke Skywalker than Han Solo; he is the "chosen one" sent to bring salvation against the forces of evil (Skywalker), rather than a rugged, romantically involved smuggler (Solo).

[18]   Such influence is also evident in the film's anti-apocalyptic name, so designated by Lucas as "eo" is Greek for "dawn." This overtly utopian title stands in contrast with the film's original name, *The Intergalactic Music Man*, which was dropped because it was considered too wordy.

States ultimately emerged "victorious" in their military, economic, and ideological struggle with the Soviet Union. The easily ignored reality, however, is that nuclear war is as much a possibility today as it ever has been. Susan Sontag, in an apt nod to Coppola, emphasizes "a permanent modern scenario: apocalypse looms—and it doesn't occur. And still it looms ... Apocalypse is now a long running serial: not 'Apocalypse Now,' but 'Apocalypse from now on.'"[19]

While it would be speculative to assert that *Captain EO* is centered on U.S.–Soviet relations, its narrative is clearly rooted in an ideological power struggle. The mission of Captain EO's crew, while ostensibly to offer a "gift" to the Supreme Leader, is actually to overthrow a presumably oppressive regime. It is significant that this mission is rooted in immediate political change, rather than trickle-down cultural influence. As Lyotard observes, "In the computer age, the question of knowledge is now more than ever a question of government."[20] Although the anonymously masked, black-uniformed troops facing Captain EO are instantly transformed into attractive, pastel-clad men and women whose faces are plainly evident, they remain exceptions in a dark world. It is only when the Supreme Leader is changed into a goddess-queen that a technicolor horizon emerges. The blackened steel that had served as the palace is replaced by Doric columns draped with ivy, and the metal planet gives way to an idyllic natural setting.

While Jackson had previously ventured into utopian-themed productions—most notably with "Can You Feel It" (1980) and the music video for "Beat It" (1983)—the production of *Captain EO* marks a notable turning point for Jackson's conceptual focus. "We Are the World," the smash charity single written by Jackson and Lionel Richie, was recorded just before the making of *Captain EO*, and over the next decade Jackson's work would often be characterized by socially harmonious themes: the introspective call-to-action "Man in the Mirror" (1987), the racially defiant "Black or White" (1991), and the utopian triumvirate of "Heal the World" (1992), "You Are Not Alone" (1995), and "Earth Song" (1995).

Of all these works, though, it is perhaps *Captain EO* that stands as Jackson's most compelling and complex utopian commentary. Jameson has elsewhere emphasized his agreement with Darko Suvin's suggestion that utopia is a "socio-economic subset of Science Fiction," rather than the other way around. Anthony Giddens' influential *The Consequences of Modernity* offers an equally interesting theory on this relationship with the concept of "disembedding," which he defines as "the 'lifting out' of social relations from local contexts of interaction and their restructuring across indefinite spans of time-space."[21] Set in the future on a different planet and populated by a cast of fantastic creatures, *Captain EO* effectively removes such local interactions and forces the audience to view its message in the

---

[19]   As cited in: Anthony Giddens, *The Consequences of Modernity* (Stanford: Stanford University Press, 1990), 134.

[20]   Lyotard, *Postmodern Condition*, 9.

[21]   Giddens, *The Consequences of Modernity*, 21.

abstract sense.[22] It does so in large part because any resolutions in a contemporary setting would be greeted with bias and bipartisanism. In this respect, *Captain EO*'s fantasy world as a tool for social commentary is both appropriate and essential. As Lyotard insists, "It must be clear that it is our business not to supply reality but to invent allusions to the conceivable which cannot be presented."[23]

The timing of *Captain EO*'s production and release further contributes to the complication of the film's utopian message. Jameson contends that:

> During the Cold War ... Utopia had become a synonym for Stalinism and had come to designate a program which neglected human frailty and original sin, and betrayed a will to uniformity and the ideal purity of a perfect system that always had to be imposed by force on its imperfect and reluctant subjects.[24]

The classic example of such dystopian recognition—George Orwell's *Nineteen Eighty-Four*—seems to offer exactly the sort of irresolution that *Captain EO* thoroughly repudiates. As Phillip Wegner observes of Orwell's conclusion, "With the only remainder being a terrible fear, *Nineteen Eighty-Four* appears to have short-circuited the very ideology of historical movement that had heretofore served as the foundation of the narrative utopia form."[25]

Captain EO was certainly not the first work to return to this foundation and to consciously reject the narrative of *Nineteen Eighty-Four*. This had already been memorably accomplished in a number of instances, including Ridley Scott's "1984" commercial (itself a forerunner to *Captain EO* as big-budget, sci-fi short film) for Apple Computer two years prior. And it is tempting to play up the contemporary harmlessness of a work like *Nineteen Eighty-Four*; after all, 1986 had already moved past the date described in Orwell's dystopia. In 1987, a critic no less than Harold Bloom would describe *Nineteen Eighty-Four* as simply a "literary period piece" whose justification "cannot differ much from a defense of period pieces of clothes, household objects, popular music, movies, and the lower

---

[22]   The film also points to a future that aligns with Lyotard's (1984) privileging of "performativity" over productivity (p. 11). This gift offered by Captain EO's crew is, appropriately, one they can "not only see ... but hear," with music and dance holding the magical keys to social transformation. This abstract revolution is again crucial to the film's utopian suggestion. As Lyotard (1984) suggests, "Given equal competence (no longer the acquisition of knowledge, but in its production), what extra performativity depends on in the final analysis is 'imagination,' which allows one either to make a new move or change the rules of the game" (52).

[23]   Lyotard, *Postmodern Condition*, 81.

[24]   Jameson, *Archaeologies of the Future*, xi.

[25]   Phillip Wegner, *Imaginary Communities: Utopia, the Nation, and the Spatial Histories of Modernity* (Berkeley: University of California Press, 2002), 191.

reaches of the visual arts."[26] It is likewise easy to pigeonhole *Captain EO* as a period piece of 1980s music, fashion, and cinematic technology.

But such dismissal misses the essential point of utopian works like *Captain EO* and dystopian works like *Nineteen Eighty-Four*. Wegner contends that, if Bloom is correct that *Nineteen Eighty-Four* is a period piece, then "it is of a period from whose repetitious history we have yet to awake."[27] In much the same way, *Captain EO*'s 2010 re-release finds America again in an escalating military situation and at ideological odds with a foreign threat on the other side of the world (in this case, Al-Qaeda). *Captain EO*'s resolution rings just as improbably easy in 2010, making the film a fantasy more than its science fiction setting ever could. Unlike *Nineteen Eighty-Four*, or even Ridley Scott's acclaimed *Blade Runner* (1982), *Captain EO* presents a way out—and an exceedingly easy one at that.

One World, One Nation

Exactly *what* it provides a way out of and *why* it does so are decidedly more complicated subjects. Is a homogeneously bright world more desirable than a dark and diverse planet? Giddens addresses the infeasibility of "an overall movement towards 'one-world,'" as "few today anticipate in the near future the emergence of the 'world-state' which many in the early part of [the twentieth] century saw as a real project."[28] One might question whether this has ever been a prerequisite for utopia (even Thomas More described his Utopia as a "world apart"), but *Captain EO*, which on the surface appears to glorify creativity and individual identity, particularly challenges this concept with its emphasis on moral binaries. The opening line of the film–"The cosmos: a universe of good and evil"–sets this trend in motion, as *Captain EO* consistently reinforces what Donna Haraway terms "certain dualisms … in Western traditions."[29]

Captain EO is termed an "infidel" by the Supreme Leader, one who "infects [her] world with [his] presence," and he is sentenced to "one hundred years of torture in [her] deepest dungeon." Although Captain EO initially accepts the punishments, on the ground that his crew has come there "uninvited and unannounced," it is quickly evident that he does not intend to submit. The presumably intended theme- that change is not easy but necessary and ultimately desirable-could just as easily be viewed as an imperialist message. The "gift" that is offered is hardly a welcome contribution, with its objective being the ideological conquest of the planet and the overthrow of the reigning administration. This begs the question: is *Captain*

---

[26] As cited in Wegner, *Imaginary Communities*, 184.

[27] Ibid., 185.

[28] Giddens, *The Consequences of Modernity*, 66.

[29] Donna Haraway, "A Cyborg Manifesto: Science, Technology, and Socialist-Feminism in the Late Twentieth Century," in *Simians, Cyborgs, and Women: The Reinvention of Nature* (London: Free Association Books, 1991), 177.

EO really about tolerance, or is it about the imposition of a subjectively "better" way of life?

The song that covers the transformative scene, "We Are Here to Change the World," bears this out in its lyrics: "We're here to stimulate, eliminate / And congregate, illuminate / ... So do surrender / 'Cause the power's deep inside my soul."[30] The necessity of "surrender" to a power that is both intellectually illuminated and morally superior rings exceedingly awkward from a post-colonial standpoint. The Supreme Leader's struggle against relinquishing her identity is clearly depicted, as she is seen in pain at the moment of transformation, while Captain EO smiles triumphantly. The ensuing celebration segues into Jackson's second song, "Another Part of Me," which proves equally reflective of this ideology: We're takin' over / We have the truth / ... This is our planet / You're one of us."[31]

The claim that the planet's inhabitants are now "one of us" raises the issue of annexation every bit as much as transformation. The result is not so much "one world" as it is simply "one nation." As Wegner contends:

> While the spatial and cultural homogeneity of the Utopian cities figures them as part of an abstract universal space, this same feature signals their unity, or shared *national* identity: for their very sameness marks their particularity, their fundamental cultural *difference* from any other such spaces found outside the bounded nation.[32]

Captain EO's conclusion shows the band of liberators exiting the scene (and the planet) to these lyrics: "The planets are linin' up / We're bringin' brighter days / ... Can't you see? / You're just another part of me."

This new national authority is left unspecified, and it should not be assumed that it is a quasi-American establishment (or a direct parallel to any other existent government). In many ways, the original industrial planet is analogous to Giddens' notion of the "juggernaut" that threatens to overthrow our own existence: "a runaway engine of enormous power which, collectively as human beings, we can drive to some extent but which also threatens to rush out of our control and which could rend itself asunder."[33] This raises the unsettling notion that the dark world Captain EO lands on offers a more realistic rendering of our contemporary Earth than the idyllic image at film's end. As Giddens explains, "In the industrialised

---

[30]   Although an integral part of *Captain EO*, "We Are Here to Change the World" was not officially released on an album until 2004, when it was included on *Michael Jackson: The Ultimate Collection*.

[31]   "Another Part of Me" was also included on Jackson's *Bad* album the following year, and was released as the record's sixth single in July 1988.

[32]   Wegner, *Imaginary Communities*, 51.

[33]   Giddens, *The Consequences of Modernity*, 139.

sectors of the globe—and, increasingly, elsewhere—human beings live in a created environment of action which is, of course, physical but no longer just natural."[34]

A Cyborg Manifesto

This trend is the focus of one of the most provocative critical articles of the time, Donna Haraway's "A Cyborg Manifesto" which was first published in 1985 during *Captain EO*'s production. Haraway argues that "the production of universal, totalizing theory is a major mistake that misses most of reality."[35] "By the late twentieth century in United States scientific culture," Haraway observes, "the boundary between human and animal is thoroughly breached. The last beachheads of uniqueness have been polluted if not turned into amusement parks."[36] Along these lines, Captain EO's entire crew is composed of animals and robots—in a film created explicitly for exhibition at an amusement park—and his superior officer, Commander Bog, is a holographic image of Dick Shawn's head.

It is, however, the Supreme Leader who presents the most obvious application for Haraway's cyborg figure, which she describes as "a condensed image of both imagination and material reality, the two joined centres structuring any possibility of historical transformation" and that is, consequently, "a creature in a post-gender world."[37] The Supreme Leader, while feminine in voice, has an upper body that is more machine than human, and has no body below the waist, as her torso gives way to a series of wires and cables that suspend her. Captain EO holds the Supreme Leader to be "very beautiful within … but without a key to unlock it, and that is [his] gift to [her]." While the film would seem to reinforce the notion of inner beauty, it just as surely (in a trend all too common for Disney pictures) quantifies that beauty in traditional physical terms.

The cyborg presents a crucial exception to such traditional notions, as it is "oppositional, utopian, and completely without innocence."[38] The moral touchstones that drive Captain EO's crew hold no appeal for the Supreme Leader and her subjects, and they are decidedly content with the order of their "world of despair." Haraway insists that "the cyborg does not dream of community on the model of the organic family … The cyborg would not recognize the Garden of Eden; it is not made of mud and cannot dream of returning to dust."[39] It does not fear the apocalypse in the same way we would because it has never been dust to begin with. In saving the Supreme Leader from this apocalyptic setting, Captain EO may have performed an unnecessary task.

---

[34] Ibid., 60.
[35] Haraway, "Cyborg Manifesto," 181.
[36] Ibid., 151.
[37] Ibid., 150.
[38] Ibid., 151.
[39] Ibid.

While the Supreme Leader is clearly cast as the villain of *Captain EO*, her role as a disembedded tool of social commentary is indispensable. A figure that is part human, part animal, and part machine plays directly into Haraway's conception of social possibility:

> From one perspective, a cyborg world is about the final imposition of a grid of control on the planet, about the final abstraction embodied in a Star Wars apocalypse waged in the name of defence ... From another perspective, a cyborg world might be about lived social and bodily realities in which people are not afraid of their joint kinship with animals and machines, not afraid of permanently partial identities and contradictory standpoints. The political struggle is to see from both perspectives at once because each reveals both dominations and possibilities unimaginable from the other vantage point.[40]

In such a way, the utopian potential of the cyborg exceeds any sort of resolution that the transformed goddess-queen might provide. As Haraway explains, "cyborg imagery can suggest a way out of the maze of dualisms in which we have explained our bodies and our tools to ourselves ... Though both are bound in the spiral dance, I would rather be a cyborg than a goddess."[41]

The dissolution of the Supreme Leader does not mean, however, that *Captain EO* rejects Haraway's theory. On the contrary, the film's namesake character provides the fullest realization of "imagination and material reality," as well as "permanently partial identities."[42] It is crucial that it is Jackson who plays the film's hero, as Jackson represents—better than any other celebrity of the time—the transcendence of race and gender. From a racial standpoint, it was clear by the time of *Captain EO* that Jackson's skin was becoming lighter, the result of both skin disorder and cosmetic surgery.[43] Prior to *Captain EO*'s filming, Jackson had undergone his third rhinoplasty and burn treatment to his scalp to offset the bodily damages from his infamous 1984 Pepsi commercial accident. This trend would see Jackson become an individual of indeterminate racial appearance in the years following the film. Michael Awkward, whose work is discussed in Chapter 4, would term Jackson's burgeoning racial ambiguity as "an important step in our efforts if not to heal the world, to begin to resolve epistemological tensions which ... often result in full-fledged intra- and interterritorial battles."[44]

---

[40]   Ibid., 154.

[41]   Ibid., 181.

[42]   Ibid., 150, 154.

[43]   Just prior to *Captain EO*'s release, Jackson had been diagnosed with vitiligo and lupus, setting off continual speculation as to whether Jackson's physical transformation was the involuntary consequence of disease or the conscious result of cosmetic alteration.

[44]   Michael Awkward, *Negotiating Difference: Race, Gender, and the Politics of Positionality* (Chicago: University of Chicago Press, 1995), 192.

Likewise, Jackson's delicate figure and feminized voice stand in stark opposition to the rugged, über-masculine figures that regularly emerge as the heroes of similar works (such as *Star Wars'* Han Solo and *Blade Runner's* Rick Deckard, both played by Harrison Ford). He does not get the girl at film's end, nor does he care to. There are no economic motivations, nor any aspirations of personal power in the wake of revolution. His sole fidelity is to his conception of universal harmony, irrespective of race, gender, or even species imperatives. Jackson's own physical transformation—the subject of so much tabloid speculation and public criticism—works to his decided advantage in this context. Jackson is the literal embodiment of the cyborg, in a manner that bypasses "bizarre" in favor of "progressive" and "utopian." For that reason, Jackson himself—even more than the character he plays—emerges as the hero of *Captain EO*, the archetypal postmodern figure of utopian potential.

The Once and Future King

The contemporary assessment of *Captain EO* will doubtlessly remain as divided as ever. At the very worst, the film provided two new Jackson songs and one of his most intricately entertaining music videos. It offers a prime test case of what Lyotard calls "the relationship of scientific knowledge to 'popular' knowledge."[45] Even if one dismisses *Captain EO* as academically or philosophically inconsequential, it represents a definitive cultural artifact of the mid 1980s.

However, the defining legacy of *Captain EO* is rooted in its treatment of the future, leaving its critical reputation to be determined. In many ways, *Captain EO* represents the fulfillment of Sergei Eisenstein's earliest desires that film not be a movement "back to the story," but rather "to the story ahead of us."[46] It is a family film that directly faces the apocalyptic possibility of the future and illustrates an effective resolution; just as surely, it stars a celebrity who continues to be redefined in popular culture. As Giddens emphasizes, "In conditions of modernity, the future is always open, not just in terms of the ordinary contingency of things, but in terms of the reflexivity of knowledge in relation to which social practices are organized."[47]

Much as *This Is It* earns Jackson "a redemptive legacy",[48] the revival of *Captain EO* offers a testament to both the transformative dimensions and the contemporary relevance of Jackson's art. In effect, the film allows us to remember our future *and* Jackson's future in a way that is dismissive of the world after 1986, rife with the freshly imaginative potential of a utopian ending. Jackson's own legacy is proof that a positive resolution is not as easy as *Captain EO* suggests, but also that the final word will always be left open to the future.

45   Lyotard, *Postmodern Condition*, 28.
46   Eisenstein, *Film Form*, 121.
47   Giddens, *The Consequences of Modernity*, 83–4.
48   Corliss, "He's Still a Thriller," 58.

Chapter 9

Tomorrow Today: Michael Jackson as Science Fiction Character, Author, and Text

Ruchi Mital

Given Michael Jackson's use of science fiction in the constructions of life and art, this poetic chapter by Ruchi Mital suggests that Jackson embodies the future in the present moment as creator/simulation, human/posthuman, and mythic hero/ classic entertainer. Mital's argument here supposes the fusion of fiction, theory, reality, and the future already encoded in an evolving history. Her proof of this becomes Michael Jackson himself, an essentially "post-human" performance of himself.

It was a bright cold day in April, and the clocks were striking thirteen.

George Orwell, *1984*

The sky above the port was the color of television, tuned to a dead channel.

William Gibson, *Neuromancer*

You close your eyes and hope that this is just imagination.

Michael Jackson, *Thriller*

The stark, discordant note struck by the first line of George Orwell's classic dystopian vision of the future no longer resonates—though it has never ceased to alarm. The clocks have been digitized. Orwell's specter anticipated the future ghost of the obsessions of cyberpunk science fiction, a genre defined by William Gibson's 1984 novel *Neuromancer*. By 1984, the future was a place in which the physical world itself was mediated. Beyond the power of media to control our thoughts, Jean Baudrillard states:

> the confusion of the medium and the message is the first great formula of this new era. The eye of TV is no longer the source of the absolute gaze ... There is no longer any imperative of submission to the model, or to the gaze "YOU are the model!" ... Such is the watershed of a hyperreal sociality.[1]

---

[1]   Jean Baudrillard, *Simulacra and Simulation*, trans. Sheila Faria Glaser (Ann Arbor: University of Michigan Press, 1994), 29.

In the postmodern, hyperreal universe—marked by relentless technological advancement that continually changes us as it changes, and the collapsed boundaries between traditional oppositions such as the public/private, organic/ inorganic, self/other—cyberpunk science fiction is the discourse that seems to best mirror our present reality. Characterized by a near-future in which virtual realities meld with physical realities and we consume our desires and identities as products, cyberpunk questions the possibility of freedom and transcendence in a simulated reality. Frederic Jameson states, "cyberpunk is, henceforth, for many of us, the supreme *literary* expression if not of postmodernism, then of late capitalism itself."[2] At this intersection of cyberpunk science fiction and postmodern theory was the beginning of a dialogue that spoke to what it meant to be human, what was to become of human *being*, in a hyperreal world where once imaginary possibilities of instant global communication and the fusion of man and machine were "real," and the real itself was becoming increasingly hallucinatory. In the moments this discussion was being born, questioning the place of man in a world dominated by multinational capitalism and mass media, one man's face dominated the media on a global scale, and continued to do so over the next 30 years. Michael Jackson.

By the late 1970s, Jackson was already a hero, having risen from a working class African American family to international fame. Yet it soon became apparent that he was more than a hero of the American dream. In 1983 he unleashed the "moonwalk," his signature dance move. With this gliding movement in which he moves backwards while appearing to move forwards, Jackson was becoming otherworldly, seemingly freed from the laws of motion. Seeing the moonwalk was like seeing the reversed wheels of a moving vehicle on film, knowing that it was somehow happening in "real life." And then came the release of *Thriller*, which, according to Griel Marcus led to "the year of Michael Jackson."[3] As Marcus notes, "*Thriller* became an image ... neither the form nor content remained tied to the record itself ... *Thriller* reinforced its own reality principle."[4]

Today, television wields "power as seduction, not (primarily) power as coercion."[5] As the distance between screen and viewer has collapsed, we have moved into the realm of the simulacrum, the image that "has no relation to reality whatsoever."[6] *Neuromancer*'s protagonist, Case, is a "console cowboy" who lives "jacked into a custom cyberspace deck that projected his disembodied

---

[2]   As cited in: Scott Bukatman, *Terminal Identity: The Virtual Subject in Postmodern Science Fiction* (New York: New York University, 1992), 6.

[3]   Griel Marcus, *Lipstick Traces: A Secret History of the Twentieth Century* (Cambridge, MA: Harvard University Press, 1989), 105.

[4]   Ibid., 105–6.

[5]   Arthur Kroker and David Cook, "Television and the Triumph of Culture," in *Storming the Reality Studio: A Casebook of Cyberpunk and Postmodern Science Fiction*, ed. Larry McCaffery (Durham, NC: Duke University Press, 1986), 232.

[6]   Baudrillard, *Simulacra and Simulation*, 6.

consciousness into the consensual hallucination that was the matrix."[7] Actions in the matrix of cyberspace affect the real world; the real world simultaneously changes the shape of cyberspace: an appropriate metaphor for the non-space of television and the Internet. Spanning the move from the twentieth into the twenty-first century, Jackson's career has been an evolving, ongoing performance we experience through the media. Applied to Jackson, the term "media circus" assumes special significance. Early in his career, as Margo Jefferson points out in Chapter 1, he famously "gave his manager a copy of a book of P.T. Barnum's 'theories and philosophies' telling him 'I want my whole career to be the greatest show on earth.'"[8] He became ringmaster, supposedly leaking wild rumors about himself, most notably the science fictional hoax that he slept in a hyperbaric chamber. Compare this to the hero of Bruce Sterling's cyberpunk classic, *Schismatrix*, Abelard Lindsay, as he describes his plan to create a circus so that he can move freely: "you will spread rumors about me: my charm, my brilliance, my hidden resources … and establish a free-wheeling, free-spending atmosphere of carefree hedonism. It will be a huge confidence trick that will bamboozle the entire world."[9] As Yuan points out, the ability to *move* and to transform are crucial to an understanding of Jackson's image. And they are at the heart of cyberpunk science function.

Transformations

"Keep all heroes going long enough, and they become gods," writes Neil Gaiman in his introduction to Alfred Bester's 1956 *The Stars My Destination*.[10] But what if we keep a hero going in a world that has since reached out to the stars, science fiction has become cyberpunk, and its concern is not only outer space, but cyberspace? In this world, we have Michael Jackson. Jackson's use of science fiction in constructions of his public self, private self, and art, and the fact that these are consumed through the mass media of television and film, expose the hyperreality which marks the postmodern universe: an implosion of fiction, theory, and the world of experience. Through the lens of cyberpunk postmodernism, we will read Jackson's work-including his films, body, and television appearances-to discover that in this game of simulation, he is both author and text, embodying the future in the present moment as science fiction itself seeks to do.

---

[7]   William Gibson, *Neuromancer* (New York: Ace Books, 1984), 5.

[8]   David Yuan, "The Celebrity Freak: Michael Jackson's Grotesque Glory," in *Freakery: Cultural Spectacles of the Extraordinary Body*, ed. Rosemarie Garland Thomson (New York: New York University Press, 1997), 372.

[9]   Bruce Sterling, *Schismatrix Plus* (New York: Ace Books, 1996), 343.

[10]   Neil Gaiman, introduction to *The Stars My Destination*, by Alfred Bester (New York: Vintage Books, 1996), x.

With this in mind we return to 1984, the year of *Neuromancer* and *Thriller*. Postmodern cyberpunk fiction is characterized by the use of recognizable, nostalgic tropes that are deployed for their charge and then subverted to create multiple meanings. The video for "Thriller" begins with an identifiable set-up: a 1950s couple ("Michael" and "Denise") drives through classic horror film woods. Even Jackson's first transformation into an agonized werewolf with blazing eyes is a familiar gothic/horror trope. Then *Thriller* takes the first of many turns that push the classic science fiction motif of anthropomorphic transformation and accompanying anxiety into the realm of the simulacrum. This is not just any transformation; Jackson is too well known to us as himself. Playfully and seductively he sings, "I'll save you from the terror on the screen / I'll make you see." "I'll make you see" implies that a truth will be revealed. It also functions as "I'll make you look." The flipside of terror is always fascination, and so we look. Through successive layers of screens-the viewer's screen, the movie screen in the film-and "real" Jacksons-the performer, the innocent main character, the monster—our capacity to define is destroyed along with objective identity and reality. Each time danger closes in, there is a flip from reality to fiction, from human to supernatural being, and back again. While the film's central metaphor may tell us that transformation and the ability to elude definition offer escape and freedom, the metaphor is contained within the intrinsic circularity of the screen: the site of a world beyond metaphor and meaning. Thus, the video operates with an awareness of the dissolution between dimensions of reality and fiction, while retaining the charged metaphor of transformation and the monstrous self/other.

Jackson's ability to transform is physical, fantastical, factual, temporal, and of the future. In his 1995 *MTV Video Music Awards* performance, Jackson presents a medley of songs with the distinctive dance moves associated with each in past performances, erasing temporal boundaries between his many self-constructions. As the "present" Jackson embodies his various selves, we must accept the fluid nature of the self as a construction. While we recognize the various Jacksons within this single performance, his new moves appear hardly human. They are stripped down to a mechanical, robotic essence suggesting that Jackson is part machine, technologically enhanced. Donna Haraway's seminal "Cyborg Manifesto," discussed in detail above by Miller in Chapter 8, defines the cyborg as "a cybernetic organism, a hybrid of machine and organism, a creature of social reality as well as social fiction": the cyborg is, of course, an essential element of the cyberpunk world.[11] In this riveting performance, the association of Jackson's body with the machine challenges the distinction between nature and technology and we observe:

---

[11]   Donna Haraway, "A Cyborg Manifesto: Science, Technology, and Socialist-Feminism in the Late Twentieth Century," in *Contemporary Literary Criticism*, ed. Robert Con Davis and Ronald Schleifer (New York: Longman, 1998), 696.

the technological capability-the mimetic ability of cyber-machine-organisms to simulate (and replace) human consciousness, the power of electronic images of the self to imitate and replicate themselves [which] endows cyborgisms with a supra-natural and a supra-physical power that transcends the merely human and that displaces the simply organic and natural.[12]

Moonwalker

"When the real is no longer what it was, nostalgia assumes full meaning. There is a plethora of myths of origin and of signs of reality—a plethora of truth, of secondary objectivity, and authenticity."[13] This drive towards rediscovering the real, of re-infusing hyperreality with reality, is exemplified by *Moonwalker* (1988), which begins with a "multi-image live performance spectacle," moves into a "retrospective of 24 years of hits," and includes music videos for the songs "Badder," "Speed Demon," and "Leave Me Alone," before arriving at the centerpiece, the short film *Smooth Criminal*.

As *Moonwalker* opens, we see the spotlight, the stage, the single sequined glove, and those magical socks: the symbols that signify the Michael Jackson myth. These are not symbols deeply imbedded in a collective unconscious; they are manufactured symbols that refer only to themselves and back to Jackson. The supernatural title *Moonwalker* appears superimposed over a massive concert crowd illuminated by the orange glow of lighters: devotees. This gives way to a montage of Jackson performance footage: mobs of people faint, dance, cry, and convulse in uncontrollable ecstasies. Performances are interspersed with images of historical figures and events as if to say the history of Jackson is one with the history of the world. The montage ends with Jackson alone on stage standing in the figure of the cross, his features first held in the expression of the martyr, then finally dissolved by the light he radiates. Through the conflation of symbols, Jackson's historical and messianic presence is established. Jackson's presence, however, is always part of a performance, revealing the performative nature of history. It is a history of clips, an edited history with a soundtrack, made more real on film than the real.

The transition from human to superhuman is crucial to cyberpunk precursor *The Stars My Destination*. Through technological enhancement, a warping of space and time, and a newly discovered love of humanity, uneducated brute Gully Foyle experiences divine revelation and becomes a messiah. He offers the masses knowledge of space-jaunting, the ability to transport oneself across previously unconquerable distances in space and time. Jackson's role as a messiah is painted

---

[12]   Louis J. Kern, "Terminal Notions of What We May Become: Synthflesh, Cyberreality, and the Post-Human Body," in *Simulacrum America: The USA and the Popular Media*, ed. Elizabeth Kraus and Carolin Auer (Rochester: Camden House, 2000), 95.

[13]   Baudrillard, *Simulacra and Simulation*, 6.

in similar terms. He expresses his love for the masses as he sings, telling them they have the power to change the world. While Gully must jaunt around the world with his physical body to reach the people, Jackson projects himself to the global audience of television and film where time is collapsed into an eternal present.

The video for "Speed Demon" plays not only with the form Jackson takes, but also those of the media and its spectators. It is a continuation of the video for "Badder" in which children replace the adult characters from the original *Bad* video, replicating their movements and expressions. The "little Jackson" walks into a cloud of smoke from which the "real" adult Jackson emerges in a Hollywood studio. A tour is in progress; the tourists on the trolley are exaggerated claymation figures. On seeing Jackson, their benign expressions become grotesque and carnivorous and they start to chase him. The paparazzi resemble military, their cameras and film, machine guns and ammunition. The media captures, yet the chase is vital.

Ducking into a wardrobe room, Jackson emerges not simply wearing a costume, but *as* the costume: a claymation rabbit in an aviator outfit. Though disguised in his new form, he cannot help but continue the game. He taunts his pursuers with his distinctive dance, by which they recognize him and resume their pursuit. The reality of Jackson, then, is beyond his form, in the essence of his movement. The pursuit ensues, the song begins, and we rush through a vivid neon cityscape. Compare the city Jackson zips through to Gibson's descriptions of Night City in *Neuromancer*: a "neon shudder" replete with criminals, everyone "swarming the street in an intricate dance of desire."[14] Characterized by sensory overload and density, these city-worlds are cyberpunk's extreme expression of capitalist technoculture. The bike is the preferred vehicle, allowing one to move freely through the twisting city grid; Chevette Washington, the bike messenger in Gibson's *Virtual Light*, knows this well:

> Sometimes, when she rode hard, when she could really proj, Chevette got free of everything: the city, her body, even time … though it felt like freedom, it was really the melding-with, the clicking-in, that did it. The bike between her legs was like some hyper-evolved alien tail she'd somehow extruded … .[15]

A transforming bike is Jackson's agent of liberation; he rides alone into the desert where he takes off his costume to become the "real" Jackson once more. It isn't over yet. The aviator rabbit comes to life and a dance battle ensues between Jackson and his alter ego. In his final move, Jackson spins and whirls, revolving through all of the characters we have seen in "Speed Demon" up until now, until the rabbit finally disappears. It seems Jackson has won; he is free because of his ability to meld and transform. But a police officer stops him and writes out a ticket, saying, "I need your autograph right here." Jackson has not escaped. As it did

---

14   Gibson, *Neuromancer*, 15, 11.
15   William Gibson, *Virtual Light* (New York: Bantam Books, 1993), 131.

for Chevette, it seemed the bike offered freedom, but it was the "melding … that did it." This is precisely what we see when Jackson enters Žižek's desert of the real. He breaks free from his pursuers and his disguise, but the disguise incarnates and challenges his identity. To survive he must "click-in," becoming more real than real, embodying multiple identities in a dance of metamorphosis. As George Slusser writes in "Literary MTV," cyberspace for *Neuromancer*'s Case "is everywhere and it is nowhere. Because he can never step outside it he ignores it."[16] Jackson cannot and does not ignore hyperreality, he plays with it. He is the cyberpunk text, character, and author.

Next is the video for "Leave Me Alone," a text further analyzed in this collection in Chapters 5 and 10. As pointed out by my colleagues here, the video is a surreal collage of animated images of the many bizarre media rumors associated with Jackson. While he may be singing, "leave me alone," the video brings the rumors to life more vividly than any tabloid: realer than the real. Both Umberto Eco and Baudrillard identify the amusement park as the pinnacle of hyperreality.[17] In *Leave Me Alone*, Jackson's body functions as a site of simulation equal to that of the screen. The Jackson that sustains the amusement part breaks free of it, standing wearily to rise above mountains as it crumbles. In this moment it is impossible to separate this image from our image of Neverland, the amusement park we know the "private" Jackson calls home. Collapsing levels of fiction and reality, *Leave Me Alone* positions Jackson's body as a contested, de-centered site of both play and possible resistance.

Our journey through *Moonwalker* leads us to the work's centerpiece, the 40-minute film *Smooth Criminal*. Within multiple frames and narrative layers, the film pits Michael and his three young friends against the evil drug dealer Lideo. In a 1930s noir setting, Michael is chased and trapped by Lideo's army of faceless foot soldiers. As they fire upon him, Michael drops to his knees in agony. The shape of his shadow changes from human to a futuristic car that fires rockets as he speeds away. Once more, when cornered, Michael Jackson transforms to gain his freedom. No longer the anthropomorphic transformation from the *Thriller* video, in *Smooth Criminal* man and machine are fused. Meanwhile, the children await Michael at Club 30s. When he arrives (in his human form once more) and steps into the door, a blinding white light pours out of the club, hopping with "guys and dolls." More than a violent gangster film, *Smooth Criminal* is self-aware in its non-threatening, old-fashioned musical and visual format. The film successfully employs the cyberpunk method of re-contextualizing familiar motifs to create new modes of understanding. Larry McCaffery notes, "*Neuromancer*'s hero, Case, is a

---

[16]   George Slusser, "Literary MTV," in *Storming the Reality Studio: A Casebook of Cyberpunk and Postmodern Science Fiction*, ed. Larry McCaffery (Durham, NC: Duke University Press, 1991), 339.

[17]   Umberto Eco, *Travels in Hyperreality*, trans. William Weaver (San Diego: Harcourt, 1986); Jean Baudrillard, "The Ecstasy of Communication," in *The Anti-Aesthetic: Essays on Postmodern Culture*, ed. Hal Foster (New York: New Press, 1998).

'detective' ... Molly is a 'moll' out of 1940s film noire ... the 'messages' ... bear similarities to ... the hero lost in a society of criminal and impersonal forces, a nostalgic longing for a more authentic, uncorrupted past."[18] He argues that within this framework of conventions, Gibson introduces the present concerns of cyberpunk postmodernism in a new discourse, including:

> the contrast between the human "meat" and metal ... the denaturing of the body and the transformation of time and space in the postindustrial world ... the "dance of data" that comprises so much of life today (a "dance" which Gibson employs as a metaphor for everything from the interaction of subatomic particles to the interactions on multinational corporations) ... the uneasy recognition that our primal urge to replicate our consciousness and physical beings ... is *not* leading us closer to the dream of immortality, but is creating merely a pathetic parody, a meta-existence or simulacra of our essences that is supplanting us ... .[19]

Since Jackson's project is not limited to what we recognize as a purely fictional mode, his presence in the film heightens this new discourse. Within a Jackson film we are always confronted with the body of Jackson, a site of simulation and much debate in the *real* world of the media and the public sphere. The infusion of one fiction within another exposes the hyperreality not only of the work, but also of the medium through—and space in which—we receive it, and consequently of reality itself.

As we enter the club, the song "Smooth Criminal" begins, and the film's narrative is interrupted by a choreographed dance format present in many of Jackson's videos. As the music reaches crescendo, the skylight explodes and glass shards cascade into the room. The internal logic of the dance sequence is interrupted as pop music is replaced by a long, low whistle. Everything is bathed in blue light. Silence. Jackson releases a long wail. The dance shifts to a slowed, primitive modern dance. The dancers are no longer aligned in rows, but crowded together, the atmosphere intensified. They writhe and arch in primal, sexual movements; they moan, controlled by an unseen force. Jackson nods his head again and again as if to say, yes, yes, yes—*this* is it. His hat covers his face; this is beyond identity. The cries gain coherence and momentum until they are chanting the chorus of the song. And then, as if this sequence never was, the song resumes, the stage lights return, and we are in the world of Club 30s and the old musical/ music video genre once more.

This startling, arresting rupture suggests Jackson's awareness of the hyperreality in which it exists. While the film is imbued with signs of a nostalgia for a clear-cut battle between good and evil, the film noir of the 1930s, the classic musical,

---

[18]   Larry McCaffery, preface to *Storming the Reality Studio: A Casebook of Cyberpunk and Postmodern Science Fiction*, ed. Larry McCaffery (Durham, NC: Duke University Press, 1991), 15.

[19]   Ibid.

and even the notion of salvation through transformation, this segment returns us to the original source of sound and movement that drives creation. As the dance sequence resumes, Jackson notices young Katie (the observer), smiles and winks at her before reassuming his tough gangster expression. He continues to embody the various levels of the narrative, but not before briefly exposing their simulated nature with a knowing look.

The army advances upon Michael, who is reborn yet again. His eyes are lasers; his face and body become metallic, showing their electronic circuitry before closing to recreate his features as a robot. The transfiguration continues as he transitions from robot into gleaming spaceship. With his victory, the spaceship Michael flies into the night sky. The children wish on the stars for his return, and the fulfillment of this wish is realized through another metamorphosis: One minute before show time, Michael returns onstage as Michael Jackson, international superstar. Viewers must accept that moments ago he was a car, a robot, and a spaceship. The imaginary Jackson is completely imploded with the real; this real is still and always an image. And yet, enclosed within the circuit of simulacra, there is a source.

HIStory: Past, Present, and Future

In the years following *Moonwalker*, what most obsessed the public was the change in Jackson's physical appearance: the progressive lightening of his skin, his narrowing nose, straightening hair. Some identified Jackson's own physical metamorphosis as an actualization of the cyborg dream. According to Victoria Johnson he is the:

> *boundary creature* residing *between* male and female, black or white, human or animal, child or adult ... [in a] cybernetic era ... [which allows] the unprecedented capacity for one to choose and autonomously *construct* one's own identity, granted one has the financial resources to do so.[20]

Perhaps Jackson was realizing the possibilities associated with the post-biological body by which his other artistic productions had already been informed.

Of course, techno-transcendence is not how most interpreted the physical transformations they observed. As many of the authors in this book point out, these physical changes were naïvely attributed to his desire to be "white," a symptom of his abuse, or the simple fact that he was a freak. This issue was central to his 1993 televised interview with Oprah Winfrey, a media event that had the fourth largest viewing audience in television history. We were told that for the first time we would learn the truth about the "private Michael Jackson."

---

[20]   Victoria Johnson, "The Politics of Morphing: Michael Jackson as Science Fiction Border Text," *The Velvet Light Trap* 32 (1993): 59–60.

Through our televisions, millions entered his amusement park home. During the interview Jackson attributed the change in his skin color to the pigment-destroying condition vitiligo. We cannot know the truth of this. As Jameson states, "the point is not to allow one of the poles of the image to settle into the truth of the other which it unmasks ... but rather to hold them apart as equal and autonomous so that energies can pass back and forth between them."[21] Holding both Jackson's changing appearance and his explanation of this change, it is not revelation to call one version of his face a lie, the other truth. There is not one Jackson the fact, another fiction; one is not tangible, the other an image on our screens. The play between them is what signifies, revealing the double helix of representation and the self.

The films *HIStory: Past, Present, and Future Disc 1* (1995) and *Disc 2* (1997) present a further evolution of the simulation game, diffusing the story of Jackson into history itself. *HISstory* destabilizes any objective, positivist reading of history. While "past" belongs to our standard conception of historical experience, the inclusion of "future" illuminates a set of events that has already happened, and exposes history to be as subjective and unknowable as the future. Of this phenomenon Jameson says:

> Note that as temporal continuities break down, the experience of the present becomes powerfully, overwhelmingly vivid and "material": the world comes before the schizophrenic with heightened intensity, bearing a mysterious and oppressive charge of affect, glowing with hallucinatory energy. But what might for us seem a desirable experience—an increase in our perceptions, a libidinal or hallucinogenic intensification of our normally humdrum and familiar surroundings—is here felt as a loss, as "unreality."[22]

While a similar invocation of history exists in *Moonwalker*, *HIStory* increases the scale of the project, making its intrusion into the *real* world more obvious, and our ability to define the *real* world more surreal and irrelevant. The cover of *HIStory Volume 1* depicts a monumental granite statue of Jackson as a "military" figure. *HIStory Volume 2* opens as Jackson leads an indefinable army, dressed in military regalia and mirrored sunglasses.[23] Jackson enters a huge square. The massive, chanting crowd gazes up at a stories-tall veiled monument. The

---

[21]   As cited in: Hal Foster, *Recodings: Art, Spectacle, Cultural Politics* (New York: The New Press, 1985), 94–5.

[22]   Fredric Jameson, "Postmodernism and Consumer Society," in *The Anti-Aesthetic: Essays on Postmodern Culture*, ed. Hal Foster (New York: New Press, 1998), 120.

[23]   In the preface of his classic cyberpunk anthology, *Mirrorshades*, Bruce Sterling writes that within cyberpunk there are "oddly common symbols, which seem to crop up ... with a life of their own. Mirrorshades, for instance ... they are the symbol of the sun-staring visionary." See Bruce Sterling, *Mirrorshades: The Cyberpunk Anthology*, ed. Bruce Sterling (New York: Ace Books, 1986), xi.

atmosphere is charged with the "historic" event. The draping on the monument falls to reveal the Jackson monument depicted on the cover of *HIStory Book 1*, released two years before the film in which the statue is realized: "the 'completely real' becomes identified with the 'completely fake.' Absolute unreality is offered as real presence."[24]

Together, *HIStory Volumes 1 and 2* illuminate the performative nature of history and the theater of politics. Jackson embodies the roles of both King of Pop and King: their essence is equalized. The film creates obvious associations with Leni Riefenstahl's *Triumph of the Will* (1935), the most salient example of a cinematic event constructed as a monumental reality. Rather than an offensive example of self-promotion and megalomania, *HIStory* functions as a critique of the fascist aestheticization of politics. In its epic grandeur it is completely absurd. In his book *Recodings: Art, Spectacle, Cultural Politics*, Hal Foster addresses the fascination with fascism, observing, "it is in fascism that one sees a culture struggle with the loss of the real."[25] Like other works that critique fascism by employing its techniques, *HIStory* "strips each form to its surface … to effects without origin or reference."[26] Through purposefully anachronistic representations, the sense of security these forms provide remains while paradoxically making us aware of their limitations. Think of Jackson's confession of two plastic surgeries, or his attribution of his changing skin color to a medical condition. These conventional explanations belie the text of his own body, which suggests something very much of the future; these inadequate responses reveal our assumptions about the body to be part of an irrelevant past. By conflating reality with fiction, the real public response to Jackson the performer with the constructed response to Jackson the totalitarian figure, fascist forms are drained of ideology, while retaining the potential force of belief.

Reality TV: Living with Michael Jackson Unmasked

What follows *HIStory*? Over a two-week period in February 2003, there was a frenzy of prime time television programming related to Jackson on three major networks. Each of these programs ostensibly had the *truth* of the *real* Jackson as its central concern; the competition for this truth only revealed truth to be unstable and irrelevant, subordinated to seduction and the simulation game. First, the already discussed *Living with Michael Jackson* documentary by Martin Bashir. Barbara Walters introduces the documentary for *20/20*, telling viewers that Jackson allowed Bashir exclusive access to his life for eight months. We learn that in viewing the piece, Walters felt "first sympathy, then shock, and finally sadness." Thus, we are told what to feel at each stage of our viewing. The program opens at

---

[24] Eco, *Travels in Hyperreality*, 7.
[25] Foster, *Recodings*, 80.
[26] Ibid., 81.

Neverland, the site of the 1993 Oprah interview. From our luck at being allowed *in* to Jackson's home (again), to revelations (already revealed) about his abusive father, this text refers more to a previous interview than any truth about Jackson's life. For example, when Bashir asks about Jackson's physical changes, Jackson repeats his response to Oprah: "no one said anything" about white people tanning to "look black, trying to be other than they are." Later he says, "People change. I was changing. I'm changing." Within the program this response is framed as defensive, deceptive. However, all our experiences of Jackson are performance: no less in documentary than any other form.

The term *documentary* presupposes a truth claim, creating the expectation of unmediated reality. However, *Living with Michael Jackson* employs the distinctive style of reality TV, itself an emptied simulation of the *cinéma vérité* form. Furthermore, immediately following his "documentary," Bashir the *filmmaker* provides his subjective opinions about his subject, informing us that Jackson "still doesn't get it." In a fluid, unquestioned transition, Bashir goes from interviewer to expert interviewee: another marker of our hyperreal, imploded universe where multiple levels of reality and fiction are in constant play. In an early scene Bashir and Jackson sit in a movie theater at Neverland, watching an old Jackson Five performance. Veronica Hollinger's reading of K.W. Jeter's cyberpunk work, *The Glass Hammer*, is relevant: "being is *defined* by its own simulation."[27] Hollinger quotes the opening of the novel, "Video within video. He watched the monitor screen, seeing himself there, watching ... everything would be in the tapes, if he watched long enough": an apt description for Jackson's "real world."[28] Jackson watching himself. Further, Jackson employed "video within video" in many of his own artistic productions, including the videos for *Thriller* and *Black or White*. Science fictional concerns presented in Jackson's work 20 years ago are played out in the science fictional *real* world of today: hence his past embodiment of a future moment, his writing of the future into *HIStory*, and his diffusion into hyperreality.

Next came two *serious* news investigations into Jackson, turning a simulation playground into a virtual amusement park. *Dateline NBC* and the *Prime Time ABC*'s, "Michael Jackson Unmasked" and "The Many Faces of Michael Jackson," interview plastic surgery experts, who present irrefutable scientific evidence, arrive at the conclusion that Jackson *must* have had more than his admitted two plastic surgeries. In the circuit of simulation, all we have is a vast network of more and more useless data; the compounding *evidence* of objective truth only make this more apparent. The emphasis on Jackson's face brings cyberpunk's focus on external surfaces into the world of experience; the inability to define his face belongs to the future. Both "news" programs include computer-generated morphing segments of Jackson's face from "black" to "white"—again, the very technique he used in his *Black or White* video years before.

---

[27]   Veronica Hollinger, "Cybernetic Deconstructions: Cyberpunk and Postmodernism," *Mosaic* 23, no. 2 (1990): 36.

[28]   Ibid.

The final installment of this series of programming was Jackson's own rebuttal of Bashir. FOX reveals that Michael Jackson had his own cameras rolling during the filming of *Living with Michael Jackson* and airs "The Michael Jackson Interview: The Footage You Were Never Meant to See." Again we are let in on the secret, this time with the chance to see through the camera behind the camera. By pointing to Bashir's program as a simulation—edited and decontextualized—this program disguises that it does the same. Positioned as the "real, secret" footage, it lays claim to authoritative truth. The ability to get behind successive lenses and frames of reference enables the claim to truth, and it is precisely this move that increases the hyperreality of the entire circuit. These media events demonstrate the collapse of fact and fiction, highlighting the impossible attempt to investigate the truth of a fiction with a fictional reality TV show dressed as unmediated documentary—itself a fiction.

The Greatest Show On Earth

While there ensues an elaborate dance of hyperreality in which we consume, observe, and comment upon Jackson, it is a hyperreality he himself has created as well as embodied. Any documentary documents a performance in which he is a player and a director; implicitly we join the dance. The news investigation that seeks to expose the *truth* he is hiding shows the same film clips, has the same soundtrack, uses the same media he uses in his artistic productions, and because of the implosion of the message and the medium, or the medium and the message, Jackson is the referential everything must refer back to. In effect, we become instruments in his symphony, actors in his play, or if you like, freaks in his circus. It seems that in any discussion of simulation or hyperreality what gets lost is precisely that statement, "in effect," and we cannot deny both effect and the power to affect. What is not simulated are the crowds, the people. The "I love you Michael," "please can I touch you," were said, over and over for the last 35 years. We are still watching, fascinated. The fainting, crying, ecstasy of people around the world happened and happens. In our hyperreal existence, perhaps this has greater meaning. In this, perhaps Jackson has been "the greatest show on earth." He has shown us the future, and yet retained something very old-fashioned as a song and dance man in the tradition of the great entertainers, the ones who can do it all with a wink and a smile.

In his article "Antimancer: Cybernetics and Art in Gibson's *Count Zero*," Ivan Csicsery-Ronay Jr. identifies the novel that followed *Neuromancer* in the cyberspace trilogy, as "Gibson's attempt to recover a place for the individual artist and work of art from the postmodern vortex that *Neuromancer* ended up affirming."[29] The tension between these two novels are the same factors at play

---

[29]   Istvan Csicsery-Ronay, Jr., "Antimancer: Cybernetics and Art in Gibson's *Count Zero*," *Science Fiction Studies* 22, no. 1 (1995). [Online]. Available at: www.depauw.edu/

within Jackson's works: the power to create and the possibility of transcendence in an image-saturated hyperreality. However, Jackson's work does not pit desire for transcendence within the matrix against the awareness that such a desire is ultimately futile. It does not put a world that is the consciousness of an artificial intelligence in polar opposition to a world that can still be shaped by human consciousness. Jackson the superstar, the superhero, the creator of the simulation, the simulation that is created, the black Jackson, the white Jackson, the victim, the victor, the human, the machine, the real and the imaginary: these operate simultaneously. They are all true. Our reading of Jackson encompasses the implosion of fiction, theory, reality, and the future already encoded in an evolving history, and shows us that within this simulated existence without a reality referential, with an awareness of this condition, the power of the artist to create and affect remains possible and vital. If Jackson's productions (especially his body) produce anxiety or fear, well, these are the emotions with which we always face the future. They are the emotions that lead to the creation of science fiction. And while it might be a hallucination, it is a *consensual* hallucination, and we, like Gibson's protagonist Case, like being jacked in.

sfs/backissues/65/icr65art.htm.

PART III
Body and Death

Chapter 10
Dancing with the Elephant Man's Bones

Raphael Raphael

Although Michael Jackson has been penned a "freak" by the mass media, Raphael Raphael uses this chapter to historicize such claims, connecting Jackson's career to a long tradition of exhibition of people with disabilities. Working through the lenses of disability studies and film studies, the author points to new interpretations of Jackson's startext, all of which centralize the performer's body as a vivid source of knowledge, critique, and discovery. Embedded in these arguments is a challenge to the reader to understand Jackson as a person with a disability, the consequences of which are many.

[P]hysical instability is the bodily manifestation of political anarchy …
Rosemarie Garland Thomson, *Extraordinary Bodies*

The last moments of Michael Jackson's 1989 music video *Leave Me Alone* take place in a sideshow. We pan through various freaks of nature: first a two-headed goat, then an alligator balancing a spinning piano on its nose, then a roaring two-headed tiger. Finally, at the very periphery of the sideshow, at its margins, comes its main event—a medium long shot of its central freak, Michael Jackson. He is wearing a ball and chain and (through the wonders of animation) dancing with the Elephant Man's bones, locked in step with history's most celebrated freak.[1] Throughout Jackson's spectacular career, his global celebrity has been linked in a dialogic chain with the chronotope of the freakshow. This chapter historicizes and politicizes this link. In so doing, it asks us to think about Jackson's global stardom in new ways.[2]

Examining the origins of his startext (which I locate in the material history of the freakshow and the visual politics of race in 1960s America) and its contradictory cultural uses (*official* and *unofficial*), I suggest Jackson should indeed be considered a freak, but with all the ambivalent cultural power the

---

[1] Joseph Merrick (1862–1890), who performed under the name "The Elephant Man," was a successful freakshow performer in Victorian England. He was memorialized in David Lynch's critically acclaimed *The Elephant Man* (1980).

[2] This chapter was originally written in the months immediately prior to the performer's death and does not address the subsequent circulation and recovery of his startext.

topos of the freak warrants. When Jackson is called *freak* in public discourse, it is usually because of a series of rumors about his health, race, and sexuality through which he is known to the public: he sleeps in an oxygen tank; he tried to purchase the Elephant Man's bones; he has undefinable gender and sexuality; and he bleaches his skin in a pathological quest for whiteness. While these rumors are intimately connected with race, health, and disability—the principal concerns of the freakshow—Jackson is generally not directly associated with material history of the actual freakshow.[3] I suggest he should be. The actual cultural work of the freakshow (and bodies in dialog with it) has been wildly multivalent. While the freak body historically often reified "official" cultural scripts about race, gender, and ability, the freak also interrupted them, imagining new identities, and as icons of resistance, invited new ways to view the (physical and political) body. This contradiction is also seen in Jackson's unstable startext.

Just as Jackson is not normally associated with the material history of the freakshow, he is incorrectly not considered an icon of political dissent. By recovering Jackson's connections to the visual politics of blackness in black pride and black power movements, as well as to the freakshow (both as historical and performative space), I flesh out and complicate popular conception of Jackson as "freak."

Jackson is often dismissed as an apolitical sign, associated perhaps with a naïve global utopianism, best reflected in the "We are the World" relief effort. This corporate-friendly utopianism indeed aligns with the needs of official global capital. In addition, as is documented throughout this book, he is associated with a series of circulated rumors about his race, health, and sexuality. He is certainly not associated with actual global resistance and protest. Again, I suggest here he should be. From early associations with black pride and the black power movement, to his use as an icon of dissent by marginalized audiences in periods of historical crisis (including 1968, the economic recession of 1982, and the crisis of the "War on Terror"), I will illustrate that Jackson's ambivalence and corporeal fluidity have made him more than merely "[America's] most successful, industrial, political and values export."[4] Jackson's radical fluidity—"neither woman, nor man, neither black nor white, neither eastern nor western, human, inhuman, colorless …"—has made him a complicated point of identification for marginalized audiences in the United States and to some extent, across the globe.[5] His unprecedented global celebrity has also, as I will illustrate, created an imperative to *fix* his fluidity, to arrest his multivalence.

---

[3]   The chapter is indebted to the work of David Yuan. See David Yuan, "The Celebrity Freak: Michael Jackson's Grotesque Glory," in *Freakery: Cultural Spectacles of the Extraordinary Body*, ed. Rosemarie Garland Thomson (New York: New York University Press, 1997), 368–84.

[4]   Ali Bulaç quoted in Gabriel Ignatow, *Transnational Identity Politics and the Environment* (Lanham: Lexington Books, 2007), 77.

[5]   Ibid.

When I refer to Jackson in this chapter, I am referring of course to his especially fluid startext, not the real person. While Richard Dyer reminds us every startext is a constellation of contradictory elements, there is something quite unique here.[6] With Jackson's unprecedented global celebrity (he is still the best-selling solo artist in history) to his virtual cultural exile, there may be no more ambivalent figure in twentieth century visual culture. This radical multivalence is perhaps the defining element of his startext. As discussed in Chapter 9, this is reflected in the crisis of his body: a series of inversions and border crossings (male/female, black/white, asexual/monstrous hypersexual). This embodied crisis has held greatest cultural power, as we will consider, in periods of crisis (both cultural and industrial). The chapter focuses on cultural uses before his death and does not address subsequent circulation and recovery of his startext. Such discussion is picked up below by Diana York Blaine and Zack Stiegler.

An Especially Fluid Startext, Inversions, and Rumors

James Baldwin is first to refer to Jackson in print as "freak." His 1985 *Playboy* article instantly zeroes in on the political threat of Jackson's body.[7] "The Michael Jackson cacophony is fascinating in that it is not about Jackson at all."[8] Jackson's principal "sins" were that he violated the most sacred of American binaries. He threatened to disrupt the inseparability of white and black and male and female as constructed categories. Baldwin was certain Jackson would not be "swiftly forgiven for turning so many tables." He identifies Jackson's principal threat: the embodied inversions we now briefly consider.

Dyer reminds us that, industrially, startext stability helps "organize the market" and assure circulation of product.[9] In contrast to this, Jackson is known for being radically unstable. His fluidity is reflective of Bakhtin's grotesque body and the ambivalent political power to which Bakhtin assigns it, constantly in transformation, threatening divisions between bodies (and categories).[10] Central to this are Jackson's ongoing body transformation and closely related issues of health and disability, especially his plastic surgery (which he claims is limited to two nose jobs and an added cleft chin). Closely related to this are transgressions of race, including persistent rumors of skin lightening. To explain why his skin

---

[6]   Richard Dyer, "Entertainment and Utopia," *The Cultural Studies Reader*, ed. Simon During (New York: Routledge, 1999), 371–81.

[7]   James Baldwin, "Freaks and the American Ideal of Manhood," *Playboy* 32, no. 1 (1985): 150–51, 192, 256–60.

[8]   See James Baldwin's "Here Be Dragons" in *The Price of a Ticket* (New York: St. Martin's Press, 1985), 689.

[9]   Richard Dyer, *Stars* (London: British Film Institute Publishing, 1998), 11.

[10]   See Mikhail Bakhtin, *Rabelais and His World*, trans. Hélène Iswolsky (Bloomington, IN: Indiana University Press, 1985).

pigmentation was dramatically lighter than at the beginning of his fame, he called upon disability, claiming changes in his complexion resulted from the skin disorder vitiligo, a claim widely disputed.

In addition to transgressing racial norms, Jackson is associated with indeterminate sexuality, with his use of make-up and delicate features appearing at least visually to privilege the feminine. Most importantly, associated with his fluid sexuality are the allegations of child abuse and pedophilia discussed throughout this collection.

It is not my intention in this chapter to consider his guilt or innocence, or to determine the truth or falsehood of any contradictory elements of his startext. On the question of his guilt or innocence, one of the few things certain is that constant speculation and intense national interest in Jackson's guilt speak to the intensity of his cultural power.[11] I am interested solely in examining this cultural power. On the one hand, his spectacle of race, gender, and disability has served the needs of "official" global capital. On the other, by making spectacles of these concerns, he has made rigid roles of identity more vulnerable to change. Because of this disruptive potential, he has offered at least a symbolic site of resistance for marginalized audiences.

For most of his solo career, Jackson has been defined by persistent rumors about his health, race, and sexuality. We can make out the basic skeleton of his startext by surveying the most well-traded of these. If there was a "Jackson Rumor Exchange Index," these half-truths and innuendos would be the blue chips. He attempted to purchase the Elephant Man's bones. He sleeps in an oxygen tank. He bleaches his skin to lighten it. These rumors all traded in concerns with Jackson's unstable health and racial identity.

While frequently concerned with border crossings in race, health and sexuality, the rumors fashioning his startext have themselves often crossed borders between high and low media. While many have circulated in respected media, including AP, UPI, and conventional news, many have their origin in the lowest form of circulated media: the tabloid and various celebrity news sites, for example, TMZ, forms many critics have dismissively associated with the freakshow.

Examining rumors that have continued to circulate, particularly around his health, can help us better understand the origins of his stardom. During the course of research for this chapter, I have closely followed a weekly Google News Alert for news about Jackson. "News" has ranged from the bizarre—a 50-foot robotic statue planned in his honor in Las Vegas—to the tragic—a rare disease left Jackson near dead, partially blind and in desperate need of a lung. (The latter rumor circulated in legitimate news, including *Reuters*, just weeks before Jackson's actual death.) These rumors provide some insight into the promotional

---

[11]   This echoes the sentiment Cynthia Fuchs expresses in her essay on Jackson. See Cynthia Fuchs, "Michael Jackson's Penis," in *Cruising the Performative: Interventions into the Representation of Ethnicity, Nationality, and Sexuality*, ed. Sue-Ellen Case et al. (Bloomington, IN: Indiana University Press, 1995), 13–33.

practices at the heart of Jackson's very global startext. A few days after this story of Jackson's grave health circulated in early 2009, his official spokesman made a statement categorically denying it, again in official news media. Not only was the story completely false but Jackson also had an exciting new project that would be announced shortly. "… Jackson is in fine health, and finalizing negotiations with a major entertainment company and television network for both a world tour and a series of specials and appearances."[12] This was not the first time Jackson appeared to "accidentally" profit from rumors about his health. To fully understand the importance of rumors of health and disability in Jackson's startext, we need to go back a century to the freakshow and its promotional practices.

Origins: The Freakshow and Visual Politics of Race

From the earliest origins of his startext, Jackson has carried on a dialog with the promotional strategies of the freakshow. His interest in the life and ideologies of P.T. Barnum has been well documented throughout this collection of essays. Barnum, perhaps the most equivocal figure of nineteenth century entertainment, capitalized on America's obsessions with race, gender, and disability. In ways generally overlooked in accounts of stardom, Barnum played an essential role in the development of modern global celebrity, helping shape the history of stardom in the process. Recognizing this largely disavowed history places race and disability at the very center of origins of global celebrity. While the freakshow is often assumed to be an exploitive practice on the fringes of culture, it was far more popular and culturally accepted. At peak popularity at the turn of the century, by some accounts, it was the most popular form of American entertainment. In its time, Barnum's quasi-respectable dime museum/house of freaks, The American Museum in New York City, was more popular than Disneyland today.[13] Key to this was the unstable capital of race. The contradiction at the heart of the freakshow is key to our consideration of Jackson's global celebrity. On one hand, the freak's arrested spectacle of otherness reified the modern subject, an embodied cautionary tale of the dangers of dissent. On the other, the freak's unruly body invited spectators (often immigrants with tenuous claims to "normal" citizenship themselves) to see—and celebrate—other possibilities of corporeality, and by inference, to envision different social and political orders.

---

12   A few weeks after these rumors brought Jackson back to public consciousness, Jackson suddenly made another official announcement. Plans were in the works for a new Broadway adaptation of the music video-movie *Thriller*, with Jackson involved "in every aspect of the creative process." (See "Michael Jackson Scares Up Broadway Thriller." [Online]. Available at: http://news.yahoo.com/s/eonline/20090126/en_top_eo/80760).

13   See Terence Whalen, introduction to *The Life of P.T. Barnum, Written by Himself*, by Phineas T. Barnum (Champaign: University of Illinois Press, 2000), xxiv.

In a period of intense national racial anxieties, the Jacksons' meteoric rise offered a spectacular and reassuring narrative of United States as fluid meritocracy. Their success seemed to offer a spectacular resolution to seemingly irresolvable racial schisms in 1960s America. While on the one hand, they enacted a conservative narrative of assimilation, this was an uneasy narrative. On the other hand, the group was always threatened by the instability of the signification of race in a period of national crisis.

The Jackson Five's rise to stardom was an all-American success story. In 1962, they began at the bottom.[14] Under the exacting tutelage of family patriarch, Joe Jackson, a steel worker and former musician, they first played regional Midwest talent shows. Young Michael, whose vocal ability didn't appear to match his age, was occasionally teased as being a "45-year-old midget." The group eventually secured regular gigs in nightclubs, often performing alongside strippers and transvestites. Within just a few years, they were among the most popular entertainers of their day.

The national circulation of Jackson's startext began in a peak year of global crisis, 1968, a period of profound anxieties about race. In addition to the backdrop of violence of Vietnam, 1968 was a year of peak concern with civil rights in America, seeing the assassinations of Martin Luther King, Jr., and Robert Kennedy. In this year of spectacular crisis, the group appeared on the national stage after signing an exclusive contract with Motown.

Many of the most iconic images that year in America were related to the visual signs of black power. Armed Black Panthers were increasingly shifting their rhetoric from "local" black concerns to connection with all oppressed peoples. This shift coincided with an acceleration of the FBI's targeted assaults upon them. Tommie Smith and John Carlos were expelled from the Olympic Village for showing the black power sign (upraised clenched fist) during the awards ceremony. The Jackson Five gain their first taste of celebrity in this peak year of spectacles of resistance. Kobena Mercer suggests the Jacksons' music was closely associated with the period's "assertive mood";[15] nurturing pride Mercer suggests was "a prerequisite for a politics of resistance and reconstruction."[16] To assure the Jacksons' "official" circulation, this association could never be made too explicit. While commodifying signs of black culture was key to the Jacksons' visual capital, Motown rather anxiously tried to keep the Jacksons' official image from being too closely associated with black power. Simultaneously, Motown deliberately borrowed from the movement's visual style, particularly dashikis and afros. In one of the group's tightly controlled press conferences, a reporter asked the Jacksons a question that threatened to make explicit their potential danger: Were the group's

---

[14]   This was incidentally the year Tod Browning's *Freaks* was re-released.

[15]   Kobena Mercer, "*Monster Metaphors*: Notes on Michael Jackson's Thriller" in *Sound and Vision*, ed. Simon Frith and Lawrence Grossberg (New York: Routledge, 1993), 80.

[16]   Ibid., 103.

afros in any way connected to black power? Motown handlers quickly interceded: the group was a "commercial product" and didn't think about such things.[17]

The central point here is that Jackson's startext has had a delicate relationship with official power. While the Jacksons' dialog with the disenfranchised was mined for its capital value, there was simultaneously a recognition of possible inconvenient meanings for the Jacksons. Put another way, industrially, there was both enthusiasm for their visual capital and concern for the necessity of containing their danger. We see these contradictions in Jackson's solo career and global circulation. Much of Jackson's solo career in the 1980s and 1990s was, by many measures, "the greatest show on earth." His album *Thriller*, released in 1982, went on to sell over 700 million records worldwide. Its success was credited with lifting the music industry out of an industrial crisis in 1982, the severest economic recession the industry and the nation had faced since the Great Depression. Jackson's high production value videos revolutionized music promotion, helping position MTV as essential promotional venue. Jackson also signed a $15 million promotional contract with Pepsi, at the time the most lucrative in history.[18]

In this successful period, Jackson's startext was especially fluid in the global marketplace, accommodating both official and unofficial uses, from Africa to Japan.[19] Some of this ambivalence was evident in uses of one of his first major

---

[17] In Jackson's retelling of the incident in *Moonwalk*, his autobiography, he claims that as the group left the room, perhaps out of mischief, they spontaneously flashed the black power sign. The truth of this claim, like many surrounding the singer, is difficult to evaluate as Jackson frequently appears to attempt to closely associate himself with the concerns of the black community when expedient; moreover, no photographs of the event appear to exist. See Michael Jackson, *Moonwalk* (New York: Doubleday, 1988), 88.

[18] See "Michael Jackson inks $15 million dollar Pepsi Pact," *Jet*, May 26, 1986.

[19] Jackson has been especially embraced on the continent of Africa. At some public events he almost appears to be an African leader or royalty, including a 1998 meeting with President Larent Fabila of the Democratic Republic of Congo as part of the world economic forum summit at Namibia in South Africa. In fact, the performer technically is African royalty: King Amon Ndoufou IV crowned Jackson a "king" of Ghana regions during Jackson's peak fame in 1995. See Adrian Grant, *Michael Jackson: Visual Documentary* (London: Omnibus Press, 1997), 178, 205. In addition, Japan has long been an especially hospitable industrial climate for Jackson. While not theatrically released in the United States, Jackson's vanity film *Moonwalk* was released and well received in the island nation. It was also where he opened the short-lived Michael Jackson Dance Studio in Tokyo in June 1999. More recently, Japan was the site from which Jackson first attempted to recover his commercial viability after the 2005 trial. It was here in one of his "favorite places in the entire world," that he attempted to make himself more palatable to an increasingly patriotic United States. In a widely publicized photo opportunity, he met with 3,000 troops (while other well-heeled guests paid $3,500 each for the chance to meet Jackson at an event in which Jackson impersonators, rather than Jackson, performed). He announced to the crowd of servicemen and women "[t]hose of you in here today are some of the most special people in the world … It is because of you in here today and others who so valiantly have given

global hits, "Don't Stop 'Til You Get Enough." In a period of local crisis in South Africa, the song was quickly co-opted as unofficial rallying cry at anti-apartheid rallies .[20] In marked contrast, in early 1980s Japan, in the months immediately before the release of *Thriller*, the song was used as part of the official launching of Jackson's global branding. Jackson was hired as spokesman for Suzuki Motor Company's "Love" scooter campaign to appeal to a local marginalized community: young women. The campaign took place in a period of local crisis of gender in Japan, a profound shift in the Japanese labor force which had women moving for the first time into positions traditionally reserved for men.[21] While serving these varied global uses, Jackson became at least equally famous for primarily North American rumors about his race, health, and sexuality. To begin to understand these contradictions and Jackson's ambivalent cultural work, we need to return to the freakshow, particularly the cultural legacy of Barnum, the author of Jackson's "bible."

Barnum's use of blackness in promotion is not widely remembered. It is important here to spend a moment with Barnum for two reasons: (1) it helps illustrate that Jackson draws upon the thematic concerns and promotional practices of the freakshow, particularly its use of the unstable mix of race and disability; and (2) for my larger argument about the disavowed cultural importance of the freakshow as mode of spectatorship, it highlights the cultural (and critical) forgetting of Barnum's role in the creation of the practices of modern stardom, a lineage Dyer and others traditionally attribute to the more respectable vaudeville.[22]

---

their lives to protect us that we enjoy our freedom." See "Jackson greets troops in Japan" *USA Today*, March 10, 2007. [Online]. Available at: www.usatoday.com/life/music/2007-03-10-2208485574_x.htm [accessed: January 2012].

[20]   Personal conversation, Elizabeth Wheeler, University of Oregon.

[21]   The early 1980s were also period of particular ambivalence about blackness in Japan. On the one hand, there was an embracing of black culture, particularly "highly commercialized and commodifiable African American street culture" (Russell 84). (See especially a discussion of John G. Russell's "the other other: the black presence in the Japanese experience" in Michael Weiner's Japan's Minorities [2008]). In the period a popular series of exploitation novels for women by the author Ami called "Trash" also explored the pleasures and danger of sexual intimacy with black men. On the other hand, it is also considered a period of peak of anti-black racism in the island nation, reflected perhaps most acutely in the popularity of Sambo and pick-a-ninny dolls in the period; a popular brand sold a million dolls a year as late as the year 2000. For consideration of Japanese culture in the early 1980s, I am grateful to conversations with Alisa Freedman, Associate Professor of English, at the Center for Asian and Pacific Studies at the University of Oregon.

[22]   Although, as we have considered, the freakshow was by many accounts the most popular form of American entertainment at the turn of the century, film history accounts generally disavow this, instead highlighting connections with the more respectable vaudeville; for example, Dyer suggests vaudeville was the principal source from which cinema "took its first audiences" (10).

Barnum is most famous today for something he never said: "There's a sucker born every minute."[23] What Barnum is not generally remembered for is the creation of modern stardom. Key to this was his fascination with blackness.[24] Looking at some of Barnum's "humbugs" (elaborate hoaxes), it is not difficult to guess what lessons Jackson's management team took as they set out to fashion the Jackson spectacle. This is clear in the successful "humbug" that launched Barnum's career. Barnum started a moral panic by claiming he had located a weed that (horror of horrors!) turned black people white. For a culture in which racial binaries were sacred, this was a dangerous claim indeed. If the most reliable visual marker for distribution of power could suddenly be made fluid, the whole social order (at least symbolically) was under threat.

Barnum was also keenly aware that adding the instability of disability to this mix could create even more profitable spectacles. Many of the freak performers he promoted became international celebrities. Among them, Henry Johnson, a.k.a. "Zip," was probably the most successful in freakshow history, performing for an estimated 100 million spectators in a career that spanned from the late nineteenth century to the early twentieth century. There was also a charged mix of blackness and disability in the performer considered "America's first freak," the elderly black woman Joice Heth. Barnum's promotion of Heth, further evaluated by Jefferson in

---

[23]   While attributed to several sources, including Mark Twain, the statement was first said, not by Barnum, but about him by Barnum's competitor David Hunnum. See Robert Kenny, *Teaching TV Production in a Digital World* (New York: Libraries Unlimited, 2004), 82.

[24]   See Eric Lott, *Love and Theft: Blackface Minstrelsy and the American Working Class* (New York: Oxford University Press U.S., 1995), 77. Barnum's use of the unstable visual capital of race can only be fully understood with an awareness of his experience with minstrelsy. Barnum hosted (and performed in) black face acts during the antebellum years. While performing in black face is now reflexively considered a visual obscenity, the visual equivalent of a racial slur, the actual cultural work of minstrelsy, like that of the freakshow, was far more ambivalent than presently remembered. By making a spectacle of race, the practice may have made racial hierarchies more vulnerable. In his *Love and Theft*, Lott notes that the performers, while acting with a "kind of ludic transgressive glee," simultaneously reified racial hierarchies, common sense notions between whites and "darkies" while at the same time making the same notions more vulnerable as the performers mocked the logic of the "fixing and classifying of racial boundaries and racial ethnography [and] eugenics" (Lott 77). Incidentally, Lott describes their performances in language that sounds remarkably similar to Bakhtin's description of the grotesque body and the utopian potential Bakhtin assigns to it: "They imagine race to be mutable; very briefly they threw off the burden of its construction, blurring the line between self and other à" (77). While taboo for decades, blackface has resurfaced recently in comedy as a means to discuss racial stereotypes; notable recent uses include Dave Chappelle's "black pixie" character and Robert Downey Jr.'s Academy-nominated appearance in blackface in the Ben Stiller comedy *Tropic Thunder* (2008). The film's representations of disability (for which it garnered an official boycott from the Special Olympics) were ultimately far more controversial than its use of blackface.

Chapter 1 of this collection, helps illustrate a promotional strategy Barnum used to make spectacles even more spectacular. It helps us understand the promotion of Jackson's own unstable startext.

A central strategy in Barnum's promotion was introducing contradictory information to the media, then denying it and profiting from the confusion and added celebrity that resulted. We can see this in his promotion of Heth. While Dyer locates the origin of modern stardom with the "Biograph Girl" incident in 1910, Barnum, in his early nineteenth-century spectacles of race, gender, and disability, initiated modern celebrity at least three quarters of a century before in his promotion of this star.[25]

As discussed by Jefferson, in 1835, Barnum claimed Heth was the 161-year-old nursemaid of George Washington. When it was proven she couldn't be older than 80, Barnum insisted he had been hoodwinked. As the controversy circulated in the press, Barnum introduced an even more outlandish claim: Heth wasn't even human; she was a very realistic robot. Barnum then promptly denied this as ridiculous, all the while profiting from the swirl of publicity. (We continually see Jackson adopting this promotional strategy.) While there is no way to be certain what particular aspects of Barnum's career Jackson was most taken by, it is not difficult to recognize Jackson's tapping into similar anxieties and successfully exploiting them. In suggesting race was fluid and contingent, Jackson, like Barnum before him, was breaking one of the central taboos of American culture, suggesting the most visible form of power distribution might not be sound after all. Consequently, concerns about Jackson's health and disability further contributed to his already charged instability.

Keeping in mind these freakshow connections changes the way that we look at Jackson, his music videos and general circulation of his startext, particularly his frequent associations with disability. Examples of direct references to freakshow tradition include the video *Leave Me Alone*, previously discussed, in which Jackson appears in a sideshow; the likeness of Barnum also appears on the *Dangerous* album cover, which also features a small man in military regalia modeled after nineteenth-century celebrity freak, General Tom Thumb.

Knowing about Jackson's "quoting" of the chronotope of the freakshow also recasts his frequent associations with visual signs of disability. In ways not generally recognized, disability, and health have been key to Jackson's startext and the crisis of his body. Key to this was his own appearance-changing plastic surgery—likely the best known elective surgery ever. I mentioned rumors before Jackson's death that he was quite ill, perhaps blind and in desperate need of lung transplant. In the last 15 years he has frequently been associated with many other signs of disability, including frequent uses of wheelchairs and surgical masks. In addition to the historical associations with the traditions of the freakshow, these associations with disability further destabilize his already unstable startext.

---

[25]   Dyer calls the incident the "first example of the deliberate manufacture of a star's image", *Stars*, 10.

Bodies of Wonder

Throughout his solo career, a key aspect of Jackson's popularity and the instability of his global startext has been his frequent association with an array of human and non-human bodies of wonder.[26] These disabled and non-disabled bodies include the diminutive Emanuel Lewis (with whom the performer frequently appeared at official industry events, for example, the Grammies) and the most famous freak of all times, John Merrick, the Elephant Man, with whom Jackson frequently associated himself through both "official" promotion and "unofficial" publicity, as we will consider shortly. Jackson was also closely associated in a high profile "official" promotional campaign with the imaginary body of wonder, E.T.

E.T. was an industrial phenomenon with which Jackson shared much.[27] Most importantly, in the early 1980s both revived their respective industries in the wake of a severe recession. They also share a commercial association. Produced by Quincy Jones, Jackson recorded a storybook version of *E.T.* for which Jackson earned a Grammy. Its critical and commercial success were quickly overshadowed by *Thriller* the following year. Jackson's music itself was increasingly overshadowed though by his own unstable celebrity.

As we have considered, at the heart of Jackson's celebrity were concerns about race and health. We turn now to an example of how these concerns were successfully commodified in another industrial crisis. In 1993, the failing NBC secured Jackson to generate revenue for two of its largest properties, the Oprah Winfrey Show and Super Bowl XXVII, the capital of race important to both.[28] In an act of industrial synergy, NBC used Jackson's appearance as the first major recording artist during a half-time show to create an extravaganza of the event. Choosing a black artist

---

[26] During the performer's "Bad" tour in Japan in 1987, Jackson actually arranged to have his monkey "Bubbles" arrive in Japan on a separate flight to the delight of 300 awaiting photographers. To intensify media attention and his own growing reputation for bizarre behavior, Jackson arranged to have the primate stay in separate accommodations in one of the nation's finest hotels. In addition, Jackson requested that the monkey's room be re-wall papered because of the monkey's supposed sensitivity to smoking.

[27] Both have grossed over $700 million: $704.8 million worldwide for *E.T.* on 1,100 screens, exclusive of the 2002 twentieth anniversary re-release on 2,500 screens (See Smith, 224); and Jackson's management claims over $750 million gross worldwide in sales over the course of his career (See *Ebony* December 2007, vol.63 no. 2, 86.) In addition, in the diegetic world of E.T., the alien is also misunderstood by adults, in some opposition to official state power, and has intense friendships with children. On their similarities, friend Liz Taylor exclaimed, "Michael is E.T.!" (Fuchs 19). See Cynthia Fuchs' "Michael Jackson's Penis" in *Cruising the Performative* (1995) for another connection; her reading of the film interprets the alien's body as site of Jackson's displaced sexuality.

[28] See Ellis Cashmore's *The Black Culture Industry* (New York: Routledge, 1997), 130. In this year of Jackson's peak capital as celebrity, he secured a contract with EMI for over $150 million over five years and also paid 70 million to control the lucrative ATV music catalog). This is also the year that allegations of abuse emerge.

may also have been related to other racial politics. The original location, Sun Devil Stadium, was boycotted because of Arizona's reluctance to accept Martin Luther King, Jr.'s birthday as holiday.[29]

Multiple intersecting corporate interests were at play. NBC's purposes for the event were twofold: first, NBC was desperate to generate advertising revenue to justify the NFL's fee for broadcasting rights, $438 million, double the previous year. So this was somewhat of an industrial crisis. Second, the event would generate publicity for the upcoming exclusive interview on other NBC product, the Winfrey show 10 days later. Additionally, the half-time show was valuable for Jackson's MJJ Productions. The event would be broadcast to 160 countries, many of which Jackson would visit in an upcoming tour. Both NBC productions were wildly successful; 133 million tuned in to the half-time show making it among the 10 most watched programs ever."[30] In its immediate wake, Jackson's live appearance on the Winfrey show was watched by an estimated 62 million, (a 39.3 Nielsen rating), making it about the twentieth watched television program in history.[31]

Garbage and Trash

> There has been so much garbage and so much trash that's written about me [that's] so untrue. They're complete lies, and those are some of the things I wanted to talk about. The press has made up so [many] god ... awful horrifying stories.
>
>   Jackson in 1993 Winfrey interview

> Sex and horrific illness are the hallmarks of any true sweeps period ...
>   *Chicago Tribune*'s Steve Daley

Toward the beginning of the Oprah Winfrey interview, Jackson announces that addressing recent rumors was a central reason for his appearance. Key to Jackson's capital was a constellation of rumors.[32] Quite pragmatically, recognizing these rumors as central to his capital, discussing and refuting them became a principal part of the program. Central to these were rumors about Jackson's health.

In 1986, photos circulated in the *National Enquirer* purporting to show Jackson sleeping in an oxygen chamber for health reasons. It was one of the most widely

---

[29] See George Thomas, "Phoenix Gets 93 Superbowl if King Holiday Goes Statewide," *New York Times*, March 14, 1990.

[30] See "Michael Jackson Gives Revealing Record Breaking Interview with Oprah Winfrey," *Jet*, March 1, 1993.

[31] See "Jackson Interview High in the Ratings," *New York Times*, February 12, 1993.

[32] Note: this is a full six months before accusations of abuse that break later that summer, so these allegations are not yet part of the rumors.

circulated of all Jackson rumors. Besides selling millions of *National Enquirer*s, because of increasing industry-wide pressure to generate revenue, the story was also a crossover success with "legitimate" newswires, including AP, IPU, "and practically every major newspaper in the country."[33] Jackson claimed this story in particular was a reason he agreed to the interview. Jackson dismissed it as absurd. "This story is so crazy," he responded. "I mean it is one of these tabloid things. It is completely made up." What Jackson neglected to add was that, while the story was indeed false, Jackson himself had been its source.

Taking promotional cues from Barnum, Jackson and his management crafted the rumor to resonate with American concerns of health (both physical and mental). According to their own accounts, they completely fabricated the story, even providing the editors with photos of Jackson in the chamber. The Jackson camp then promptly dismissed the story as ridiculous, while a frenzy of speculation and further interest in Jackson ensued. According to Jackson's former manager, Frank DeLio, their sculpting of the spectacle was so complete that one of Jackson's explicit stipulations was that "Bizarre" appear in the headline.[34] So Jackson and his management made strategic use of interest in the performer's health to circulate Jackson's unstable global image.

In the interview, Jackson also associated himself with disability by addressing rumors he had attempted to purchase the Elephant Man's bones. Looking genuinely hurt, Jackson quipped, "Where am I gonna put some bones?" Insisting it was just "another stupid story," he took the opportunity to contribute to his own branding as freak by clearly identifying himself with the famous disabled performer. "I love the story of the Elephant Man [in David Lynch's 1980 film]," Jackson explained. "It made me cry because I saw myself in the story." Like the oxygen chamber rumor, the rumor about purchasing the Elephant Man's bones also appears to have been a calculated promotional strategy by the Jackson camp. It was leaked to the press, then publicly denied in a successful promotional attempt to heighten interest in Jackson, while also making his startext even more unstable by associating him directly with the freakshow.

The rumors with the highest capital, though, concerned race. Echoing the panic caused by Barnum's race-changing weed, Jackson was rumored to be bleaching his skin white. The rumor on the one hand appeared to reify dominant racial hierarchies that privilege whiteness. At the same time, like Barnum's race-changing weed, it threatened to expose race as something dangerously fluid. Responding to the rumor, Jackson reaffirmed his racial identity, again calling upon health and disability, ultimately revealing them to be interconnected. Jackson claimed he inherited a disease from his father (later revealed to be vitiligo) causing

---

[33]   For an overview of the industrial restructuring and revenue pressures that lead to the "mainstreaming" of tabloid discourse in national news, see in *A Companion to Television*, 272–4.

[34]   See Charles Melcher et al., eds., *The "National Enquirer": Thirty Years of Unforgettable Images* (New York: Melcher Media, 2002), 243.

involuntary pigment loss. Moreover, he affirmed to Oprah Winfrey "I am proud to be a black American. I am proud of my race." So in the highly publicized event, Jackson again heightens his associations with the freakshow, particularly the intersecting issues of health and race, to make his startext even more fluid. We turn now to see how this instability has made the performer a powerful point of identification for marginalized audiences, especially in times of crisis.

"Fixing" Jackson

While *Thriller* is widely remembered and considered in cultural criticism, Jackson's 1992 music video *Black or White*, until this collection was published, has largely been neglected. It, however, is an especially useful text for our discussion, as it suggests ways in which Jackson's startext has invited identification with marginalized audiences in times of crisis. This powerful identification creates an imperative to "fix" and contain Jackson's fluidity. To understand the danger of this identification, the cultural context of the video's reception is especially important. It premiered simultaneously in 27 countries to an estimated 500 million. Most importantly, in the United States, it premiered in the fragile months between the spectacular beating of Rodney King and subsequent popular uprising in Los Angeles' urban black community when the arresting officers who had beaten the nearly unconscious and restrained King were acquitted of all charges.

The video is somewhat of an anomaly for Jackson. While he is frequently associated with videos like the one for *Thriller* that have a fairly clear narrative frame, the video for *Black or White* offers no discernible narrative. Jumping from spectacle to spectacle, it is closer in form to a cinema of attractions. As pointed to above by some of my colleagues, in the video's first half, Jackson dances in several sequences with various ethnic dancers: first African, then Native American, then Thai and East Indian. To underscore an apparent uncritical praise for globalization, Jackson appears in a medium close-up singing atop the torch of the Statue of Liberty. We pull out to an extreme long shot of a CGI-generated landscape with iconic landmarks from various nations all in the same space—the Eiffel Tower, the Taj Mahal, the ruins of the Coliseum, Big Ben—all happily orbiting around Jackson, one big, happy global family/marketplace.

These spectacles are consistent with the naïve global utopianism often associated with Jackson (best reflected in the "We are the World" project). As he dances, he repeats the refrain, "If you want to be my baby, it don't matter if you're black or white."

The video is best remembered for a morphing sequence developed by Pacific Data Images further illustrating this global and racial fusing. A series of medium close ups of ethnic bodies fluidly morph into each other as spectacular multicultural allegory. While this memorable sequence is rightly remembered by anyone who has seen it, more radical aspects of the video, particularly those consistent with Jackson's uneasy dialog with the visual rhetorics of race (and black power) are largely forgotten. I am especially interested in a final sequence in which Jackson appears in an abandoned urban street scene;[35] it clearly speaks to the danger of his fluidity. Jackson first morphs from a literal black panther, immediately evoking associations with his early relationship with the visual politics of black power and black pride in late 1960s America. After an intertextual reference to Gene Kelly's "singing in the rain"—a high angle long shot of Jackson dancing next to a lamppost—in a long shot, Jackson inexplicably attacks an abandoned vehicle, smashing in windows with his fist (Figure 10.1). This is clearly not the Jackson of "We are the World." He then climbs atop the vehicle, picks up a crowbar left conveniently on the trunk, and proceeds to smash in remaining windows. What takes place next is the most explicitly sexual dance sequence of his entire *oeuvre* of videos. In a low-angle long shot, Jackson rubs his chest, and then appears to rub his genitals. We cut to a close-up of his crotch area as the performer known for gender-bending appears to rub himself as if he had a vulva (see Figure 10.2).

Figure 10.1   *Black or White* music video screenshot, 1991

<hr />

[35]   The set is reused from his video of the same album, "The Way You Make Me Feel," in which the locale is clearly coded as a black, lower middle-class, urban neighborhood.

Figure 10.2   *Black or White* music video screenshot, 1991 (2)

Immediately after the provocative sequence, Jackson picks up a trash can in a long shot and throws it through a store window, quickly running out of frame. The trash can through the window is a brief intertextual reference to Spike Lee's *Do the Right Thing* (1989). In the film, the character Mookie initiates a riot by throwing a trash can through the window of Sal's Pizzeria. This violence that ends *Black or White* puzzled many viewers, and in fact simply does not make sense unless placed in dialog with the cultural context of responses to the King beating and the subsequent uprising. The obvious danger of representations of a black panther initiating violence in an urban landscape helps explain why great effort was taken to contain the sequence's potential danger.

In the flurry of controversy surrounding the airing, Jackson promptly denied advocating violence. We considered the early delicate balance between using the visual capital of black resistance movements and avoiding the danger of being too closely associated with them. With this cultural memory in mind, Jackson's morphing from a literal black panther and then proceeding to inexplicably destroy property takes on heightened importance. Jackson maintained that his choice of using perhaps the single most visual symbol of black power and armed resistance—the black panther—had no significance whatsoever.

In addition to its dialog with a history of resistance, a series of inversions in the text further add to his instability. Mulvey suggested in her oft-neglected "Changes" that such inversions, even if eventually contained within the narrative, may bleed into larger culture.[36] She suggests this is especially true for a populous unaccustomed to articulating its political longings. These inversions in representations can help an audience begin to imagine radical political change. The video opens with a clear inversion of family power. Macaulay Culkin (as thinly veiled proxy for Jackson) overcomes his father in a struggle over turning the music down. Culkin, aged 11 at the time (the same age Jackson was when he first became a star in The Jackson Five), was already associated with family inversions from the 1990 box office hit *Home Alone*.[37] In the scene, Jackson's music is framed as catalyst for the inversion. Culkin glances in a cutaway shot at a concert poster of Jackson before turning to the camera in a close-up and literally blasting his father out of the house with music. These inversions in this period of unrest create an imperative to "fix" Jackson's fluid meaning.

Especially considering Jackson's potentially dangerous identification with marginalized audiences, in this time of cultural crisis, great effort was taken to contain his image and its fluidity. The black panther sequence, the most problematic of the video, was surreptitiously digitally altered.[38] Racist graffiti was added to the urban landscape to narrativize Jackson's actions, to make his violent actions seem to make sense, to justify it. A window suddenly reads, "Hitler lives!" Another, "Wetbacks, go home!" There are also other racial epithets and spray-painted swastikas, the straw dogs of racism. These digital changes attempt to shore off the "terror of uncertain signs" Barthes suggests is the danger of multivalent text, fixing the "floating chain of signifieds" Jackson's fluidity might represent.[39]

Other text is added in a further attempt to "fix" the sequence's meaning. In the last moment of the original video, Jackson stares at the camera in a medium close-up, expressionless. Particularly because of the violence preceding it, the stare is difficult to interpret. Is it a threat? A warning? To further reinforce that it is neither, in the altered version, words are superimposed at the bottom of the frame. The text "Prejudice is ignorance" makes certain Jackson's ambiguous glare does not take on any inconvenient significance. Perhaps the most effective way that

---

[36]   Laura Mulvey, "Changes," *Discourse*, Fall 1985: 11–30.

[37]   See Janet Wasko, *How Hollywood Works* (London: Sage, 2003), 228. The film remains among the 20 most successful films in the industry's history. With $285,761,243 in receipts, *Home Alone* (1990) was the 17th biggest domestic grosser ever (as of 2003).

[38]   The digital changes were likely made immediately after the controversy surrounding the initial broadcast of the video when an edited version was released. I have been unable to determine with certainty who was responsible for the digital alterations (whether Epic records, parent company Sony, Jackson's MJJ Productions or Jackson himself). See *Seattle Times* November 16, 1991 article "Jackson Alters His New Video," published immediately after the original airing. All official circulating versions (and "unofficial ones" on video sharing networks, for example, Youtube) appear to reflect the digital changes (or delete the entire sequence), save for the video's inclusion unaltered in a 1995 release of "Michael Jackson Video Greatest Hits HIStory" in VHS format.

[39]   Roland Barthes, *Image-Music-Text* (New York: Hill and Wang, 1977), 39.

the problematic sequence was contained was by omitting it altogether, which is generally done whenever the video is broadcast in the United States.

While the reception of the video for *Black or White* speaks to Jackson's ambivalence and the need to contain his image, the widespread circulation of one of the most spectacular images of his career, his November 2003 arrest, attempted to "fix" or arrest Jackson's dangerously fluid meaning once and for all. Douglas, Turner, and Bakhtin have all suggested the cultural power of oblique bodies is greatest in times of crisis. Their symbolic importance is most pronounced when existing power structures appear to be under threat. We close this section with a look at the cultural work of Jackson as freak in the period of the greatest threat to the so-called "War on Terror" in early 2003.

On November 20, 2003, the image of Jackson in handcuffs or in a mug shot was ubiquitous. Here we clearly see the importance of the shift in news coverage considered earlier. For the American legitimate press, Jackson's arrest for accusations of abuse against a 13-year-old was covered as the top national news story; for many smaller regional papers, it was identified as top international story. The spectacular event appears to freeze, once and for all, Jackson's ambivalent and disturbingly fluid image. This "arrest" again is especially important if we keep in mind Jackson's long history of at least symbolic associations with dissent and anti-authority. To fully understand the importance of this, it is essential to place the moment of the arrest and the circulation of the image in historical context.

The arrest took place in a period of a profound global crisis that went largely unnoticed in the United States: an unprecedented event that threatened to undermine the legitimacy of the "War on Terror," the greatest challenge to its authority the effort had yet faced. In the months immediately before Jackson's arrest, the largest coordinated global uprising/anti-war protest in human history took place in thousands of cities across the world as people gathered to protest the United States' attack on the people of Iraq. (Just the portion occurring in Rome with 3 million protesters was recognized by *Guinness Book of World Records* as the single largest anti-war protest in history). Estimates of the whole event vary wildly from 6 to 30 million worldwide.[40] As George W. Bush prepared to visit Britain in late November, there was frequent discussion in the British press about the political danger and potential embarrassment to the visiting leader and to the British government, as they prepared to face what was planned as one of the largest protests the nation had ever seen. On November 20, 2003, the day Bush was scheduled to have official public receptions with Prime Minister Tony Blair and the Queen, some of the largest protests in Britain's history did "welcome" him to Great Britain. By organizers' estimates, 300,000 in London protested the United

---

[40]   See "Millions join anti-war protests worldwide," *BBC News Online*, February 17, 2003. [Online]. Available at: http://news.bbc.co.uk/1/hi/world/europe/2765215.stm.

States' attack and British complicity.[41] The event threatened to (at least potentially) undermine the legitimacy of the unpopular effort.

While American newspaper covers were saturated with the arrest of the "King of Pop," papers throughout much of the world featured the single most spectacular image from the protests in London: the felling of a giant plaster statue of Bush.

The street theatre made ironic commentary on the earlier, carefully stage-managed, felling of Saddam Hussein's statue in Iraq. As planning for the protest was discussed by political commentators in Europe, some wondered what the political impact for Bush and the larger "War on Terror" would be from this potentially humiliating spectacle of resistance. There were no such discussions in the dominant American press, where the protests received little attention. Images both of the protest and of this spectacular image of inversion were not widely circulated. Consequently, in the United States, the event is not widely remembered by American citizens, certainly not as well as Jackson's arrest the same day.

I am not using the relationship between these images to suggest a media critique of distraction politics. Nor am I suggesting some kind of deliberate coordinating between the two events. Instead, I read the juxtaposition of the circulation of these two images (Jackson's arrest on the one hand and the symbolic defeat of Bush on the other) as speaking to Jackson's cultural power as freak. It speaks to the impossibility of Jackson's revolutionary body (fluid and inscribed with inversions and, as considered, implicit threats to official power) in a time of crisis known for binary certainties ("Either you are with us or you're with the terrorists")[42] and unprecedented concerns over protecting sacred borders, both of the body and of the nation. In these widely circulated images, Jackson as (at least potentially) symbolic revolutionary symbol was "fixed" as pathological at precisely the same moment resistance itself was pathologized. So it was in such a moment that this constantly changing body, perhaps the ur-text of otherness, was politically contained. Within popular discourse, this was clearly reflected in the conflating of the "terror" of Jackson as unstable sign and the "official" enemies of the "War on Terror," namely Saddam Hussein and Islam.

The Freak's Return

Until after his death, Jackson's startext circulated in what might have been considered a kind of cultural exile (at least from the United States). Nonetheless, his continued cultural power could be seen bubbling up in circulated popular media, especially at is periphery in interactive media. This included the widely

---

[41]   Reuters estimated the crowd at around 100,000. See "Over 100,000 March Against Bush in London," November 20, 2003. [Online]. Available at: www.commondreams.org/headlines03/1120-07.htm.

[42]   See "Gulf divides US and Europe," *BBC News*, January 18, 2003. [Online]. Available at: http://news.bbc.co.uk/2/hi/programmes/from_our_own_correspondent/2666283.stm.

popular viral video of inmates in the Philippines staging a full performance of the song "Thriller." We have also considered the recent renewed interest in Jackson's health. I read these continued unofficial uses and rumors of Jackson's return to the public eye as speaking both to his continued cultural power and implicitly to the unstoppable power of popular resistance.

Summing up, in this chapter, we have rooted much of Jackson's power in his unstable connection with freakshow history. In addition to recasting how we consider the performer's global celebrity, and the role of race and ability concerns in its construction, examining this link with the most debased mode of spectatorship has also invited us to consider Jackson's ambivalent relationship with power as especially fluid and "uncertain sign." We have seen the circulation (unofficial and official) of his startext take on especially charged meaning in uncertain times, periods of dramatic cultural and industrial transitions—whether his initial debut in 1968, his revitalization of the music industry in the recession of 1982, or his vacillating dance with power during the "War of Terror." While not the subject of this chapter, the renewed circulation (and recovery) of Jackson's startext after his death, in a period with its own pronounced rhetoric of crisis and change, surely speaks to the continued cultural power of the freak.

Chapter 11

Cultural Anxiety Surrounding a Plastic Prodigy: A Performance Analysis of Michael Jackson as an Embodiment of Post-Identity Politics

Julie-Ann Scott

In a chapter that offers a disability and performance studies perspective of Michael Jackson, Julie-Ann Scott posits that a post-identity body transcends cultural categories, performing humanity void of social markers and the meanings assigned to them. She points out that in a culture that largely embraces the idea of entering a post-identity space where race, gender, and, age are irrelevant in assessing individual worth and potential, Jackson's evolving embodiment reminds us of our dependency on these cultural signifiers and our anxious response to bodies that disrupt them. Such a conclusion challenges not only our assumptions about the dichotomy of normal versus abnormal, but also our albeit unconscious participation in cultural cleansing.

June 25, 2009

I learned that Michael Jackson had died as I was adjusting the snaps of my life jacket, preparing to white water raft down the Pacuare River in Costa Rica. My rafting guides, Alex and Luis (who shared the news as they loaded our supplies into dry bags) lived in the small rain forest village adjacent to the eco-lodge I had stayed the past four days. Despite the distance from American popular culture their surroundings indicated, both had grown up with American music and television and spoke of the deceased performer and celebrity in detail over breakfast before we started down the river. For the rest of the day, as we paddled through the rapids, they sang familiar lines from the star's popular songs as we entered into the rapids ("Just beat it" on our way through and "I'm bad, let me tell you once again who's bad," once we had triumphed over the waves in) all to honor the "King of Pop's" passing. As we stopped to eat on the side of the river, Alex and Luis continued to discuss Jackson's death. Alex noted that it was "sad" that he died, that he was "an amazing singer and dancer." With a pause he continued that Jackson looked "scary," and "not right" as Luis and I nodded in agreement. We all shared a look of sadness, perhaps pity, before Alex ended the conversation with a seemingly rhetorical question, "Why would such a talented person do that to himself?" With that we all rose off the embankment and started toward the raft. The words Alex chose to describe his feelings toward the body of the American star stayed with me as we floated down the jungle river under the bright sun, and still now, as I sit quietly at my desk six months later, looking out the window as the snow falls out of an overcast sky.

From Icon to Spectacle: Jackson's Physical Transformation as Performance of Identity

I did not ask Alex to explain to me what exactly he found "scary" and "not right" about Jackson's face. I knew. I cannot remember a time I did not know. Like Alex, I was born around the height of Jackson's superstardom, just a few years after he released *Thriller*. I watched the face that graced television, T-shirts, and lunch boxes throughout my childhood change over time. I listened intently as media personalities, medical and psychological professionals sought to explain it. The amount of media attention given to Jackson's face over the course of his life indicates that many people shared the questions and unsettling feelings about the change in Jackson's face that Alex, Luis, and I discussed over lunch on the day of his death.

Through this analysis, I will not seek to provide answers as to why Jackson's face morphed, as an article in the September issue of *Allure* described, "from adorable child of obvious ethnicity to boy-man with an otherworldly visage."[1] I am not a psychologist, medical professional, or Jackson's acquaintance. I cannot provide any *expert* or *inside* opinion regarding what surgeries Jackson underwent or the reasons he chose to do so. Rather, as a performance scholar, I will turn the gaze toward Alex, Luis, me, and the rest of the cultural members that deemed Jackson an international sensation, catapulting him to a level of stardom that spanned five decades. I am interested in how our attention shifted between celebrating his music and grieving his changing face.

Jackson's physical transformation has been analyzed from a medical perspective, as cultural speculators sought to map the surgeries needed to morph his features. His ever shifting skin color, hair styles, and physique have also been analyzed from a psychological perspective, as the physical evidence of Jackson's inner pathology. Both of these perspectives focus their attention on Jackson's identity, seeking to answer questions through diagnosing his body. From a performance perspective, Jackson's changing face is a participatory event, a performance co-constituted in cultural time and space with an audience that included millions of spectators. Because of his superstardom, spectators across national boundaries

---

[1]   Joan Kron, "Michael Jackson's Dermatologist and Former Plastic Surgeon Talk," *Allure: The Beauty Expert*, 2009, 9.

are able to collectively engage with Jackson, struggling together to co-create his identity as a cultural icon.

Jackson's transformation left us collectively confused and unsettled. In response, through multiple media forms, we enacted counter performances that sought to expose and explain his performance as the manifestation of personal psychoses. Through shifting our attention from Jackson to the cultural discourses we draw upon to interpret Jackson's personal performance, I will argue that our anxiety surrounding Jackson's changing form stems from our desire to resist the potential dismantling of meanings and understandings upon which we come to "know" others and ourselves. Jackson's face unsettles us because of its ambiguous performance of race, gender, and age. It draws us in, seduces, intrigues, and frightens us, compelling us to face the fragility of the identity categories on which we base our own personal and cultural identities. In response, over the course of his adult life and after his death, we struggled with Jackson, media personalities, psychological and health professionals to resist the shared vulnerability of the morphing Jackson's body illuminated. Our diagnoses of his body and mind are not simply attempts to explain that which we deem inherently *unnatural*, but the reiteration of dominant cultural narratives surrounding what it means to be human in a post-identity culture that performs resistance both to the importance of assigned race, gender, and age to bodies and to bodies that blur their assigned boundaries.

In this analysis, I will first trace the cultural performances that emerged in response to Jackson. I will then situate them within historical cultural spaces in which we attempt to revise our narratives surrounding race, gender, and age. In the wake of national legislation, human rights movements, and medical advances we are compelled to pronounce the end of the cultural power surrounding racial, gender, and age and the beginning of a post-identity cultural space in which these cultural categories no longer determined one's perceived worth, opportunities, or cultural experience. In closing, I will offer insights into what we can learn about post-identity politics in our cultural performances surrounding the life and death of Jackson, a cultural icon. To begin, we must understand what it means to perform and re-perform culture into existence

Co-Constituting Cultural Identity through Performance

Bauman asserts that performance offers "a cultural means of objectifying and laying open to scrutiny culture itself."[2] Performance research creates a space to trace the formation of shared cultural realities, to render dominant ideologies, truths, values, and understandings as fragile creations of the humans that define

---

[2]   Richard Bauman, "Performance," in *Folklore, Cultural Performances, and Popular Entertainments: A Communication Centered Handbook*, ed. Richard Bauman (New York: Oxford University Press, 1992), 47.

themselves by them. In performance, each human interaction is not simply a discovery or exchange of preexisting knowledge and truths, but sites of struggle where identity and culture take shape, forever vulnerable to dismantlement and reinterpretation. Through ongoing daily interactions, members of a culture momentarily crystallize performativity, "... the reiterative and citational practice by which discourse produces the effect that it names."[3] Performativity is never confined to one interaction but materializes across interactions.

The surfacing and re-surfacing performativities act our personal and collective identities into being. In each human exchange, cultural members cite past performances, reiterating and resisting them as they constitute the present and offer possibilities for the future. Knowledge, truths, and realities exist because we continually perform them in our daily interactions, breathing, seeing, hearing, speaking, and moving them into tangibility. As Hamera asserts, performance "[engages] culture as an embodied process, not a thing, text, or set of variables."[4]

In turn, from a performance perspective, Jackson's face is not *naturally* unsettling; rather, it *becomes* unsettling through repetition, through the re-surfacing of performativities in our daily encounters with one another. Within our ongoing struggles to constitute that which is real, good, right, valuable, and true, Jackson's face emerges in opposition, defiant and disruptive to our ideals. Deemed wrong, we engage in resistive performances, demanding explanations that allow us a means to dismiss it as pathological and therefore non-threatening to our reiterated dominant cultural ideals.

Through positioning culture, identity, and meaning in a continual state of "production," and therefore continually vulnerable to being dismantled, revised, and reproduced, performance highlights the vulnerability of even or most deeply embedded cultural truths.[5] Butler argues that the foundations upon which we come to know and understand ourselves and others (such as categories of gender, race, and age) are "real only to the extent they are performed" and re-performed by cultural members.[6] That said, the perpetual re-surfacing of performativities in cultural performances allow them to become so familiar that we accept them as natural preexisting truths, eternally fixed, and therefore strong enough to serve as

---

[3]   Mary S. Strine, "Articulating Performance/Performativity: Disciplinary Tasks and the Contingencies of Practice," in *Communication: Views from the Helm for the 21st Century*, ed. Judith S. Trent (Boston: Allyn & Bacon, 1998), 314.

[4]   Judith Hamera, *Opening Acts: Performance in/as Communication and Cultural Studies*, ed. Judith Hamera (Thousand Oaks: Sage Publications, 2006), 240.

[5]   Kristen M. Langellier and Elizabeth Bell, "The Performance Turn: Poiesis and Praxis in Postmodern Times," in *A Century of Transformation: Studies in Honor of the 100th Anniversary of the Eastern Communication Association*, ed. James. W. Chesebro (Oxford: Oxford University Press, 2009), 108.

[6]   Judith Butler, "Performative Acts and Gender Constitution: An Essay in Phenomenology and Feminist Theory," in *Performing Feminisms: Feminist Critical Theory and* Theatre, ed. Sue-Ellen Case (Baltimore: Johns Hopkins University Press, 1990), 278.

the bedrock upon which we build our personal and shared identities and beliefs upon without reflection. Cited and re-cited performativities become shared cultural performances, shared narratives of who we are, "lodge[d] ... so fully in collective memory" that they become "points of ongoing reference and return."[7] Foucault refers to these shared cultural stories as "major narratives, told, retold, and varied, formulae ... ritualized texts to be spoken in well-defined circumstances, things said once and conserved because people suspect some hidden secret or wealth lies buried within."[8] Performances that challenge these narratives, such as Jackson's changing face, disrupt categories of race, gender, and age are met with resistance as we collectively struggle to defend that which we *know* to be *true*.

Cultural conversations surrounding Jackson's face focus on how and why Jackson chose to undergo a transformation that unsettles us. This lack of reflection over why it makes us unsettled potentially indicates that the cultural truths, values, and understandings his face disrupts are deeply embedded within us, interwoven within the fabric of our personal and shared identities. In our questioning and rejection of Jackson's face, we reiterate our culture's major narratives that re-perform meanings thickly entangled within our shared discourses, the "dynamic constellation of words and images that legitimate and produce a given reality."[9] Through marginalizing his embodied performance we protect the shared beliefs and values that Jackson's face could potentially render vulnerable. Through our questions and explanations surrounding *what happened to him*, "*what happened to us*, individually and collectively" in our ongoing creation and re-creation of identity and culture becomes apparent.[10] In performance, through our reactions to Jackson's body, we struggle to constitute meaning and identity. I will sketch a brief history of cultural performance surrounding Jackson's plastic surgery before situating these interactions within cultural discourses.

[7]   Della Pollock, "Memory, Remembering, and the Histories of Change," in *Sage Handbook of Performance Studies*, ed. D. Soyini Madison and Judith Hamera (Thousand Oaks, CA: Sage, 2006), 93.

[8]   Michel Foucault, "The Discourse of Language," in *The Routledge Language and Cultural Theory Reader*, ed. Lucy Burke, Tony Crowley, and Alan Girvin (New York: Routledge, 2000), 234.

[9]   Elizabeth J. Allan, "Constructing Women's Status: Policy Discourses of University Women's Commission Reports," *Harvard Educational Review* 72, no. 1 (2003): 46.

[10]   Michael Bowman, "Toward a Curriculum in Performance Studies," in *The Future of Performance Studies*, ed. Sheron J. Dailey (Annadale: National Communication Association, 1988), 113. Author emphasis.

Something is *Wrong* with Him: Cultural Reactions to Jackson's Changing Face

Through a series of cosmetic surgeries, Jackson's body occupied an increasingly liminal identity space. As many of my fellow authors have argued, his taut pale skin, delicate facial features, wide eyes, strong cleft chin, and frail body blurred boundaries between race, gender, and age categories. This blurring unsettles the society that fell in love with the entertainer's former body, compelling us to continually ask why he would choose to forsake the identity categories we embraced him within. Media personalities repeatedly conducted investigative interviews with the star, his friends, family, dermatologists, plastic surgeons, and psychological health professionals.[11] At times, conversations with Jackson shifted to interrogative performances in which interviewers sought confessions from Jackson about the *truth* of his body, which Jackson continually evaded.[12]

In his biography, Jackson addressed his surgeries, offering the simple explanation that he desired the surgeries and therefore was entitled to them, "I can afford it, I want it so I'm going to have it."[13] However, Jackson's desire was not enough to justify the personal performance that simply confused the culture that mourned the loss of the face that they first fell in love with and made famous. Ironically, the culture that normally celebrates the changing of appearance to increase attractiveness and self-esteem rejected Jackson's surgeries as an attempt at individual enhancement, instead speculating that he wished to erase the very identity they fell in love with, a talented, African American, male entertainer.[14]

Jackson, backed with the testimony of his medical doctors, admitted that he had undergone plastic surgery and skin bleaching in an effort to hide the effects of two autoimmune diseases: vitiligo which causes one to lose skin pigment in patches and lupus which causes both hair loss and the appearance of legions on the face.[15] Jackson's diagnoses offer a potentially familiar cultural narrative: that the star was a victim of a physical, pathological fate. The changes to his face were tragic and inevitable, the result of his attempts to conceal the breakdown of a body that society had once embraced and celebrated for its voice and movement. In

---

[11]   See Kathy Davis, "Surgical Passing: Or Why Michael Jackson's Nose Makes 'Us' Uneasy," *Feminist Theory* 4 (2003): 73–92, and Macarena Gómez-Barris and Herman Gray, "Michael Jackson, Television, and Post-Op Disasters," *Television & New Media* 7, no. 1 (2006): 40–51.

[12]   Ibid.

[13]   John Randall Taraborrelli, *Michael Jackson: The Magic, The Madness, The Whole Story* (Boston: Grand Central Publishing, 1991), 420.

[14]   See Leora Farber, "Skin Aesthetics" *Theory, Culture, & Society* 23 (1998): 247–9, and Meredith Jones, "Mutton Cut up as Lamb: Mothers, Daughters and Cosmetic Surgery Continuum," *Continuum: Journal of Media & Cultural Studies* 18, no. 4 (2204): 525–39.

[15]   See Gina Kolata, "Doctor Says Michael Jackson Has a Skin Disease," *New York Times*, February 13, 1993.

turn, his unsettling performance emerges as an attempt to mitigate the effects of another socially anxious performance. Like the slightly askew wig or noticeably plastic false limb a cancer patient may wear to conceal the effects of disease and treatment, Jackson's pale skin emerges as an unsuccessful performance of normality, an inevitable tragedy to pity and mourn rather than despise.

However, many cultural members did not accept Jackson's revelation of medical diagnoses as a worthy explanation, instead judging his chosen performances in response to his illnesses as deviant and unnecessary, an inappropriate response to the breakdown of his body.[16] These questions centered predominantly on the lightening of his skin.[17] According to the Mayo Clinic, vitiligo patients usually opt for treatments to restore color to the paling areas rather than stripping color from the unaffected skin.[18] In addition, the choice to widen his eyes and put a cleft in his chin cannot be easily explained as a response to the potential symptoms of either physical disease.[19] In response, media stories circulated with speculations that his atypical performance of identity stemmed from a psychological rather than physical condition, "body dysmorphic disorder."[20]

The Mayo Clinic defines body dysmorphic disorder as:

> a type of chronic mental illness in which you can't stop thinking about a flaw with your appearance—a flaw either that is minor or that you imagine. But to you, your appearance seems so shameful and distressing that you don't want to be seen by anyone.[21]

Psychologists speculated, based on Jackson's testimony of his childhood, that his father's constant teasing about his large nose and facial acne[22] brought on the disorder that eventually caused his face to bear "no resemblance to the cute, dark-skinned child of the 1970s with African features dressed in flower-power pants and a sporting a huge afro."[23] The diagnosis of body dysmorphic disorder distances Jackson's personal performance of identity from that which is deemed normal. With body dysmorphic disorder, 'normal' vanity is taken to an extreme, unhealthy space that 'healthy' people know not to go.

---

[16]   See Kron, "Michael Jackson's Dermatologist and Former Plastic Surgeon Talk."

[17]   Ibid.

[18]   Mayo Clinic, "Research, M.F. f. M.E. a.," Mayo Clinic: Medical Education and Research. [Online]. Available at: www.mayoclinic.com/health/vitiligo/DS00586 [accessed: January 3, 2009].

[19]   See Kron, "Michael Jackson's Dermatologist and Former Plastic Surgeon Talk."

[20]   Ibid.

[21]   Mayo Clinic, "Research, M.F. f. M.E. a."

[22]   See P. Sheridan, "The Cosmetic Surgery Addict," *Express.co.uk: Home of the Daily and Sunday Press*, January 3, 2010. See also Taborelli, *Michael Jackson*, 420.

[23]   Davis, "Surgical Passing," 82.

Body dysmorphic disorder is often compared to anorexia because both diagnoses focus on a preoccupation and distortion of bodily appearance.[24] Davis offers an alternative way to view psychological disorders in which the patient is diagnosed as having an inaccurate perception of her/his body.

The Mayo Clinic defines anorexia nervosa as:

> an eating disorder that causes people to obsess about their weight and the food they eat. People with anorexia nervosa attempt to maintain a weight that's far below normal for their age and height. To prevent weight gain or to continue losing weight, people with anorexia nervosa may starve themselves or exercise excessively.[25]

Like anorexia, body dysmorphic disorder is defined as a disease of the mind that is revealed through the body. A distorted perception compels patients to harm their body, causing them to appear grotesque in their pursuit of physical, cultural ideals. Although environmental factors such as exposure to media ideals, disapproval from parents or lovers, and/or traumatic life events are interpreted as catalysts for the onset of such illnesses, ultimately, the patient's susceptibility is linked to her or his chemical make-up, positioning the victim's embodied identity as the ultimate cause of the illness.[26]

Performance allows us a means to shift our gaze from the individual body to cultural discourses, to see the performances of bodies deemed grotesque as emerging from past performances and performativities, citing dominant cultural meanings, even in their deviance from and resistance to them. Kuppers explains, "the word 'grotesque' stems from the Latin of Rome's 'grottos'—hidden places, caves, places where the aesthetic eye can rest from order, symmetry, and can lose itself in the folds and baroque display of detail and ornamentation that characterizes grotesque style."[27] The grotesque performance deviates from mainstream expectations, taking that which is deemed aesthetic to an excess, displaying cultural values to a degree deemed unwarranted, creating a spectacle. In turn, the grotesque body, in its performance of spectacle exposes the underlying dangers of our cultural ideals, forcing us to confront that which we would rather leave in the *ghettos* of our cultural meanings.

Spitzack interprets anorexia as a performance of resistance rather than personal disorder. According to Spitzack, the severe anorexic's embodied performance disrupts dominant performances of femininity, by taking the esteemed slender

---

[24]   See "Body Dysmorphic Disorder in Anorexic Patients," *Nutrition Research Newsletter* 10, 2002.

[25]   Mayo Clinic, "Research, M.F. f. M.E. a."

[26]   See *Nova: Dying to be Thin*, directed by Larkin McPhee (2000; St. Paul: PBS, 2004), DVD.

[27]   Petra Kuppers, *Disability and Contemporary Performance: Bodies on the Edge* (New York: Routledge, 2003), 45.

feminine figure to an extreme that leaves us uncomfortable.[28] As spectators to the anorexic's performance, that which we value as good and beautiful is exposed as dangerous and ugly. In turn, anorexia emerges as a performance of resistance that forces cultural members to face the *grottos* of our ideals and confront the grotesqueness that lurks beneath the coveted slender body. She or he embodies the cultural fixation with both consumption and its denial. The performance of anorexia exposes the desperation that lurks within our deep-rooted puritan values of self-restraint, forcing us to face that in our obsession with bodily control through diet and exercise we are always on the brink of chaos.[29]

Through diagnosing the anorexic as disordered, her daily performance can be marginalized as a deviation from normality rather than a performance of our own ideals taken to an extreme. From our safe space as *non-disordered* cultural members, we can watch her with interest, wince at her bones and look pityingly into her sunken eyes without interrogating our own values. We perceive ourselves as distant spectators, rather than participants in her ongoing performance. "Distance is retained by the spectators, assurance of [the anorexic's] otherness is evidenced by the performance: they are not spectacles."[30] As a result, our shared cultural preoccupations with the size of our bodies and performances that follow (dieting, exercising, discussing struggles with weight with one another) are deemed normal and natural while her self-imposed starvation is considered deviant, unnatural and in need of treatment and restoration.

Deeming Jackson a "freak," who is potentially suffering from body dysmorphic disorder, arguably allows cultural members to take on a similar spectator role, distancing ourselves from his personal performance. In our sensationalizing and marginalizing of his changing body, we perform the anxiety his body evokes within us. Our fixation with Jackson's deviant performance indicates that, like the anorexic, he threatens deep-rooted cultural values that through our rejection of his performance we defend and reiterate. In order to illuminate these values, we must look at the cultural ideals of the time and space of Jackson's ongoing performance of identity.

Jackson as Post-Identity Ideal and Spectacle

As an international phenomenon, Jackson was celebrated and idolized before his bodily transformation. As discussed in Chapter 10, The Jackson Five released their premier record the same year the Civil Rights Act was passed, prohibiting discrimination in any public facility, in government, and in employment and

---

[28]   Carole Spitzack, "The Spectacle of Anorexia Nervosa," *Text and Performance Quarterly* 13, no. 1 (1993): 1.

[29]   See Sharlene Janice Hesse-Biber, *Am I Thin Enough Yet?* (Oxford: Oxford University Press, 1997).

[30]   Spitzack, "The Spectacle of Anorexia Nervosa," 19.

making it illegal to compel racial segregation in the workforce, schools, or housing. Consequently, audiences who embraced The Jackson Five arguably embodied this new national ideal, one that enhanced their belief that black people can overcome financial hardship with raw talent, and family support.[31] In 1971 Jackson began his successful solo career as both the civil and women's rights movements continued to advocate for equality with the support of the still relatively new legislation. By 1982, when Jackson released *Thriller*, many had begun to argue that racism and sexism had been overcome and that anyone could now achieve success despite their race or gender.[32] Celebrities of color like Jackson, who appealed to both black and white audiences, served as symbolic, embodied evidence of the success of the legislation and political movements of the 1960s and 1970s.

Josef refers to this cultural mindset as "post-racism" and "post-feminism," asserting that "despite the racialized and gendered nature of all aspects of American life, including media coverage, twenty-first century U.S. culture is replete with the idea that we are beyond, past, or 'post' notions of race-, gender-, and sexuality-based discrimination."[33] Josef ties these perspectives both to legislation such as anti-affirmative action measures in the form of California's Proposition 209 and Washington's Initiative 200 and "from the wider variety of racialized and gendered representations in the media today," including Jackson's reign as the King of Pop in the post-racism era.[34]

In addition to society arguing that we had reached a post-race era, the 1980s and 1990s marked an era in which cosmetic surgery became more mainstream, so that those who could afford surgeries could opt to enhance their appearances. With these new technologies, one no longer is expected to grow old gracefully; in contrast, cultural members, particularly women, are expected to extend youth as long as possible with diet, exercise, and plastic surgeries.[35] In turn, cultural members with the financial means to afford cosmetic surgeries and treatments are able to embody a sense of agelessness that spans decades. Jones coins the term "stretched middle age" to define the life period created by a cultural in which one is expected to continue to attend to their body with a regimented diet, exercise, wardrobe, cosmetics, and even surgery. As she notes, "in this paradigm, contrary to appearances, it is less about reclaiming or reinventing youthfulness and more about attempting to create a look of indeterminate age or 'agelessness.'"[36] Those embodying the "stretched middle age" distort cultural expectations of aging so that

---

[31]   See Davis, "Surgical Passing," 73–92.

[32]   See Ralina Landwehr Josef, "Tyra Banks is Fat: Reading (Post-)Racism and (Post-)Feminism in the New Millennium," *Critical Studies in Media Communication* 26, no. 3 (2009): 237–54.

[33]   Ibid., 238.

[34]   Ibid.

[35]   See Leora Farber, "Skin Aesthetics," *Theory, Culture, & Society* 23 (2008). See also Jones, "Mutton Cut up as Lamb," 525–39.

[36]   Jones, "Mutton Cut up as Lamb," 527.

people are expected to move from youth to a space where one cannot tell if they are in their thirties or sixties. Through reiteration in the media and those around us, expectations surrounding the performance of age shift to expect bodies to maintain the smooth skin and thin body for decades longer than they were expected to in prior generations.[37]

Through the social advancements made by the civil rights and women's rights movements, as well as technological and medical advances made that allow us to preserve youth, we have entered an era of post-race, post-feminism, and post-age, in which one's race, gender, and age do not impact one's daily life or opportunities;[38] indeed, we perform these beliefs on a daily basis. Yet, as we perform and re-perform the irrelevance of these categories into existence, our discomfort with and resistance to Jackson's personal performance reveals our ongoing struggle with them. When a body threatens to blur the boundaries of these categories we are compelled to fight against their dismantling, providing diagnoses that marginalize a disruptive body from our own, uncovering just how much we depend on these categories that are deeply embedded in cultural discourses and our understandings of ourselves and others.

Jackson's pale smooth skin, delicate nose and mouth, wide eyes, tattooed make-up, broad cleft chin, frail form, long wig, and high voice successfully blurred identity categories. The ambiguity surrounding his performance of race, gender, and age left cultural members fixated on his motives, speculating if he was trying to become white, a woman, or regress back to childhood, refusing to allow his body to enter an ambiguous space that defied fundamental categories upon which we understand and interpret human beings. As we strive to prove racism is behind us, that we have entered a space where color does not define our worth, that we are socially color-blind, we aggressively resist a body that erases its color and in turn, perceivably its racial identity. Similarly, as we strive to claim that sexism is behind us, that there is no need for feminism because women have achieved equality, a body categorized as male speaking in a high voice, with tattooed make-up, evokes negative judgments. In a time when we expect adults to defy age, a man whose ageless skin is accompanied by a falsetto voice that never matured is met with suspicion.[39]

One's performance of race is irrelevant, until it disappears. One's performance of gender is immaterial until we cannot confirm which side of the binary it falls. One's performance of age does not matter until we are left questioning if a seemingly adult body has ever left childhood to mature to deemed culturally acceptable sexuality. In turn, our unease, suspicion, and judgment of Jackson's performance of identity crystallizes our dependency upon binaries we attest we

---

[37]   See Farber, "Skin Aesthetics," and Jones, "Mutton Cut up as Lamb," 525–39.

[38]   See Josef, "Tyra Banks is Fat," 237–54.

[39]   Jackson's relationships with young boys and accusations of child molestation offer another opportunity for performance analysis of Jackson but cannot be effectively addressed within the confines of this analysis.

have moved beyond and rendered irrelevant in our enlightened, post-identity space.

A Conception of a Productive Post-Identity Performance Space

McRuer asserts that when we perform the irrelevance of social categories, refusing to acknowledge their pervasiveness, we reference "the ugly historical and ideological realities from which they emerged."[40] He goes on to explain that "identity depends on degradation in the other, redoubled sense: to the extent that identity-movements are rehabilitated identities."[41] For example, from McRuer's perspective, in popular slogans that seek to celebrate identities that are historically marginalized in society such as "Black is beautiful," "grrrl power," and "age is just a number," cultural members reiterate the dominant meanings they seek to resist, that colored, feminine, and aging bodies have been devalued and victims of cultural prejudice across history. When we are compelled to perform something into irrelevance, we are inescapably performing the pervasive relevance we seek to dismantle without confronting its continued power that we seek to challenge. McRuer calls for us to acknowledge this struggle rather than seeking to ignore it because through confrontation of the underlying, continued presence of power structures, we can cause their embedded marginalizing meanings to surface, making them vulnerable to dismantlement.

In our interrogations of Jackson, asking him if he is trying to be white, feminine or childlike, we are performing our own struggles surrounding these categories. When a body defies that which is deemed natural, we are forced to question meanings we have come to depend upon, to grapple with the fragility of that which we achingly wish to be true. Our berating of Jackson for defying identity categories crystallizes the importance we place upon them in our daily performances of self and culture, reminding us that the categories we struggle to render irrelevant still matter to us, and matter deeply in our daily performances of self and culture. As our ongoing response to Jackson's performance indicates, the possibility of a raceless, genderless, ageless world frightens and unsettles us. Our diagnosis, judgment, and pity toward Jackson, can be understood as a performance of resistance, a means to marginalize his embodied performance as outside of the boundaries of normal humanity and therefore non-threatening to the categories of identity it defies.

Shildrick asserts that we should acknowledge that we fixate on human bodies that we deem deviant, not out of fear of their difference from us, but our acknowledgment that they are part of us; in our fear, intrigue, hatred, and judgment there is inescapable identification. In short, as humans, we know

---

[40]   Robert McRuer, *Cultural Signs of Queerness and Disability* (New York: New York University Press, 2006), 141.

[41]   Ibid.

humanness and respond to it. She explains that we recognize bodies we seek to marginalize as "component[s] of all humanity, deeply embedded within the fantasies, sociocultural, interpersonal and even intrapsychic level of experience."[42] She goes on to explain that in the "hostility and paradoxically the fascination that greets [human difference] we might sense self-recognition. It is as though each one knows but cannot acknowledge that the ... other is a difference within, rather than external to, the self." Drawing upon Shildrick's insights, in our harsh judgments of those we stigmatize and deem other, a level of self-identification exists. From this perspective, our sense of aversion is not to that which is apart from us, but that which is in us. In looking at the bodies/spectacles we seek to marginalize we come to know part of ourselves. Consequently, from Shildrick's perspective, our resistance to Jackson's body is arguably a resistance to ourselves. Our fixation on his form allows us to avoid confronting the vulnerability of the social categories deeply embedded in our collective histories, written into our shared cultural narratives, and reiterated across our daily performances. In our focused questions about why he would choose to transform his body, we perform our resistance to the possibility of embodied performances that transcend cultural categories upon which we gauge ourselves and others.

In his arguments against post-identity cultural space, McRuer offers an alternative post-identity politics, one that acknowledges the continued pervasiveness, power, and privilege associated with identity categories. He argues for "a postidentity politics that allows us to work together, one that acknowledges the complex and contradictory histories of our various movements, drawing upon and learning from those histories rather than transcending them."[43] Within McRuer's post-identity politics, we do not seek to ignore past performances and the meanings that emerge from them. Rather, we seek to confront and dismantle them, realizing the potential to transform them through ongoing performances of resistance.

We fixated on Jackson's ongoing performance throughout his life, and continue to do so now, after his death. A performance perspective allows us to shift our gaze from Jackson's psyche to his ongoing performance of identity that he revised throughout his lifetime, inescapably in an ongoing struggle with cultural members to co-constitute meaning, identity, and truth. Our reactions to Jackson, naming him a freak, or "Wacko Jacko" as he was referred to by the press, stem from historical, cultural performances that he challenges, defying our expectations and forcing us to defend our deeply embedded notions of human identity, or acknowledge them as vulnerable to dismantlement. In turn, we do not seek to diagnose Jackson as medically and psychologically ill simply out of curiosity or concern but rather to mitigate the unsettling power of his performance, to relegate him to the margins of society, stigmatized as mentally ill / physically disabled and therefore

---

[42] See Margrit Shildrick, "The Disabled Body, Genealogy, and Undecidability," *Cultural Studies* 19, no. 6 (2005): 755–70.

[43] McRuer, *Cultural Signs*, 202.

non-threatening to the performances of normal, rational humanness. By deeming his relationship to his body's race, gender, and age pathological, the by-products of an abusive, exploited childhood, we can pity his tragic life rather than confronting how important it is to us to be able to distinguish which of these categories those around us embody. In turn, asserting that while we have moved to a cultural space where race, gender, and sex are not important markers, clearly the disordered star is tragically fixed upon them. As this analysis indicates, a performance perspective offers an alternative interpretation of Jackson's changing face.

Conclusion: Reinterpreting Jackson's Embodied Performance as Cultural Innovation

After Jackson's death we celebrated his life, his amazing talent, and prolific career. We deemed him a musical genius capable of performances that would forever immortalize him as the "King of Pop." In contrast, we mourned and pitied the private life and illness that compelled him to morph the face we once loved into one we found grotesque. Perhaps, Jackson's performance of self was as innovative as his musical performances, as creative, and as captivating. Through shifting the performance gaze from Jackson to his cultural audience, we can see that Jackson forced us to confront the vulnerability of identity categories, by shifting his performance of self. By defying our expectations of his racial-, gender-, and age- identity, he illuminated that such categories were only real to the extent they were performed and re-performed. As we longed for a performance of restoration, for him to admit his changing body was the result of personal pathology and therefore distanced from ourselves, we remained attentive to him, intrigued by the possibilities he offered. Jackson's embodied performance forced us to confront a cultural space in which identity categories were rendered nonexistent. As we accused him of not accepting himself, we were forced to confront the vulnerability of our own identities.

Chapter 12

The Unbearable Lightness of Being Michael: The Religious Witness of Michael Jackson

David Dark

Michael Jackson never made a secret of his spirituality, yet never fully articulated his religious beliefs in public. David Dark uses this chapter to philosophize about the ways in which religion played out in the person of Jackson, pointing to the ways in which religiosity and cultural performance are inextricably linked when celebrity, disgrace, and death are brought together by art.

> The human being does not, in general, enjoy being intimidated by what he/she finds in the mirror.
>
> James Baldwin, "Here Be Dragons"

> He thought of experience as, potentially, a dramatic poem: circumstance the matter, conflict and imagination the instruments, poetry the end. As for truth itself, he believed it could not be stated, could not be known, but might be enacted. Truth lives in the mode of action, not of knowledge: it is enacted in the temporal form of play, and only that form is true.
>
> Denis Donoghue, *William Butler Yeats*

> MICHAEL, ON BEHALF OF MANKIND, WE'RE SORRY.
> Inscription on a sign spotted at the scene of Jackson's acquittal on June 14, 2005

Amid the commentary generated by news of the death of Michael Jackson on June 25, 2009, there was an especially apt word on offer through the English author Andrew Sullivan, who published the following sentiment on his blog: "I grieve for him; but I also grieve for the culture that created and destroyed him. That culture is ours and it is a lethal and brutal one."[1] What's especially helpful about Sullivan's assertion is the way it resists the temptation to keep Jackson's controversial life and his tragic death at a distance. The culture that created Jackson, sustained his career, and, in no small measure, destroyed him is *our* culture. At the time of his

---

[1]   Andrew Sullivan, accessed June 2009, "Thinking about Michael," *The Atlantic*, June 25, 2009. [Online]. Available at: http://andrewsullivan.theatlantic.com/the_daily_dish/2009/06/thinking-about-michael.html [accessed: August 9, 2010].

passing (and perhaps even now), he remained such a galvanizing figure within our popular discourse, so often situated somewhere between the issues of race and sex, that few public voices knew quite what to say about him or whether or not their professional careers could shoulder the cost of having said it. Nevertheless, Sullivan reminds us that a sane assessment will not indulge the myth of critical distancing when it comes to Jackson. He is our familiar. His concerns and his contradictions are ours. He is one of us.

And it is in the interest of resisting the myth of critical detachment that we do well to consider an account of Jackson as a religious figure. Religion, as I cast it, is a kind of neutral social fact (*religare* as "tying together") even as religion, as a category, can be deployed, as I intend to do, as a critical tool. We can readily note, with Marx, that religion can serve as a form of otherworldly consolation which anaesthetizes the popular imagination into submission. But there's also the broader account in which religion names nothing less than the stock inventory of word and image on offer for narrating historical processes, an assemblage of ways of putting matters, explaining the *hows* and *whys* of life and how it might yet (or should) be lived. As Marx has it:

> Religion is the general theory of this world, its encyclopedic compendium, its logic in popular form … The wretchedness of religion is at once an expression of and protest against real wretchedness. Religion is the sigh of the oppressed creature, the heart of a heartless world, and the soul of soulless conditions … [2]

This language recasts religion as not merely the opiate of the masses but, more broadly, the poetics of the people. And it is a necessarily religious space within which Jackson, as a commercial entity, person, and a performer, plays and preys. And religion, in this sense, isn't something one can be for or against or decide to somehow suddenly engage or isolate, say, in the form of a strand, an influence, or a component, because religious traditions, the myriad fables, legends, myths, and stories that bind, are always already underway. We're soaking in them. Their engagement precedes us, having already formed our imaginaries in one way or another. It is in this sense that Marx insists that critiquing religion is prerequisite to every critique. Religion is that with which we have to do (or the way we do everything we do or think we do). It binds us for better and worse till we begin to critique it religiously and relentlessly, in view of the possibility of better boundedness, different and more redeeming orientations, or, to put it a little strangely, less bad religions. Religiosity, in this sense, is a sort of non-optional sociality, an open-ended form which funds the more settled forms we have in mind when we speak of religions.

If religion names the trajectory of our animating concerns and sometimes radically uncritical and largely unconscious adorations, our positing of Jackson

---

[2]   Karl Marx, Critique of Hegel's "Philosophy of Right," trans. Annette Jolin and Joseph O'Malley (Cambridge: Cambridge University Press, 1977), 131.

as a religious figure will serve both to celebrate his power as a pioneering, poetic and prophetic witness and to problematize and redemptively critique his lifelong relationship with his public. Considered religiously, these two sides to his story cannot be neatly separated.

As we take in a broad sketch of Jackson's development as a performer within The Jackson Five, we recall that he was cultivated for and plugged into an ambivalent but powerful covenant with his audience long before the relationship could be considered consensual. What do the masses derive (then and now) from giving ear to an eight-year-old child dancing among his older brothers and singing, with as much passion as he could manage or mimic, lyrics of sexual longing? What do we, the audience, give back, relationally, or as Chapter 11 would have it, performatively, beyond the paradoxically positive reinforcement of strangers in his years of ostensible emotional development? How do we characterize this transaction? As is the case with many a child-star, it was an operation of psychic stripmining, we might say, as we recall images of Jackson smiling, in his late twenties, with an arm around E.T., dangling a child out a window in Berlin in his forties, or, at the age of 50, greeting his fans in his final public appearance with the words that peppered his interactions with collaborators and strangers alike: "I love you."

But our recognition of the public drama in which Jackson's lifelong, commercial successes were accompanied by what appeared to be the gradual diminution of the possibility of his emotional health must not exclude the skill, artistry, and courage with which he grabbed hold of his impossible situation and sought to lift more voices than his own. Cornel West's description of a political-spiritual continuum is especially evocative here:

> [Michael Jackson was] the international emblem of the African-American, blues-spiritual impulse … part of that tremendous wave in the ocean of human expression … Any great artist is wrestling with their sadness and loneliness, their fears, anxieties and securities, and they're transfiguring those into complicated forms of expression that affect our hearts, minds and souls and remind us of who we are as human beings, the fragility of our human status and the inevitability of death.[3]

While it will depend upon an ear willing to hear and an eye determined to see beyond (or in spite of) the more tabloid-worthy aspects of Jackson's life so completely critiqued in this present collection of essays, West is noting the ways in which Jackson sought to meaningfully metaphorize his experience, casting it in the direction of a proffered human universal epic (*His*tory). In keeping with the lyrical, prophetic tradition West has in mind, it can only be received and discerned in the mode of call and response. And we might be moved to note that Jackson's confidence, however outlandish, that *his* story is somehow *our* story

---

[3]   Interview on *The Tavis Smiley Show*, June 30, 2009.

too, *everyone's* story, is inextricable from the childlike hopefulness from which, by all appearances, he never entirely emerged. "I believe in me," he cried. "So *you* believe in *you*" ("Wanna Be Startin' Somethin'"). Everything rode on reciprocity. For Jackson, this circle of self and other, at his most joyous moments, remained unbroken.

On the one hand, this was all vanity, and Jackson's delusions of global, communal grandeur were simply his way of accessing his one avenue to what he perceived to be reality by drawing unto himself the collective attention of countless strangers. A Lewis Lapham adage is, in this sense, applicable: "Because the public image comes to stand as the only valid certification of being, the celebrity clings to his image as the rich man clings to his money—that is, as if to life itself."[4] But doing justice to Jackson's religious witness requires a more dialectical form of representation. Tragically (but not, it must be said, atypically), his own sense of self seemed to demand the dysfunctional hyperbole of advertising language and branding (*The Legend Continues, Bad, Dangerous, Invincible*), and there is certainly a witness of sorts to be discerned in the tale of a man who, like many others, only profited dissolution and disfigurement upon gaining a world of image-driven successes, forfeiting, in large part, the possibility of localized, person-to-person, unself-conscious soul. But in the same sense, hi-tech, theatrical decor aside, Jackson skillfully sought to narrate his own sad journey in image and song, insinuating himself again and again into the popular mainstream, crowning himself its king, refusing the scapegoating mechanism that would transmogrify him, always working his way through constraining spaces into wide open ones, conjuring them, in fact.

In this sense, especially with songs like "We Are the World," "Earth Song," "Man in the Mirror," and "Heal the World," his recasting of his own image was a re-assertion of harmony, a *re*-citation of love and good order in spite of his own psychic fragmentation. In more ways than one, as my colleague Diana York Blaine discusses below in Chapter 13, he consistently played the role of shaman as he sought to be a popular and energetic communicator of the sacred to his society, summoning the public and one presidential administration after another to turn its attention to global famine, the AIDS crisis, and environmental devastation years before other pop artists got on board. And lest we view his humanitarian endeavors as self-serving, it's important to note that a vision of his own personal brokenness lurks throughout the script. While it's admittedly awkward to put such a question to the listening audience, he asks "Have you seen my childhood?" in the theme from *Free Willy 2* (1995), and his confessional lamentation concerning his own emotional deprivation, a life in which there was often neither community nor communication, is palpably, if often surreally, felt.

And here, we turn to the rawer, non-lyrically transmitted, expressions of his hopes, dreams, and self-understanding. In a televised public statement concerning

---

⁴   Quoted in David Loy, *A Buddhist History of the West: Studies in Lack* (Albany: State University of New York Press, 2002), 66.

the allegations of child sexual molestation and his body searches at the hands of the LAPD, Jackson had this to say: "If I am guilty of anything, it is of believing what God said about children: 'Suffer little children to come unto me and forbid them not, for such is the kingdom of heaven.' In no way do I think that I am God, but I do try to be Godlike in my heart."[5] With such assertions in mind, the mystic imagination of Michael Jackson, bordering on the blasphemous by some standards, moves into view.

This testimony can be illuminatingly juxtaposed with Jackson's conversation with Bashir, discussed by Amy Billone and others in more detail above; Bashir asks whether or not Jackson wants to grow up.

"No," he replies. "I am Peter Pan."

Bashir: "No you're not, you're Michael Jackson."

Jackson: "I'm Peter Pan in my heart."

And by way of elaboration, Jackson politely observes, "You've never been where I've been mentally."

A moment's thought can confirm that this assertion is incontestably true, and, while receiving it as an honest, illuminating description of Jackson's own mental state seems to be outside of Bashir's sphere of concern, it sits squarely within the task of discerning and appreciating Jackson's religious witness and his fitful, fevered role as an accidental *and* self-consciously mystic figure. While the psychic trauma of his unique existence might be beyond our reach (save perhaps via the robust, powerfully orchestrated, nightmare vision of show business available to us in David Lynch's *Mulholland Drive* (2001)), we can nevertheless consider the sacred space Jackson occupied, fell into, and, from another angle, personally conjured. Needless to say (and this might also be asserted concerning many of his celebrity-brand contemporaries), this space and his presence within it exceed, to some degree, the span of his natural life.

By considering this space, we begin to catch a glimpse of Jackson's understanding of his own religious vocation as a performing artist. Both are uniquely on display in the documentary film of his final days preparing what was publicized as his last tour ("The final curtain call," he deemed it): *Michael Jackson's This Is It*.

Through Jackson's own stage directions and the reminiscing of his collaborators, a vision of his sense of calling, the cultural task he viewed as ever before him, forms. As he envisioned it, the show was to begin with various images of landmark moments in world history (hopeful, progressive, violent) projected on orbs, one of which would eventually land in the hand of a giant robot ("Light

---

5 Jackson, live from Neverland, December 22, 1993. [Online]. Available at: http://findarticles.com/p/articles/mi_m1355/is_n10_v85/ai_14947357/.

Man") reminiscent of Gort in *The Day the Earth Stood Still* (1951). The image of Light Man holding the orb in his outstretched hand was intended to evoke the scene from *Hamlet* in which the Prince of Denmark contemplates death by way of the skull of his old friend, the jester Yorick. Light Man would eventually open up and be shown to contain (surprise, surprise) Jackson himself; but not before, the "awesome video experience," in the words of director Kenny Ortega, was to "then [be] transferred to his body." The universality of Jackson's own person (whether psychosis or religious vision) was unmistakable essential to the production and, given where he's been mentally, never in doubt.

While watching the rehearsals for the *This Is It* tour which wasn't to be, one notes the invigoration Jackson feels as the outcast whose vindication is within reach even as the stakes feel heartbreakingly high. In what was to be the introductory video for "Smooth Criminal," Jackson is dropped, Zelig-like, into the middle of scenes in *The Maltese Falcon* (1941). "What's *he* doing here?" Mary Astor asks Humphrey Bogart, as if she knows *his kind* doesn't belong there. In his zoot suit and with his eyes and hoary face uncovered, Jackson stares ahead defiantly before making his getaway. He brings the same spirited antagonism to his practiced performance of "Human Nature." Let the prosecution be satisfied with his plea of humanness, he argues in song. And he indulges a proud growl on behalf of any and everyone deemed freakish, deviant, or beyond the pale when he intones, "I like livin' this way, I like lovin' this way." It's as if he recognizes all too well his kinship with Gloria Swanson's Norma Desmond in *Sunset Boulevard* (1950) and knows better than anyone the terrible things show business does to the human spirit, but he has a job to do. And he'll kick against mortality to the bitter end.

His feedback and his cues to his fellow performers make it clear that he has more in mind than a mere jump-starting of his brand; he means to minister, to undertake what Van Morrison calls "The Healing Game." As he admonishes the keyboardist on "The Way You Make Me Feel" to slow it all down, he explains, "You have to feel totally nourished by it, you know?" And at the conclusion of the prepared video for "Earth Song" which features a child risking being run over by a bulldozer to save the last plant in sight in a scene of environmental devastation, Jackson explains that he'll confront an actual bulldozer on the stage, putting an end to its damage with his own body. The oneness, the interdependence of all life forms (a fact on the ground, not a big idea), he explains, is to be the guiding trope of the tour: "It gives some sense of awareness and awakening and hope to people." Observing this scene on the heels of his lively rendition of "Black and White," my wife remarked, "He's really a utopian, isn't he?"

And that he was. As a poetic and ethical summons, Jackson's work might be best understood as a form of public service announcement, an experiment in making people aware and therefore mobilized toward compassion, toward seeing what their negligence was doing. The distance between ourselves and the people we see in images of war and deprivation, he constantly argued, is a construct that must be overcome. His call to see ourselves (and ineluctably *him*self) anew is simultaneously a call to see poetically *and* to perceive reality as it is. Each performance and, in some sense, his every public appearance were infused with the hope that it might be understood as one more assertion of goodwill, a space-making enterprise in which healing and renewed consciousness might occur.

If we can resist the temptation to reduce Jackson's witness to a strict either/or stand-off (Angel or Devil ... Wacko Jacko or Christ-figure), we can appreciate—and even receive instruction from—the ethical and poetic heft of his work while sustaining a redemptive critique of the celebrity, psycho-covenant that destroyed him and continues to destroy so many (audiences and performers alike). This is the strange worship traded back and forth between media personalities and, in *Sunset Boulevard*'s Joe Gillis' amazing phrase, "those wonderful people out there in the dark." The psychic toll, we understand, is exacted from all parties.

The struggle of Jackson's existence was a live demonstration (as victim and practitioner) of the damage our fixations do. Our fixations generate suffering (our own and others) by constantly sabotaging the possibility of love and life even as we mistake our fixations (fan to public figure and vice versa) for our only hope for love, life, and ultimate significance. These fixations are what Buddhist thinker David Loy calls (drawing the phrase from Otto Rank) "immortality projects."[6] They are in some sense synonymous with our avowed *and* unavowed religious commitments, though religion, as a pejorative term, is popularly used to describe the immortality projects of others.

Grounded in his understanding of Buddhism, Loy is able to name our drive to "immortality projects" as "a sense of ontological *lack*." This lack names the anxiety generated by "two opposed but complementary fears ... Life fear is anxiety in the face of standing out from nature, thereby losing connection with a greater whole. Death fear is anxiety in the face of extinction, of losing individuality and dissolving back into the whole."[7] Or as Loy so effectively puts it in his description of the lack that drives the people of the West individualistically, politically, and spiritually, our immortality projects are funded by our misapprehension of the intuition that informs the feeling that "*'I' am not real right now.*"[8]

The intuition is explained by the Buddhist notion of *anatta* (no self) and Loy draws on this teaching as he describes the immortality project that is the ego-self (the big one that drives all our little ones): "The ego-self is this never-ending project to realize oneself by objectifying oneself, something consciousness can no more do than a hand can grasp itself, or an eye see itself." Out of the "perpetual failure" of this project, a failure no amount of money, fame, or accomplishment can prevent, we develop a fear of the shadow of this "sense-of-lack" from which we're forever on the run.[9] While few public figures seem to fit the bill for "Man in the Mirror on the Run" quite so powerfully as Michael Jackson, in caricatured

---

[6]   David Loy, *Lack and Transcendence: The Problem of Death and Life in Psychotherapy, Existentialism, and Buddhism* (New Jersey: Humanities Press, 1996), 3.

[7]   Ibid., 62.

[8]   Loy, *A Buddhist History of the West*, 3.

[9]   Ibid., 4.

form anyway, I'd like to risk reminding the reader of the hazards of casting the first stone, prematurely *other*-ing or scapegoating Jackson, and indulging the aforementioned myth of critical distancing. While Jackson was doubtless a captive of an immortality project or two, I'd like to argue that, at his serene and mystic best, he often comes off as a practitioner of mindfulness, an awakened one, a bodhisattva of sorts. His movement, in this sense, is a steadfast refusal to become attached to a single, death-dealing concept: a life that was poetry in motion.

In light of Jackson's movement, consider the Zen teaching of Huang Po in which the immortality project (or projects) is described as the formation of concepts or the making of forms:

> When all such forms are abandoned, there is the Buddha. Ordinary people look to their surroundings, while followers of the Way look to the Mind, but the true Dharma is to forget them both. The former is easy enough, the latter very difficult. Men are afraid to forget their minds, fearing to fall through the void with nothing to stay their fall. They do not know that the Void is not really void, but the realm of the real Dharma. This spiritually enlightening nature is without beginning, as ancient as the Void, subject neither to birth nor to destruction, neither existing nor not existing … It cannot be looked for or sought, comprehended by wisdom or knowledge, explained in words, contacted materially or reached by meritorious achievement. All the Buddhas and Bodhisattvas, together with all wriggling things possessed of life, share in this great Nirvanic nature … You cannot use Mind to seek Mind, the Buddha to seek the Buddha, or the Dharma to seek the Dharma. So you students of the Way should immediately refrain from conceptual thought. Let a tacit understanding be all![10]

To the extent that we make of Buddhism (or any religion, celebrity cult, or ideology) an attempt to transcend the realm of tacit understanding, to leap past the sense of finitude that informs our existence, to somehow definitively overcome our sense of lack, we condemn ourselves to never seeing the world and our place within it properly, to never entering the realm of real dharma. According to Loy, the attempt to transcend religiosity (a self-consciously tacit understanding) is another doomed immortality project. "If that lack is a constant, and religion is understood as the way we try to resolve it, we can never escape a religious interpretation of the world."[11]

What kind of religion are we talking about? A religion of awakened insights that don't presume to expiate the lack, insights recorded and put into engaged and engaging practice of constant interrogation with an eye toward further insight. As Morny Joy testifies, these insights "represent neither a nihilistic nor determinist description of reality, but a radical interrogation of the assumed self-sufficient status

---

[10]   Huang Po, *The Zen Teaching of Huang Po on the Transmission of Mind*, trans. John Blofeld (New York: Grover Press, 1958), 41–2.

[11]   Loy, *A Buddhist History of the West*, 8.

of any entity—be it a person or an object."[12] As Loy maintains, this is the religious interpretation (the way of life) the Buddha taught. In view of *anatta* ("the strange but essential Buddhist claim that our sense of subjectivity does not correspond to any real ontological self")[13], this interrogation, an interrogation whose end is compassionate practice, is what we have (all we have) to do, a pilgrimage that involves, over and over again, "the deconstruction and reconstruction of the fictive sense of self."[14] It is a journey of new and ever-renewed awareness, a journey I believe Jackson, at his best, invites us on. As Joy describes it, "What is needed is a new way of relating to the world: a different sense of self. This would be a version that both critiques and constructs its practice with insights born of self-questioning honesty, that is, by a mindfulness of our selves, in whatever guise they are manifested."[15]

Jackson's music, videos, and live performances privilege, again and again, a sense of mystery (of knowing that we are not knowing) in all of our dealings. And Jackson himself, like a child (for better and worse) remained perpetually open to the unforeseen possibilities in the way he sought to organize the world. As a humanitarian, he assumed, as a given, that the status quo never goes far enough in imagining further, in widening the sphere of humaneness and hospitality, in refusing to settle for the deadened and deadening practice of already-made-up-minds. His was a radical open-endedness hell-bent on seeing what it has yet to see. His lifelong performance of alive and signaling wonder is in keeping with Loy's description of enlightenment:

> Buddhist awakening does not grasp or otherwise resolve the essential mysteriousness of our being in the world. It opens us up to that mystery, a mystery that is an essential aspect of the meaning of "sacred." In practice, this means that the broadest context for all our intellectual efforts is a wonder in the face of a world that always exceeds our ideas about it. That excess does not signify any defect in our understanding. Rather, it is the source of our understanding, allowing for a perpetual bubbling-up of insights and images—when we do not cling to the ones that we have already become comfortable with.[16]

Jackson never tired of reminding us (and himself) that damaging activity originates in our equally damaging, perverting imaginations which are founded, in Buddhist terms, in a deluded sense of duality that can only be overcome by an awakening

---

[12]   Morny Joy, "Mindfulness of the Selves: Therapeutic Interventions in a Time of Dissolution," in *Healing Deconstruction: Postmodern Thought in Buddhism and Christianity* (Atlanta: Scholars, 1996), 78.

[13]   David Loy, *The Great Awakening: A Buddhist Social Theory* (Boston: Wisdom, 2003), 22.

[14]   Ibid., 5.

[15]   Joy, "Mindfulness of the Selves," 97.

[16]   Loy, *Great Awakening*, 27.

to our "interpenetrating non-duality with the world, which is wisdom."[17] "We are all one," he insisted to the dancers, musicians, and the production team of the *This Is It* tour. The goal is soul. Our fortunes are not separate. There are no unrelated phenomena. The tour, in this sense, was nothing less than a religious revival for Jackson, a staging of grace and love and mindfulness. Partially but not *merely* deluded, we might say, but this is the way it goes with immortality projects near and far.

Whether we deem him primarily a pilgrim, a pervert, a mystic practitioner, or a madman, there is no escaping Jackson as a storyteller and a bringer of song, stories and songs which will inform and enrich our popular consciousness for the foreseeable future, and, with this in mind, we return to the question of Jackson's witness and what we aim to do with it. Is it false, faithful, true? The story he tells and the story he *is* can't be received from a distance. The story inhabits and haunts and speaks again as stories will. Or as Michel de Certeau has it: "The story does not express a practice. It does not limit itself to telling about a movement. It *makes* it. One understands it, then, if one enters into this movement oneself."[18] Insert soul here.

---

[17]   Ibid., 29.

[18]   Michel de Certeau, "Story Time," in *The Practice of Everyday Life*, trans. Steven Rendall (Berkeley: University of California Press, 1984), 81.

Chapter 13

"We Are Going to See the King": Christianity and Celebrity at Michael Jackson's Memorial

Diana York Blaine

Like every element of his life, the death of Michael Jackson was a consumable, public event. Millions of people across the world were invited, via television broadcast and Internet streaming, to attend the memorial of the late star. Diana York Blaine, who attended the funeral services in Los Angeles on July 7, 2009, outlines the manner in which Jackson's death became an opportunity for not only cultural re-imagination but also for social deification. In death, she explains, Jackson's star image, subjective signifier, and cultural position finally found a stability which was never offered him in life.

Following Michael Jackson's death, a massive memorial service was held for the pop star in downtown Los Angeles. In some respects this ritual followed normative expectations, including the eulogizing of the dead by friends and family, the employment of music and images to memorialize, and the use of religious discourse. However this was no ordinary event, for this was no ordinary man. Jackson epitomized fame in a culture-indeed world-that has increasingly come to rely heavily upon celebrity in order to stabilize itself and to produce meaning. Jackson's death, therefore, posed a problem: the disintegration of a symbol of fabulous success, personal satisfaction, and true intimacy. So in order to recuperate the power of Jackson as a sign, and to recharge the validity of these concepts key to the functioning of modern society, the memorial service ultimately offered a hybrid of celebrity culture, late capitalism, and Judeo-Christianity.

In this chapter I will explore the challenges posed by Jackson's celebrity persona not just in death but during his life as well, including those related to race and sexual orientation, and demonstrate how the memorial service strove to resolve them, ultimately erasing his queer identity, striving to exonerate him of charges of pedophilia, and portraying him as a symbol of both the success and the failure of the civil rights movement.[1] Next I will examine how this ritual worked to solve the problem of death itself, increasingly a conundrum in modernity, by offering the ethically recuperated Jackson as immortal Christ figure, eternally alive via his status as legend in the entertainment industry as well as in a transcendent realm beyond. Thus celebrity culture does not merely replace religion, as some critics have suggested it does, but inhabits the very same space, both infusing conventional theology with the attributes of modern secular society, and simultaneously infusing secular society with the presence of the sacred.[2] In this ritual context, Jackson's vaunted strangeness becomes not a sign of his perversity but of his status as sacred object.

The Paradoxes Presented by Jackson's Life and Death

Modern celebrity requires that the star's persona be an embodiment of oppositions, and Jackson certainly fulfilled this mandate. He was from a working-class family yet lived a breathtakingly lavish existence. He was a childlike figure, a scrupulous master of his own brilliant career, engineering carefully scripted performances and projects. He was an ordinary guy, one of the people, capable of reaching out with most humble deference to those who were suffering, yet also infamously strange, wearing one glove, hanging around with gussied-up monkeys, and supposedly sleeping in a hyperbaric chamber. He was an energetically sexual performer, with hip-thrusts and crotch-grabs, and yet seemingly asexual as well, becoming what one critic has termed "a symbolic eunuch," insofar as he was "valuable though non-persuasive."[3]

It is been argued throughout this collection of essays that his popularity actually emerged out of these very contradictions, that our inability to fix him in a single category kept Jackson's identity enthralling. Richard Dyer notes that this "extreme ambiguity/contradiction … concerning the stars-as-ordinary and the stars-as-special" is what makes them stars in the first place.[4] As modern life has become more complex, and definitions of identity less grounded by traditional social structures, people look to celebrities to help construct a self. According to one study, "Fans develop self-defining relationships with celebrities and seek to adopt their perceived attributes, resulting in powerful forms of personal and social

---

[1]   I was in attendance at the service, held at the Staples Center in downtown Los Angeles, on July 7, 2009. My observations are based upon personal observation as well as a videotaped version. [Online]. Available at: www.abcactionnews.commediacenterlocal. aspxvideoId=16111@wfts.dayport.com&navCatId =3&rss=823 [accessed: December 12, 2009].

[2]   For a discussion of how celebrity culture mirrors, but ultimately falls short of, the dynamics of traditional religion see Chris Rojek, *Celebrity* (London: Reaktion Books, 2001) 51–99.

[3]   Ellis Cashmore, *Celebrity/Culture* (Abingdon: Routledge, 2006), 163.

[4]   Richard Dyer, *Stars* (London: British Film Institute, 1998), 43.

transformation."[5] Therefore a figure such as Jackson, who offers the promise of breathtaking personal transformation and progress apparently unbounded by conventional, mortal limitations, seems inviting indeed. Instead of rejecting him based upon his lack of a singular identity, fans, particularly those experiencing their own sense of powerlessness or marginalization, can hope that they too will be accepted in spite of, or perhaps because of, their difference.

But the ability of any celebrity to transgress normative boundaries of identity and behavior can only go so far. Thus, a sex scandal might enhance a performer's image as long as it still falls within the bounds of socially acceptable coupling. Paris Hilton, for example, appears to have suffered no long-term consequences for the release of a sex tape showing her in a night of heterosexual passion. Jackson's scandals, on the other hand, insofar as they involved alleged intergenerational and homosexual desire, could not simply be incorporated into the standard, naughty-star narrative. These were transgressions for which he could not apologize, or go to rehab, for that would only confirm his guilt in a culture that currently ranks pedophilia as a worse crime than murder.[6] While Ellis Cashmore claims that Jackson's ability to resurface after each accusation, fans seemingly intact, suggests that his scandal has "a happy ending," these charges undeniably had an enormous impact on his popularity—he simply never achieved the same sales successes as he had previous to each round of accusations—as well as on his physical and psychological health.[7] Indeed Jackson's increasing exiles to various countries in the Middle East must certainly be ascribed in part to his need to escape the revulsion that he encountered from mainstream America.[8] Being a liminal figure simply was not enough to transcend the taint of child molestation in a country that James Kincaid suggests has become obsessed with the idea of innocence defiled.[9] Indeed in Jackson's case, his lack of a mainstream identity undoubtedly

---

[5]   As cited in Cashmore, *Celebrity/Culture*, 82.

[6]   Tiger Woods reputedly attended rehab for having multiple sexual partners while married. He also issued an apology on his website. While these affairs were intragenerational and heterosexual, the sheer volume of them has seriously tarnished his image in a country that tends to view adultery with hysteria, even impeaching a president over it. Woods, it seems, has rebounded unscathed from this scandal. As to the ranking of pedophilia over murder, the Adam Walsh Child Protection Act of 2006 permits sex offenders to be incarcerated indefinitely in spite of having completed their sentences. No similar laws pertaining to murderers have been suggested. For more on this legislation, see www.ncsl. org/issues-research/civil-and-criminal-justice/hr4472-adam-walsh-child-protection-and-safety-ac.aspx.

[7]   Cashmore, *Celebrity/Culture*, 163.

[8]   Such scandals usually reveal the racial divide in America as white citizens find themselves more convinced of the guilt of a black celebrity than do African Americans. The cases of Kobe Bryant and OJ Simpson reveal this schism. See Cashmore, *Celebrity/ Culture*, 159.

[9]   See James Kincaid, *Erotic Innocence: The Culture of Child Molesting* (Durham, NC: Duke University Press), 1998. Here, he ascribes the popularity of the film *Home*

contributed to the public's uncertainty about his inclinations once the charges were filed.

Similarly, as many of the chapters above have attested to, Jackson's apparent transgression of his own African American ethnicity turned him into a figure of morbid fascination. While in some sense his decreasingly African features and skin color perhaps permitted him to function as a post-racial symbol of unity, for the most part media coverage of these changes excoriated "Wacko Jacko." No mercy was shown to him in spite of his own protestations that the obvious lightening of his skin was due to vitiligo rather than any desire to become a white man. However, the changes in his facial features were not as easily passed off as symptoms of disease. As fascinated viewers watched over the years, his nose become smaller and smaller and his chin and cheekbones sharper and more prominent. Tabloids frequently ran side-by-side images documenting the startling transformation he underwent from child to teen to adult. Jackson married two white women, nor were his own children apparently African American. Cumulatively, he became less identifiable as a member of his own marginalized race, but as to be expected in a racist society, not more of a member of the dominant one either. No longer was his personal success unproblematic proof of the end of racial barriers and the possibility inherent in the American Dream: young black boy makes good through luck and pluck. Instead, he increasingly seemed to embody a kind of self-loathing that left him neither white nor black, man nor boy, straight nor gay.[10]

And then he died, this final loss of power contributing to the myriad contradictions threatening to imperil Jackson's status as *great*. Someone once known for his ability to transcend bodily limitations—Barry Gordy said at the memorial service that the moonwalking Jackson "went into orbit and never came down"—he had indeed come down most decisively, to the ignominious end awaiting all mortals. Nor was his demise particularly heroic. News coverage extensively documented

---

Alone to the audience's desire to watch the young and comely Macaulay Culkin assailed by would-be molesters. Culkin, of course, was one of Jackson's companions around the same time. Apparently people distinguish between their own voyeuristic enjoyment of the threat of pedophilia with the presumed actual deployment of it. Yet while the charges against Jackson may have affected his record sales, they never affected mainstream interest in his life. He became part of the spectacle of child molestation that Kincaid argues we currently construct and consume. For another instance of this fascination with presumed pedophilia see also Diane Blaine, "Necrophilia, Pedophilia, or Both?: The Sexualized Rhetoric of the Jon Benet Ramsey Case," in *Sexual Rhetoric: Media Perspectives on Sexuality, Gender and Identity*, ed. Meta Carstarphen and Susan Savoina (Westport: Greenwood, 2006), 21–61.

[10]   Beyond the scope of this current discussion would be a consideration of the way that white consumers view black celebrities as representing "a new type of whiteness that makes the racial hierarchy invisible or at least opaque" (Cashmore, *Celebrity/Culture*, 138). Jackson's popularity with mainstream audiences can perhaps be attributed in part to this dynamic, but his visual transformation away from his original roots was itself the subject of intense speculation. Because of this I would argue he remained a marked racial subject rather than being allowed to assimilate into normative white identity.

his final hours: pathetically ingesting a surgical anesthetic designed to knock him into oblivion; frantically resuscitated for hours by a desperate private physician, Dr. Conrad Murray, who would be convicted of involuntary manslaughter on November 7, 2011 due to his involvement in Jackson's final moments; finally transported to an awaiting ambulance with some providential bystander snapping a last blurry image of his decrepit corpse in his own driveway. Southern California local news stations even ran a live broadcast of his body, decisively shrouded by a white sheet, being removed from the hospital and into an awaiting sheriff's helicopter. The official announcement of his death at UCLA Medical Center was followed by days of coverage of the coroner's handling of the body, extensive autopsy rumors contributing to the image of the wasted body of the entertainer being repeatedly and handily disemboweled.

No, it was not going to be possible to imagine Jackson alive somewhere, cavorting in glee with Elvis. He was clearly dead. And if our celebrities can die, so can we. Thus Jackson's death ushered the problem of the mortal body into our living rooms in a major and spectacular way. Anthropologist Geoffrey Gorer has argued that denizens of modernity no longer have a certainty in the afterlife, therefore fearing natural death and turning it into a taboo akin to that of sex for the Victorians. He says that people focus on unnatural deaths in order to deflect away from the reality of their own geriatric and decidedly unsexy demises, and thus prefer representations of death that are what he terms "pornographic": sensationalized, violent, and divorced from the emotions normally associated with the event.[11] Certainly Jackson's death falls into this category in a number of ways. He died an unnatural death, his death was sensational, and he represented the other sufficiently to reassure mainstream middle class viewers that this was not something they had to worry about happening to them.[12] But, crucially, Jackson was a celebrity with whom many people closely identified due to his "growing up in our living rooms."[13] Additionally, his poignant loneliness and longing for acceptance and love struck at the heart of the perils of identity in an age of individualism and meaningless consumption. Jackson's own elastic relationship to his race, sexual orientation and gender mirror the confusion of many who similarly labor under the *you can be anything you want* fiction of modernity. Jacko may

---

[11]   Geoffrey Gorer, *Death, Grief and Mourning in Contemporary Britain* (Garden City: Doubleday, 1965), 192–9.

[12]   For an in-depth discussion of these issues, including the salience of race and gender in media representations of death, see Blaine, "Necrophilia, Pedophilia, or Both?"

[13]   A phrase I hear over and over, even from my students, who were certainly not alive to watch him "grow up." This suggests that Jackson has been separated from chronological time and become mythic. Nor can it be argued in any reasoned way that occasionally viewing someone on television performing staged intimacy truly constitutes a sharing of their childhood even if the viewer were present during the original broadcast. No one watched him grow up who was not present in his life a majority of the time.

have been wacko, but he was, as my colleague David Dark argues in Chapter 12, also us.

Stabilizing Jackson's Identity: The Memorial Rhetoric

Throughout this collection we have seen how Jackson's success was predicated on the slipperiness of Michael Jackson as a sign. We have also considered ways in which his reputation and success suffered due to related extremes of behavior and appearance. Now we will examine they ways in which his memorial service served to mitigate the damage caused by those elements of Jackson's persona that could not be recuperated into an identity acceptable to mainstream consumers in the United States, a move necessary to protect Jackson, and the Jackson family, as a valuable brand. The stabilizing also serves to support the metanarrative of individual success crucial to the social structure in the United States and strives to exonerate blackness as a problematic racial category. Finally, we shall see how these attempts varied in their efforts, ultimately producing the contradictory image of Jackson as a man who both overcame the barriers of race and class and was simultaneously thwarted by them.

Thus, the memorial service had an agenda that surpassed that of the average funeral. Participants at this event clearly evinced the need to legitimate Jackson in the eyes of the audience despite his enormous popularity and worldwide reaction to his death. Normative eulogies may be considered persuasive only insofar as they seek to keep community intact following a death, but in this case a number of speakers at the memorial actually invoked a second kind of rhetoric not traditionally deployed in eulogies to argue that Jackson had been unjustly accused of crimes.[14] Standard eulogies, as epideictic rhetoric, are a ceremonial kind of speech conventionally offering only praise of the dead and avoiding any negative appraisals of the deceased's character. Generally one's indiscretions, if any, go unmentioned altogether in a funeral setting.[15] Jackson's memorial, however, was filled with speakers using *judicial* rhetoric to insist upon the innocence of the fallen star, clearly invoking the criminal prosecution in order to argue for his absolution. Judicial rhetoric operates on a completely different level of persuasion

---

[14]   Donovan Ochs, *Consolatory Rhetoric* (Columbia: South Carolina University Press, 1993), 30–31. Ochs discusses the persuasive nature of the conventional funeral elegy in detail. Because most funerals avoid any controversy, there is simply no need for argument. They perform a more invisible annealing of the rent in community caused by a death. Exonerating the deceased from alleged misdeeds is not typically the goal.

[15]   See Ochs, *Consolatory Rhetoric*, 32. Ochs demonstrates the need to praise the dead in order to keep community intact. While this was not Jackson's funeral, as a separate rite was held for close family and friends, the memorial nonetheless functioned quite conventionally as a funeral, including by having the body present, something more traditionally associated with funerals and not memorials.

than that of the epideictic insofar as it attempts directly to persuade an audience of someone's guilt or innocence. As epideictic rhetoric, eulogies generally only strive to assuage anxiety about mortality and the health of the community following the loss of a member. This violation of the standards of decorum in the context of a funeral demonstrate a clear desire to wash Jackson's image clean of any taint of pedophilia whatsoever in this most public of settings.

While never specifically mentioned, the legal problems were directly alluded to in a number of ways. "There were words cast about," regarding Jackson, said Congresswoman Sheila Jackson Lee. These "words" referred to a history in which Jackson faced criminal prosecution. "There are those that like to dig around in mess," noted Al Sharpton. "Mess" here refers poetically to the morass of allegations regarding the celebrity's presumed penchant for sex with young men. Jackson made some "questionable decisions," said Barry Gordy. Presumably these decisions involved his avowed sharing of his bed with boys.

In each case, following the invocation of the sex scandal that dogged Jackson, the speaker's rejoinder was decisively exculpatory. Lee, who said she had come on behalf of the House of Representatives, intoned that "… as a member of the United States Congress, we [sic] understand the constitution, we understand laws, and we know that people are innocent until proven otherwise, that is what the constitution stands for." The audience responded to this assertion of Jackson's innocence by a member of the federal government with a standing ovation. Al Sharpton took a more metaphorical approach to judicial rhetoric, saying, "But millions around the world are gonna uphold his message. It's not about mess; it's about his love message." He added that when one climbs "steep mountains, sometimes you scar your knee. Sometime you break your skin." Clearly these tropes allude to Jackson's pedophilia charges, here reduced to scabs rather than illegal acts against minors. As for Gordy, he noted that while there were those "questionable decisions," he added that "Michael Jackson accomplished everything he dreamed." Left unexamined was whether or not achieving goals ameliorates those socially problematic choices. Or perhaps more accurately, the assertion here seems to be that as long as one climbs mountains and accomplishes personal dreams—and is never found guilty in a court of law—no stigma should accrue to the star persona.

These clear invocations of judicial rhetoric in a setting conventionally inhospitable to its use reveal a strong need not just to praise Jackson but to purge his image of the taint of pedophilia. Doing so would permit him to stand as an unimpeachable example of African American success rather than an embarrassing reminder of the racist accusations hurled against black men in a country historically willing to associate non-normative ethnicity with sexual perversion and criminality. And most certainly the memorial service was a celebration of African American community, privilege, and celebrity. Only a few of the speakers or performers were white; much of the praise of Jackson focused on his transcending racial barriers; the funeral itself reflected conventions of African American ritual, including the presence of a gospel choir.[16] The attendance of Stevie Wonder, Lionel Ritchie, Magic Johnson, Usher, inter alia, signaled that this occasion represented the heights of black status and achievement. In this sense Jackson himself was not being feted as an individual but as the representative of the race.

That blackness needs sanitizing as a symbol even in the presence of African Americans who have enjoyed fantastic celebrity and monetary success-including political power-speaks to the pervasiveness of racism. Unlike most rituals attended by African Americans *for* African Americans, this one was going to have an audience of millions of white people. The occasion became therefore not just an opportunity to praise the dead but to convince an audience of potential skeptics as to the legitimacy of black identity. To this end Jackson himself became an important object of identification, the common link between the disparate ethnic groups conventionally at odds in the United States. Kenneth Burke notes that "you persuade a man [sic] only insofar as you can talk his language by speech, gesture, tonality, order image, attitude, idea, *identifying* your ways with his."[17] In the case of this memorial service, playing up Jackson's positive qualities and exonerating him of negative ones permits him to function as a symbol of the excellence of African Americanness. And while Aristotle, quoting Socrates in his *Rhetoric*, notes that "It is not hard to praise Athenians among Athenians," it is much harder to do so when you are with Lacedaemonians.[18] Therefore, the Jackson constructed by the rhetoric at the memorial service portrayed him not just a black success story, but an *American* success story, thus offering a crucial form of identification for the audience who might not share the ethnic identity but do share the national one.

To this end, the rags-to-riches tale of the Jackson family was repeated by a number of speakers, identifying their lives as the American Dream par excellence. Al Sharpton, in a heavily emotive speech, described the poignant story of:

> a mother and father with nine children that rose from a working-class family in Gary, Indiana. They had nothing but a dream. No one believed in those days that these kinds of dreams could come true but they kept on believing. And Michael never let the world turn him around from his dreams.

Sheila Jackson Lee said while she cannot write music, dance or sing, "I do know an American story." She then referred to the Jackson family, including Jackson's own children, as "all these wonderful, beautiful symbols of America." Pastor Lucius Smith, who began and ended the memorial service, testified that "Michael Jackson was and always shall be a beloved part of the Jackson family and the family of

---

[16]   See Charlton McIlwain, *Death in Black and White: Death, Ritual, and Family Ecology* (Cresskill: Hampton, 2003). Here, you will find a detailed discussion of the distinct characteristics of African American and white funeral rituals.

[17]   Kenneth Burke, *A Rhetoric of Motives* (New York: George Braziller, 1955), 55. Emphasis in original.

[18]   Ibid.

man." The repeated emphasis on his talent, drive, and success, all in the context of the American Dream, serve to transform him from individual to Everyman, an allegorical figure reflecting the inherent possibility of achievement in a country that poses no barriers to enormous accomplishment for anyone.

In this same vein, Jackson was presented as a civil rights leader who strode with the greatest names in U.S. history and beyond.[19] The service itself began with Smokey Robinson reading a letter from Diana Ross immediately followed by a statement from Nelson Mandela. This procedural move from Ross, a black singer who had close ties with Michael Jackson at certain points in his early life, to a political figure whose actions helped bring down apartheid in South Africa, conflate the categories of entertainer and civil rights leader, thus setting up a forum in which Jackson's lack of participation in any political cause or resistance movement could nonetheless be interpreted as heroic intervention into the realms of discrimination and oppression. Speakers repeatedly credited him with personally ending racism in the United States, from Magic Johnson claiming that Jackson allowed "Kobe and I to have our jerseys in people's homes across the world because he was already there," to Sharpton's belief that Tiger Woods, Oprah and Obama all succeeded because Jackson "broke down the color curtain" and made people "comfortable" enough with blackness to ultimately "vote for a person of color to be the President of the United States of America." The adult children of Martin Luther King Jr. spoke, their very presence, like the letter from Mandela, elevating the entertainer to heights of political activism and racial emancipation. King's daughter said:

> throughout the ages few are chosen from amongst us to use our gifts and talents to demonstrate God's love in an effort to bring the world together in a true sister and brotherhood. Michael was such a one.

Clearly the echoes of Martin Luther King Jr. also being "such a one" infuse Jackson's biography with mythic and heroic overtones.

Yet there was also the clear sense at the memorial that in spite of his monumental stature and success, Jackson had been plagued by persecution. He seemed both a symbol of the ability to overcome racism—indeed was directly credited with ending it in a variety of ways—*and* a symbol of its omnipresence. While Jackson's "sad times," as Barry Gordy referred to them, were never specifically attributed to prejudice, the sense that he was being unfairly attacked resonated with the history of unfair prosecution of African Americans, and every single voice who

---

[19] Beyond the scope of this current discussion would be consideration of what specific contributions Jackson made to the erosion of racism in entertainment and beyond. The one clear instance in which his presence made a difference was when CBS insisted that MTV play the *Billy Jean* video. Previously the channel had resisted broadcasting work by black entertainers. This moment, spurred by CBS's desire for profit rather than any political sensibility, is viewed as pivotal for the breakthrough of the appearance of African Americans on this popular and powerful station.

spoke out to exonerate him was closely associated with black culture and politics. Congresswoman Lee noted that she came "on behalf of the Congressional Black Caucus." She later added that she had gotten to know "his story and it has not been told by all of what you've heard." Al Sharpton said that he first met Jackson at the Black Expo in Chicago in 1970, then proceeded to praise the singer for his refusal to "let people decide his boundaries for him." After crediting Jackson with being responsible for "our" videos being shown and "us" being on the cover of magazines, he later said Jackson "dealt with" what he had to "deal with" for "us." The "us" seems clearly to refer to African Americans rather than people in general or those accused of criminal activity. Martin Luther King Jr.'s daughter decried the fact that he was "embroiled in accusations and persecutions." Marlon Jackson told that audience that "we will never understand what he endured ... being judged, ridiculed." In a poignant moment directly addressing his late brother, he added "maybe now Michael they will leave you alone." It is unclear exactly who "they" might be. Charges were brought against him by the people of the State of California. Fans were unwilling to "leave him alone." The media attention of course made Michael Jackson possible.[20] Apart from these groups—none of which would make a logical target for direct attack—remains an amorphous sense of inequity, one certainly related to the specifics of Jackson's life but seemingly freighted as well with the baggage of a people who continue to struggle for recognition and validation in a culture entrenched in institutionalized racism. In spite of Jackson's lack of overt political activism during his life—his calls for love and tolerance were generic and undirected at any source—he became a politicized figure in the rhetoric of the memorial service, symbolizing both success over and continued attack by an unnamed and unseen nemesis.

The final way Jackson's persona underwent stabilizing during the event involved the assertion of his overall humanity. This man who did so much to alter his visage and live a life of spectacular splendor was represented as a normative African American with working-class tastes. Much was made of the idea that he was just a kid from a family that had no material advantages, only talent and "a dream." While the very word "star" implies a creature who resides above the hoi polloi, "anchoring the celebrity's image in relation to a "real moment before fame" invites us to feel closer to celebrities and to suggest our proximity to their emotions."[21] Throughout the event, photos of him as a child with his natal features intact were displayed at key moments on the enormous screen at the back of the stage. Two separate speakers, Magic Johnson and Barry Gordy, both spoke

---

[20]   See Stephen Hinerman, "(Don't) Leave Me Alone: Tabloid Narrative and the Michael Jackson Child-Abuse Scandal," in *The Celebrity Culture Reader*, ed. P. David Marshall (New York: Routledge, 2006), 454–69. Hinerman's discussion of the relationship between Jackson's image in the press before and after the accusations of molestation is quite helpful.

[21]   Littler as cited in *Framing Celebrity: New Directions in Celebrity Culture*, ed. Su Holmes and Sean Redmond (New York: Routledge, 2006), 37.

nostalgically of softball games at the Jackson family home. A number of those who remembered him asserted that he was "real" even after he became a huge star. For example, Johnson told an anecdote about being summoned to Jackson's mansion in later years to be asked to perform in a video. He says he needed to check with Jackie to be sure the call was "really" Michael. This narrative situates Jackson as the unreal, unobtainable celebrity in relation to Magic Johnson, one of the most famous sports figures in the modern era here reduced to merely another fan. But once at the home of his "idol," Johnson was stunned to find Michael Jackson eating a fast food stereotypically aligned with black culture:

> I said "What? Michael, *you* eat Kentucky Fried Chicken?" That made my day. That was the greatest moment of my life. We had such a good time sitting on the floor eating that bucket of Kentucky Fried Chicken.

The message was clear: Michael Jackson was real. Magic Johnson assured the audience that the man they thought was of a different species was just like them. Others echoed this same message. Brooke Shields insisted that while their friendship "may have seemed very odd ... we made it real." Al Sharpton thundered to Jackson's children, "... wasn't nothing strange about your daddy. It was strange what your daddy had to deal with." Pastor Lucius Smith began the service by insisting to an arena and a broadcast audience of hundreds of millions of people who had never met the "idol," that "first and foremost this man before us today was our brother, our son, our father, and our friend." We shall see in the next section how this assertion of his humanity prepared the audience for his canonization as savior.

"I'm Alive and Here Forever": Jackson as Celebrity Christ Figure

The current craze for idolizing famous entertainers offers a space for ecstasy, worship, and transcendence, thus operating, as David Dark also suggests in Chapter 12, much like a religion. Secular society has gained dominance over theocracies in the modern west. But the decline of conventional theology due to the rise in moral individualism was not replaced by a corresponding rise in state-sponsored holidays, as Emile Durkheim predicted it would. Therefore, celebrity culture "establishes the main scripts, presentational props, conversational codes and other source materials through which cultural relations are constructed."[22] People participate in secular rituals of community that are similar to religious ones insofar as "they replicate clear principles of inclusion and exclusion, they are faithful to transcendent spiritual beliefs and principles, and they identify sacred and profane values."[23] Thus the sense of belonging that comes from being a fan

---

[22]   Gabler as cited in Rojek, *Celebrity*, 393.

[23]   Ibid., 57.

of a particular star can provide order, identity, and meaning. "Modern fame," according to Leo Braudy, "is always compounded by the audience's aspirations and its despair, its need to admire and to find a scapegoat for that need."[24] This dynamic clearly parallels that of religiosity as figures like the martyred Christ offer points of connection for the pious and his bloody sacrifice becomes the center of obsessive attention and ecstasy. Today's fan looks to their mass media idol just as "the Puritan in the seventeenth century looked to Christ for comfort and inspiration."[25]

This convergence of religious piety and celebrity worship works most effectively in the realm of musical entertainers. Rock stars frequently become iconic heroes for their fans, who weep, sob, and faint in their presence.[26] Sheila Whiteley sees audiences as particularly engaged by the agonies of their idols, figures who are addicted to drugs, living lives of excess, "heroes ... whose emotions have broken out of prescribed limits, endowing them with a godlike eminence which is curiously enhanced by their often ignoble deaths."[27] This adulation of entertainers who seem to be able to resist conforming, even to the point of dying unnaturally, reflects their status as shaman figures, according to Rojek. Seeing continuity between the worlds of religion and celebrity, he notes that "all cultures possess rites, myths, divine forms, sacred and venerated objects, symbols, consecrated men and sacred places."[28] But today's shaman figures are more often mass-media celebrities rather than conventional priests. Drawing on the work of anthropologist Mircea Eliade, Rojek observes that in order to function as shamanistic, modern celebrities must offer some element of transgression in a spectacle "associated with revelation and rebirth." The shaman "possesses the power to conjure different collective intensities of being that, through the metaphor and experience of the ecstatic journey, admit transcendence."[29]

Jackson surely functions as such a shamanistic figure, both in life and in death. His physical abilities seemed to defy nature, a key attribute of the venerated priest

---

[24] Leo Braudy, *The Frenzy of Renown* (New York: Oxford University Press, 1986), 9.

[25] Rojek, *Celebrity*, 74.

[26] Of interest but beyond the scope of this discussion is how Michael Jackson differs from the conventional rock idol like Jim Morrison. Jackson's drug use, for example, involved substances available via prescription rather than the street, thus softening and feminizing his addiction. His proclivities in the bedroom were seen as perversions rather than enviable transgressions. And the musical genre he excelled in was exceedingly mainstream. Instead of "sex, drugs and rock and roll," one might say Jackson represented "pedophilia, Propofol, and pop."

[27] Sheila Whiteley, "Celebrity: The Killing Fields of Popular Music," in *Framing Celebrity: New Directions in Celebrity Culture*, ed. Su Holmes and Sean Redmond (New York: Routledge, 2006), 331.

[28] Rojek, *Celebrity*, 53.

[29] Ibid., 56. Also, for more discussion of the role of the blues performer in this shamanistic role, see Rojek, *Celebrity*, 68.

figure. The fact that his iconic move was termed the "moonwalk" suggested he traveled beyond the realm of the earth. The shaman, Rojek notes, "partially asserts and reinforces his power through the performance of various tricks and undertakings."[30] Jackson's career was marked by such tricks, including those like the changes in his appearance that gained him notoriety for his strangeness. In fact, insofar as he was non-normative in his presentation of race and gender, he operated as a marginal figure who thereby opened up possibilities for transgressing conventional categories of meaning.[31] In his very freakishness he makes possible things which are not of this world, thus operating as a port to a reality beyond this one. During a class discussion of his death, one of my students said "there's nothing ordinary about Michael Jackson." It is precisely this perception that makes him available to the audience as a magical figure. Images of him being worshipped by tens of thousands of fans are commonplace. One of his brothers noted at the service that he could not walk across the street, such was the adulation and hysteria he invoked. When Jackson visited Prague on tour in 1996, an enormous inflatable replica of the star was placed at the former site of an enormous statue of Stalin. The message was clear: Jackson is a cult figure who commands worship.

Because the shaman figure must not be bound by conventions of mortality, Jackson's death did not undermine his status as miraculous figure. Indeed in many ways it rehabilitated and reinvigorated his godlike persona. The very dynamics of shamanism require ascent, descent and redemption. Jackson surely ascended in life, being lifted above the normal human being and associated with magical qualities. He descended as well, his humiliating association with pedophilia marring the purity of his image as harmless trickster who merely played with children. This was not a fall that he could take responsibility for; in the current U.S. climate there would be no forgiveness for someone who acknowledged having sexual contact with children. Therefore his death offered the clearest possibility of redemption for Jackson, a chance to purify his mythos from the taint of sexual perversion. Whiteley notes that for celebrities, "death is no barrier to their perceived status as 'gods.'"[32] In the case of Michael Jackson, I would argue that death was actually a requirement for the reinstatement of that status. In this sense, the many voices at the memorial insisting upon his innocence were redeeming a deity, burning off the taint of criminal behavior and leaving instead the image of an innocent scapegoat. As Al Sharpton argued, there wasn't anything "strange" about Michael Jackson— nothing, that is except for the fact that he was not a mortal human being but a god who visited the earth to save it.

This invocation of Jackson as a deity was constant and overt through the memorial service. While Judeo-Christian eulogies conventionally include descriptions of the deceased living on in a paradisiacal afterlife, Jackson's service

---

[30]   Rojek, *Celebrity*, 77.

[31]   In this way he parallels Valentino, who gained his popularity from his non-normative representation of race and masculinity. See Rojek, *Celebrity*, 71.

[32]   Whiteley, "Celebrity," 329.

went much further, overtly conflating him with Jesus Christ as an immortal and generative source of love and healing. This canonization took place from the outset. As a gospel choir sang "Soon and very soon, we are going to see the King," Jackson's casket was carried into view. The parallel was unmistakable: Michael Jackson was not just the King of Pop, but the King of Kings. In speaking of his charitable acts, Jackson Lee thundered that "the king, yes the King, the KING, stopped and said 'I care about you.'" This emphasis on his sacred qualities was continued by Maya Angelou, who asserted in her elegy that "He came to us from the Creator, trailing creativity in abundance." Jackson not only brought creativity, he "taught the world how to love," according to Al Sharpton. Bernice King said to the family "My prayer is that no one or nothing, public or private, fact or fiction, true or rumored, will separate you from the love of"—here it seemed she was going to say Michael Jackson, but instead continued with—"God, which is in Christ Jesus, because ultimately at the end of the day, it is only God's love that will anchor and sustain and move you to a higher ground, for above the noise of life, there you will find the peace, comfort, and joy necessary to advance"—here it would seem she would say "God's will," but instead she said "Michael's legacy." This confusion added to Jackson's mythic status. She continued that like her father and mother, "Michael's life and work is inspired by the love of God." This legacy of unconditional healing and love, inextricable from that of God and Christ Jesus, was illustrated by frequent images of him robed in white, arms outstretched as if crucified, that appeared on the giant screen at the back of the stage at the Staples Center.

Continuing with this Christlike apotheosis, speakers also identified Jackson as a healer throughout the service. Fans often attribute "magical or extraordinary powers" to celebrities; in this case, Jackson's status as mystical healer was continually invoked.[33] Pastor Lucius Smith told the gathered crowd that "Michael did so much to try and heal the world." At the end of the service he added that in "some small way he did." Jackson Lee, explaining that the "hearts of entertainers" are misunderstood, explained that "they heal the world on behalf of America. When we're at war, our icons like Michael sing about healing the world." Offering him a title that certainly recalls those granted to sacred figures, she said "I call him Michael Jackson Who Cared and Loved for the World." Shahin Jafargholi, the next boy wonder discovered on England's version of *American Idol*, thanked Jackson for "blessing me and every single human being on earth with his amazing music." In a world in which there has been "a collapse in the belief of the goodness or purity of things and a corresponding increase in irony and skepticism," the young man's prayerful invocation of Jackson as a source of "blessing" rather than one of corruption, constructs celebrity culture as the site of the sacred and a force of good.[34] Kenny Ortega, invoking the rhetoric of the Second Coming, claimed that Jackson's comeback concert tour "was, I promise you, his triumphant return to the

[33]   Rojek, *Celebrity*, 53.
[34]   Holmes and Redmond, *Framing Celebrity*, 289.

world." The show, he continued, was "living testament to his ability to be timeless and timely, musical and magical, living in our hearts for always, heal the world, make this a better place." Such testimony recalls those of the disciples in the New Testament, speaking in awe of the miracles they witnessed Christ perform. This miraculous resurrection, albeit discursive, completes Jackson's role as shaman figure, able to descend into and then return from the underworld unscathed.

As befitting a Christ figure who was able to rise from the dead, Jackson was figured in the rhetoric of the service as immortal. Rojek notes that along with elevation above the norm and the attribution of magical powers, immortality is the third characteristic of the shaman.[35] The speakers at the service insisted upon his immortality, even to the point of discursive excess. Jackson will be honored "forever and forever and forever and forever and forever," said Jackson Lee, to a rousing ovation. "Because he gave so much to so many of us, Michael Jackson will be with us forever," Kobe Bryant claimed. "As long as we remember him," said Pastor Smith, "he will be there forever to comfort us." Smokey Robinson asserted his belief that Jackson "will live on forever." Later he said:

> I believe so much in God. I believe so much that this is not it. We have life after this is done. So my brother's in a place where he is most certainly going to live forever in the hereafter.

Brother Marlon portrayed the dead Jackson as "the voice of our angelic trumpets [who] will continue to be an angelic voice in heaven with our creator."

These depictions of Jackson suggest he has not so much taken the place of a religious figure, but that he has actually become one. While celebrity culture cannot generally offer "an encompassing grounded view of social and spiritual order," the conflation of Jackson's unique talents with the metanarrative of Judeo-Christianity create a hybrid that is neither one nor the other.[36] The stability critics attribute to celebrity culture in what Rojek terms "post-God" society here actually infuses religion with the energy and immediacy of mass media stardom.[37] Jackson's celebrity status elevates—not simply mirrors—Judeo-Christianity, which receives a needed boost from association with an iconic figure able to incite worship and ecstasy. At the same time Jackson becomes infused not just with the cache of celebrity, itself already another ontological order of being, but with the very stuff of the sacred. This potent combination of Jackson's celebrity and Christian theology provides a powerful ordering imperative necessary in times of imbalance, here precipitated by the death of an individual and the rise of a secular culture that has displaced certainty about the afterlife.[38] And so the rhetorical acts performed this memorial, as at all funeral services, strive to console the audience,

---

[35]   Rojek, *Celebrity*, 403–406.

[36]   Ibid., 98.

[37]   Ibid., 393.

[38]   See Gorer, *Death, Grief and Mourning in Contemporary Britain*.

making "less ominous" the "inevitability of their own death."[39] Thus this Michael/
Jesus figure who enjoys eternal life offers the hope that we shall as well.

Since the service represents a convergence of Judeo-Christianity with late
capitalism and celebrity culture, the venue itself became a sacred space in spite
of its conventional role as secular entertainment arena. "Because they bring an
individual into contact with the sacred," funerals "must be set apart in special
times and places."[40] As audience members entered the Staples Center, there was a
hushed and reverent mood. Yet there was some tension between the usual joyous
attendance of a concert and the somber behavior expected at a funeral. People were
surprised not to find vendors offering Jackson paraphernalia for sale, for example,
and there was clearly uncertainty as to whether to applaud the performances of
stars like Mariah Carey. But producers strove to make clear that the ritual was a
religious one and the arena was for this occasion a church. As the gospel choir
sang its first number, an enormous image of a stained-glass rose window was
projected onto the screen at the back of the stage. This religious iconography was
repeated at key moments throughout the service, always underscoring Jackson's
depiction as spiritual being. Having the perimeter of the Staples Center completely
devoid of traffic save those pedestrians with tickets in hand added to the sense of
this being a pilgrimage to a holy site.

The transformation of a commercial venue into a sacred one and a secular idol
into a religious one provided a powerful denial of both the reality of mortality
and the alienating effects of consumer culture.[41] Jackson became the ideal brand
for our age, a god who can be bought. Audience members did not need to choose
between a jaded material culture and a transcendent spiritual one. These were
inextricably bound together by the miraculous, magical Michael and his healing
message of love. The seemingly insurmountable problems of life—and death—
can be solved by accessing him/Him, just as Jackson's own mortified body has
been resurrected and perfected. Indeed the final picture on the giant screen was of
an ecstatic Jackson with the words "I'm alive and I'm here forever" superimposed
on the image. And while the pastor made a final attempt to differentiate the King
of Pop from the King of Kings, noting that the former must "bow his knee to the
latter," the ultimate impression of the memorial overwhelmed this late assertion
of the pop star's mere humanity. Indeed the pastor himself bade the audience to
carry Jackson's message—not God's—out into the world, to reach out to others
"with the love Michael taught us in his music." Through death, divorced from his
problematic, desiring body, ritually cleansed of his transgressions, and offered up as
a scapegoat, Jackson becomes an unimpeachable symbol of love and redemption.

---

[39]   Ochs, *Consolatory Rhetoric*, 21.

[40]   Rothenbuehler as cited in Ochs, *Consolatory Rhetoric*, 25.

[41]   See James Green, *Beyond the Good Death: The Anthropology of Modern Dying*
(Philadelphia: Pennsylvania University Press, 2008). Green's discussion of perceptions
about death in the United States server as a good context to understand this point.

Chapter 14
Remember to Always Think Twice: The Reconciliation of Michael Jackson

Zack Stiegler

For the last 20 years of his life, Michael Jackson was the subject of consistently negative portrayals in the mass media, with allegations of sexual abuse, financial troubles, eccentric public behavior and a constantly changing physique becoming the focus of his media persona. Yet when Jackson died, traditional and social media coverage of the pop singer changed dramatically. In this chapter, Zack Stiegler navigates how and why, upon his death, the mass media jettisoned Jackson's tabloid image focusing instead on the cultural impact of Jackson's creative work, his iconic status in the 1980s, as well as his historical significance and legacy as "the greatest entertainer of all time."

Months after Michael Jackson died, Madonna opened the 2009 MTV Video Music Awards with a heartfelt speech eulogizing Jackson. Most poignantly, Madonna shared her reflections upon his passing:

> When I first heard that Michael had died, I was in London, days away from the opening of my tour. Michael was going to perform in the same venue as me a week later. All I could think about in that moment was I had abandoned him, that we had abandoned him. That we had allowed this magnificent creature that once set the world on fire to somehow slip through the cracks. While he was trying to build a family and rebuild his career, we were all busy passing judgment. Most of us had turned our backs on him. In a desperate attempt to hold on to his memory, I went on the Internet to watch old clips of him dancing and singing on TV and on stage. And I thought, "My god, he was so unique, so original, so rare and there will never be anyone like him again." He was a king. But he was also a human being. And alas, we are all human beings, and sometimes we have to lose things before we can truly appreciate them.

Madonna's words were more than a simple tribute from one member of pop royalty to another. Her contention that we "abandoned" Jackson and that "sometimes we have to lose things before we can truly appreciate them" encapsulates the trajectory of his career and cultural reputation.

From the moment that The Jackson Five became a pop sensation in 1969, Jackson was a fixture in American mass media. His media presence grew over the ensuing years, and he became a bona fide global pop phenomenon by the early 1980s. Even with Jackson's alleged legal transgressions beginning in 1993, he remained a constant media presence, although framing of Jackson changed substantially. In contrast to the overwhelming critical and cultural praise heaped upon him for decades, Jackson's relationship with the mass media became tumultuous to say the least.

For the final two decades of Jackson's life, his representation in mass media was overwhelmingly and consistently negative. Allegations of sexual abuse, financial troubles, eccentric public behavior, and a drastically altered appearance made Jackson a source of derision in the tabloid as well as the mainstream press. An August, 1996 cover story from the *National Enquirer* proclaimed "Jacko's Nose Drops Off—Now His Docs Scramble to Fix It." *The Daily Mirror* claimed a "showbiz exclusive" in its October 13, 2006 issue with a cover story asserting that Jackson had a sex change operation. Such stories were not confined to the pages of tabloid publications. A string of *Rolling Stone* articles in 2001–2002 chronicled the singer's allegedly mounting financial problems, claiming that "the Jackson empire is in disarray," citing millions of dollars in unpaid legal and investment fees, missed concerts, and the star's extravagant spending habits.[1] Placing Jackson atop their list of "Rock's 50 Greatest Meltdowns" in 2002, the same publication chastised the singer in the caption of a photo with ex-wife Lisa Marie ("already plotting her escape") and another of Jackson's televised statements during the 1993 molestation allegations ("Live from Neverland: 'Hello, children!'").[2] In the same period, *Vanity Fair* columnist Maureen Orth claimed that the singer was involved a series of voodoo rituals that had Jackson bathing in sheep's blood to absolve his debts and slaughtering cows in Switzerland in a ritual intended to curse Stephen Spielberg and David Geffen.[3] These are but a few examples of the ways in which for 20 years, the mass media presented Jackson as a sort of pop cultural sideshow freak.

All of that changed on June 25, 2009. With Jackson's passing, media coverage of the pop star took an immediate and dramatic turn. Suddenly, media focus was not on Jackson's eccentricities, physical appearance or alleged sexual improprieties, but rather on the cultural impact of his creative work, his iconic status in the 1980s as well as the singer's historical significance and legacy as

---

[1]   Peter Wilkinson, "Is the King of Pop Going Broke?" *Rolling Stone*, 2002a, 25; Peter Wilkinson, "Jacko's Money Woes Deepen," *Rolling Stone*, 2002b, 39; Peter Wilkinson, "The Truth about Jackson's Money," *Rolling Stone*, 2003, 17.

[2]   Robert Sheffield, "Rock's 50 Greatest Meltdowns," *Rolling Stone*, 2002, 54.

[3]   Maureen Orth, "Losing His Grip?," *Vanity Fair*, April 2003. [Online]. Available at: www.mjfiles.com/allegations/losing-grip-maureen-orth. [accessed: July 20, 2010].

"the greatest entertainer of all time."[4] Where coverage of Jackson's death did address his fall from grace and troubled personal life, it was most often framed in a sympathetic light. *People* and *Rolling Stone* called Jackson's latter days those of "a broken man"; *Time* labeled his final years "sad"; *Vanity Fair*'s cover declared Jackson a "tragic icon," and bid farewell to "a fallen king."[5] Countless outlets in broadcast, online and print media reverently referred to Jackson as "the King of Pop," Jackson's self-appointed title.

This was a curious turn of events. For nearly 20 years, Jackson played the role of mass media's celebrity whipping boy. Now suddenly, much of the discourse about Jackson venerated rather than chastised him, and traditional mass media were not alone. Web traffic reached unprecedented levels as news of Jackson's death spread. Twitter, Wikipedia, Google and TMZ all experienced site crashes due to droves of Web visitors seeking information on Jackson's death.[6] Days after his death, sales of Jackson's back catalog skyrocketed, culminating in his *Number Ones* collection ranking as the third biggest seller of 2009, while he topped year-end tallies of best-selling artists.[7]

In the weeks following his death, Jackson vigils and tribute events sprang up across the country. Much like the early 1980s, Jackson's music once again became inescapable for the entirety of the summer months: bars, dance clubs, summer festivals, karaoke nights, jukeboxes, car stereos in traffic—all allowed Jackson's music to reclaim a sense of ubiquity in the wake of his death. Much like the mass media, the public too had suddenly shifted its perception of Jackson from ambivalence or negativity to reverence and tribute.

---

[4] The "greatest entertainer of all time" title was most emphatically stated by Berry Gordy at Jackson's public memorial service as well as press interviews around that time. Other public figures granting Jackson this superlative include Star Jones, *American Idol*'s Randy Jackson, and Tiger Woods. See, for example, Jessica Robertson, "'Idol' Judge Calls Michael Jackson the 'Greatest Entertainer of All Time'," *Spinner*, June 25, 2009. [Online]. Available at: www.spinner.com/2009/06/25/idol-judge-calls-michael-jackson-the-greatest-entertainer-of/ [accessed: April 17, 2010].

[5] Joey Bartolomeo, et al., "The Accused," *People*, July 13, 2009, 87–8; Brian Hiatt, "What Went Wrong," *Rolling Stone: A Tribute to Michael Jackson*, July 30, 2009, 80–87; Richard Lacayo, "Deformed by Surgery. Warped by Fame. The Sad End of an American Icon," *Time*, July 2009, 48–50; see also cover of September 2009 issue of *Vanity Fair*.

[6] Phoebe Ayers, "Jackson's Death, New Data Center, More," *The Wikipedia Signpost*, June 29, 2009. [Online]. Available at: http://en.wikipedia.org/wiki/Wikipedia:Wikipedia_Signpost/2009-06-29/News_and_notes [accessed: April 17, 2010]; Linnie Rawlinson and Nick Hunt, "Jackson Dies, Almost Takes Internet with Him," *CNN.com*, June 26, 2009. [Online]. Available at: www.cnn.com/2009/TECH/06/26/michael.jackson.internet/index.html [accessed: April 17, 2010]; Maggie Shiels, "Web Slows after Jackson's Death," *BBC News Online*, June 26, 2006. [Online]. Available at: http://news.bbc.co.uk/2/hi/technology/8120324.stm [accessed: April 17, 2010].

[7] Nielsen Company, *The Nielsen Company 2009 Year-End Music Report* (Nielsen, 2009), 2.

This chapter examines the recuperation of Michael Jackson's reputation following his death. In doing so, it draws upon rhetorical approaches to apologetic discourse as a means of understanding the shift of media and popular opinion about Jackson that occurred literally overnight. Through this conceptual lens, I argue that media coverage of Jackson's death may be read as dually apologetic, at once an atonement for past media treatment of Jackson and, through artistic, cultural, and historical praise, an effort to fortify his legacy. However, Jackson's posthumous comeback is not solely a product of mass media coverage. As Internet activity surrounding Jackson's death indicates, social media played a large role in recuperating Jackson's image, facilitating the production of mediated discourse about Jackson's death, life and legacy. Michael Jackson's death is thus an exemplary moment of the increasing interrelation between traditional mass media and user-driven social media online, both of which operate as apologetic discourses working to restore Jackson's public image.

Conceptual Background

As a point of analysis, apology dates to at least ancient Greece and the rhetorical concept of *apologia*, a speech act in which the rhetor defends his or her character in response to a specific charge or accusation.[8] As a genre of speech, *apologia* contains at least two basic elements-the charge or accusation against an individual's character or moral worth (*kategoria*) and the accused's self-defensive response (*apologia*). The literature of apologetic discourse emphasizes that to be considered apologia, discourse should follow this basic charge/response format.[9]

Twentieth century scholars rightly understood that in the contemporary environment of mass media, *apologia* need not be confined to oratory.[10] As such, rhetorical critics employed *apologia* in analyzing mass mediated apologetic discourse, including Nixon's "Checkers" speech, Ted Kennedy's Chappaquiddick

---

[8]   Sharon D. Downey, "The Evolution of the Rhetorical Genre of Apologia," *Western Journal of Communication* 57, no. 1 (1993): 6, 42–3; Noreen Kruse, "Motivational Factors in Non-Denial Apologia," *Central States Speech Journal* 28, no. 1 (1977): 13; Noreen Kruse, "The Scope of Apologetic Discourse: Establishing Generic Parameters," *Southern Speech Communication Journal* 43 (1981): 280, 290; see B.L. Ware and Wil A. Linkugel, "They Spoke in Defense of Themselves: On the Generic Criticism of Apologia," *Quarterly Journal of Speech* 59 (1973): 273–83; Cf. Plato's *Apology*, Isocrates' *Helen* and Aristotle's *Rhetoric*.

[9]   Downey, "Evolution," 42–3; Kruse, "The Scope of Apologetic Discourse," 284–6; Halfor Ross Ryan, "Kategoria and Apologia: On their Rhetorical Criticism as a Speech Set," *Quarterly Journal of Speech* 68 (1982): 254.

[10]   Kruse, "The Scope of Apologetic Discourse," 291.

speech and Billie Jean King's self-defense following the exposure of her extra-marital, lesbian love affair.[11]

Media coverage of Jackson's death does not explicitly follow a charge/response format, as it did not develop in relation to any specific charge or accusation against Jackson's character, nor does Jackson's death coverage apologize for any specific act, at least not directly. Kruse notes that "works that attempt to repair the rhetor's reputations, but which are not generated in response to actual situations" may not fit into the defined parameters of *apologia*, but are apologetic discourses nonetheless, and must be accounted for.[12] Additionally, the very nature of apologetic discourse has changed considerably in the last half century. Downey notes that the significant growth in knowledge and technology in the twentieth century fundamentally changed apologetic discourse to focus on image management more so than strict self-defense.[13]

To that end, Benoit reshaped *apologia* into what he termed "image restoration." Benoit's theory views communication as a goal-oriented activity, one of the key objectives of which is to maintain a reputation favorable to oneself.[14] Building upon the existing literature, Benoit primarily applied his theory to a variety of mass mediated contexts including athletes, celebrities, corporations and politicians.[15]

---

[11]   See Sherry Devereaux Butler, "The Apologia, 1971 Genre," *Southern Speech Communication Journal* 37, no. 3 (1972): 281–9; Jeffrey Nelson, "The Defense of Billie Jean King," *Western Journal of Communication* 48, no. 1 (1984): 92–102; Laurence Rosenfield, "A Case Study in Speech Criticism: The Nixon-Truman Analog," *Speech Monographs* 35, no. 4 (1968): 435–50.

[12]   Kruse, "The Scope of Apologetic Discourse," 287.

[13]   Downey, "Evolution," 53–4.

[14]   William Benoit, *Accounts, Excuses, and Apologies: A Theory of Image Restoration Strategies* (Albany: State University of New York Press, 1995), 63.

[15]   See William L. Benoit, *Accounts, Excuses, and Apologies: A Theory of Image Restoration Strategies* (Albany: State University of New York Press, 1995a); ibid., "Hugh Grant's Image Restoration Discourse: An Actor Apologizes," *Communication Quarterly* 45 (1997): 251–67; ibid., "Richard M. Nixon's Rhetorical Strategies in His Public Statements on Watergate," *Southern Speech Communication Journal* 47 (1982):192–211; ibid., "Sears' Repair of Its Auto Service Image: Image Restoration Discourse in the Corporate Sector," *Communication Studies* 46 (1995b): 89–105; William L. Benoit and Susan L. Brinson, "AT&T: Apologies Are Not Enough," *Communication Quarterly* 42 (1994): 75–88; ibid., "Queen Elizabeth's Image Repair Discourse: Insensitive Royal or Compassionate Queen?" *Public Relations Review* 25 (1999): 145–56; William L. Benoit and Anne Czerwinski, "A Critical Analysis of USAir's Image Repair Discourse," *Business Communication Quarterly* 60 (1997): 38–57; William L. Benoit and Shirley Drew, "Appropriateness and Effectiveness of Image Repair Strategies," *Communication Reports* 10, no. 2 (1997): 153–63; William L. Benoit and Robert Hanczor, "The Tonya Harding Controversy: An Analysis of Image Repair Strategies," *Communication Quarterly* 42 (1994): 416–33; Willaim L. Benoit and Dawn M. Nill, "Oliver Stone's Defense of JFK," *Communication Quarterly* 46 (1998): 127–43; Willaim L. Benoit, Paul Gullifor, and Daniel Panici, "President Reagan's

Throughout this body of work, Benoit examines the ways in which public figures utilize mass media as a vehicle for apologetic discourse in an effort to restore their public image following an event that tarnishes that image.

Burns and Bruner argue that existing models of image restoration are both simplistic and presumptuous. The authors point out that the very term "image restoration" assumes that following the deployment of image restoration strategies, a person's damaged reputation fully returns to its prior state.[16] Noting that complete restoration is unlikely, Burns and Bruner suggest the broader label "image restoration discourse."[17] Benoit also addresses the semantic issue, eliminating "restoration" completely, opting instead for the term "image repair."[18] The term "image repair" avoids the absolutism of "image restoration" while acknowledging that the process is much more complex than any linear mode would suggest. In this chapter, I adopt Benoit's revision for the mere fact that it is a less absolute term, and thus provides greater flexibility in application.

In analyzing coverage of his death, it is important to note that although Jackson's reputation is at stake, he is not the rhetor in this particular discourse, but its subject. This is in contrast to previous mass media *apologiae* such as Nixon's Checkers speech, or even Jackson's videotaped statements in response to allegations of sexual abuse in 1993 and 2005. Whereas in these examples mass media are merely a technological conduit for individual apologetic rhetors, coverage of Jackson's death situates mass media themselves as rhetors. The mass media's function as a third-party apologetic rhetor is not unprecedented.[19] However, it does present an atypical rhetorical situation, particularly in the context of apologetic discourse. As such, I view mass media's apologetic discourse following Michael Jackson's death on two levels. The first reads the death coverage as an apology, while the second more specifically views the mass media as working to repair Jackson's public image.

Defensive Discourse on the Iran-Contra Affair," *Communication Studies* 42, no. 3 (1991): 272–94; Joseph R. Blaney and William L. Benoit, *The Clinton Scandals and the Politics of Image Restoration* (Westport: Praeger, 2001); Joseph R. Blaney, William L. Benoit, and LeAnn M. Brazeal, "Blowout! Firestone's Image Restoration Campaign," *Public Relations Research* 28 (2002): 379–92; Susan L. Brinson and William L. Benoit, "The Tarnished Star: Restoring Texaco's Damaged Public Image," *Communication Quarterly* 12 (1999): 483–510.

[16]   Judith P. Burns and Michael S. Bruner, "Revisiting the Theory of Image Restoration Strategies," *Communication Quarterly* 48, no. 1 (2000): 30.

[17]   Ibid., 31.

[18]   William Benoit, "Another Visit to the Theory of Image Restoration Strategies," *Communication Quarterly* 48, no. 1 (2000): 40.

[19]   See for example Nelson's analysis of Billie Jean King's defense following the exposure of her extramarital affair. Nelson, "The Defense of Billie Jean King."

Jackson Death Coverage as Apology

One way to interpret mass media coverage of Jackson's death is as an atonement for their representations of Jackson in preceding years. Jackson's relationship with the tabloids began in the mid 1980s with reports, well documented and critiqued by my colleagues in this collection, of an attempted purchase of Elephant Man John Merrick's bones, sleeping in a hyperbaric oxygen chamber and stories of similarly eccentric, but harmless behavior. Some, as Raphael Raphael suggests in Chapter 10, even allege that Jackson planted these stories himself to generate personal publicity.[20] From around the time of his 1991 *Dangerous* LP, media speculation and tabloid reports became more personal as Jackson's sexuality, surgical procedures, and skin tone came under increasing scrutiny. Here, Jackson's cultural reputation took a sharp but consistent downfall in the United States, in part driven by his image as presented in mass media, whether accurate or not. Following an out of court settlement in the 1993 child abuse and molestation allegations, the latter portion of that decade saw Jackson marry and divorce twice and father three children, whose paternal lineage continues to be a point of speculation even after his death.

As the new millennium dawned, Jackson's reputation further spiraled out of control. First came his crusade against then CEO of Sony Music, Tommy Mottola. Jackson's claims that poor sales of his 2001 album *Invincible* were due to racial discrimination by Mottola were jeered by the press and the public, regardless of their veracity.[21] Jackson received additional criticism when he dangled his infant son over a Berlin hotel balcony in 2002, raising questions over his suitability for parenthood.[22] The well-discussed 2003 television interview with journalist Martin Bashir furthered speculation about the pop star's character and soundness of mind, showcasing Jackson's extravagant spending habits and stirring controversy when Jackson defended sharing a bed with children. Following the broadcast, a second set of sexual allegations emerged, leading to a 2005 criminal trial, which while

---

[20]   Alan Light, "Jackson's Dangerous Game," *Rolling Stone*, 1993, 17.

[21]   See for example Anthony Breznican, "Erratic Behavior, Appearance Again Cast Doubts on Michael Jackson's Image and Career," December 2, 2002. [Online]. Available at: http://media.www.elvaq.com/media/storage/paper925/news/2002/12/02/Entertainment/ Erratic. Behavior. Appearance.Again.Cast.Doubts. On.MichaelJackson0146s.Image. And-2533623.shtml [accessed: April 17, 2002]; Michael Saul Daily, "Jacko Whacks Biz, Calls Sony Boss Racist," *The Daily News*, July 7, 2002. [Online]. Available at: www. nydailynews.com/archives/news/2002/07/07/2002-07-07_jacko_whacks_biz_calls_sony_. html [accessed: April 17, 2010]; and Fred Goodman, "Michael Jackson's Meltdown," *Rolling Stone*, August 8, 2002, 19–20.

[22]   "Jackson Sorry for Baby Stunt," *BBC News World Edition*, November 20, 2002. [Online]. Available at: http://news.bbc.co.uk/2/hi/entertainment/2494249.stm [accessed: April 17, 2010]; and Jennifer Vineyard, "Michael Jackson Calls Baby-Dangling Incident a 'Terrible Mistake,'" November 20, 2002. [Online]. Available at: www.mtv.com/news/ articles/1458799/20021120/jackson_michael.jhtml [accessed: April 17, 2010].

acquitting Jackson, damaged his public image seemingly beyond repair. The unfavorable media coverage of Jackson during this period—deserved or not—undoubtedly helped to reframe him as a sort of tabloid freak, while his artistry and talent became at best secondary considerations.

In light of this history, we may read the mass media's reappraisal of Jackson's character as an atonement, an apology for the many stories over the years that contributed to the construction of a public image of Jackson that was visually inhuman, psychologically unsound, and sexually devious. Here, an obsession with Jackson as a tabloid figure superseded the artistry and talent that transfixed popular culture years earlier. Whatever the mass media's intent may have been in covering Jackson during the 1990s and into the twenty-first century—be it journalistic integrity or consciously aiming to cut down his cultural reputation—coverage of Jackson during this period was generally negative. In light of this, we may read the press's overwhelmingly positive treatment of Jackson following his death as a *mea culpa* for the negative image of Jackson that multiple mass media outlets helped to construct.

In his sociological examination of apology, Tavuchis notes that "an apology, no matter how sincere or effective, does not and cannot *undo* what has been done. And yet, in a mysterious way and according to its own logic, this is precisely what it manages to do."[23] The positive and sympathetic media coverage of Michael Jackson's death does not erase the turbulent relationship Jackson shared with the press for decades; however, Jackson's death coverage has had just that effect. Working through the broadcast and print coverage of Jackson's death, it is easy to forget his on accusations that the mass media demonized him and destroyed his reputation, calling them "garbage, "junk food," "liars," "misleading," "parasitic" and "trash."[24] As far as coverage of Jackson's death is concerned, this contentious relationship and his troubled personal life are at best a footnote to the record-breaking, audience-thrilling superstar of the 1980s.

Viewing the mass media coverage of Jackson's death as atonement is an interesting line of inquiry; however, whether or not the media intended to achieve this goal is a purely speculative discussion. More concretely than the atonement hypothesis, however, is the postulation that media coverage of Jackson's death actively works to repair his public image, which it initially helped to dismantle.

---

[23] Nicholas Tavuchis, *Mea Culpa: A Sociology of Apology and Reconciliation* (Stanford: Stanford University Press, 1991), 5.

[24] See Michael Jackson, interview by Ed. Bradley, *60 Minutes*, December 2003. [Online]. Available at: www.cbsnews.com/stories/2003/12/28/60minutes/main590381. shtml; History: the Michael Jackson interview, VH1 (1996); See also Jackson's 1989 video for "Leave Me Alone" (directed by Jim Blashfield and Paul Diener) as well as songs such as "Tabloid Junkie" (1995) "Scream" (1995) and "Privacy" (2001).

Repairing Jackson's Image and Securing His Legacy

Ware and Linkugel's landmark essay provides the basis for Benoit's theory of image repair, and thus is essential to understanding the concept and application of image repair strategies.[25] Ware and Linkugel expand existing models of apologetic discourse by identifying four modes of resolution and postures of self-defense that a rhetor may take: denial, bolstering, differentiation, and transcendence. Of these, bolstering is most relevant to the current conversation.

In bolstering, the rhetor "attempts to identify himself with something viewed favorably by the audience."[26] As a strategy of image repair Benoit explains that:

> bolstering may be used to mitigate the negative effects of the act on the actor by strengthening the audience's positive affect for the rhetor. Here those accused of wrong-doing might relate positive attributes they possess or positive actions they have performed in the past ... increasing positive feeling toward the actor may help offset the negative feeling toward the actor and may help offset the negative feelings toward the act, yielding a relative improvement in the actor's reputation.[27]

Acting as rhetors in their coverage of Jackson's death, the mass media minimized the problematic public image that he had held for the last two decades. The Michael Jackson of tabloid fame took a backseat to another Michael Jackson: the child-cum-soulman leading the Jackson Five, the real "thriller"; the electrifying performer and pioneering visual artist of the MTV era.

It is this image of Jackson—young, sexy, successful, talented, dignified—that the media used to bolster his image in the wake of his death, rather than the ghostly, surgically altered visage that graced TV screens and magazine covers for the last 20 years. *Vanity Fair*'s cover story on Jackson's death resurrected the star's 1989 photo shoot with the magazine, complemented by interview excerpts from 1972–88; *Newsweek*'s cover featured a close-up shot from the Jackson Five days; *Time* and *People* chose photos from the early 1990s around the time of *Dangerous*; *Entertainment Weekly* and *New Musical Express* went with regal shots from the *Thriller* era; *The Village Voice* cover was a shot of Jackson in 1976; the covers of *Maclean*'s and *Rolling Stone* depicted Jackson in iconic onstage poses from his "Billie Jean" routine. Local newspapers similarly focused on images of Jackson at his prime, generally avoiding photographs from the post-*Dangerous* era in favor of images depicting Jackson as a budding pre-teen pop star or at the height of

---

[25] See B.L. Ware and Wil A. Linkugel, "They Spoke in Defense of Themselves: On the Generic Criticism of Apologia," *Quarterly Journal of Speech* 59 (1973): 273–83.

[26] William Benoit and Shirley Drew, "Appropriateness and Effectiveness of Image Repair Strategies," *Communication Reports* 10, no. 2 (1997): 156; Ware and Linkugel, "They Spoke in Defense of Themselves," 277.

[27] Benoit, *Accounts, Excuses, and Apologies*, 77.

his fame in the 1980s. For example, *The Kansas City Star* chose a cover image that had Jackson in an onstage shot from the *Bad* tour, *The Boston Globe* and *Detroit Free Press* depicted the King of Pop striking a triumphant pose during his 1993 Super Bowl performance, *The Atlanta Journal Constitution* showed him cradling his eight awards at the 1984 Grammys, while the front page of the Chesterton-Valparaiso *Post-Tribune* shared an image of a pre-pubescent Jackson from the Motown days. Through their graphical representation of Jackson and the substance of their reporting, the media chose to associate Jackson with his achievements, successes, and talents, despite the fact that these were confined to a bygone era that preceded his more troubling identities and images.

Bolstering Jackson's image through his distant rather than recent past makes a case for the singer as an artistically, culturally, and historically significant figure. With his breakthrough artistic achievements left in decades past, Jackson's legacy was in danger. The accused child molester, the man-child with the alien appearance, threatened to overcome the Michael Jackson that set the popular music and culture on fire decades ago. The media's bolstering of Jackson in coverage of his death chose instead to associate him with "something for which the audience has positive affect"—namely, the music, performance, and record-breaking achievements Jackson attained from the 1960s through his phenomenal solo success in the 1980s.[28]

In addition, bolstering here functions as a survival strategy for Jackson's cultural reputation, one of the primary functions of *apologia* and associated discourse.[29] It may seem odd to speak of a rhetorical survival strategy in relation to someone who has passed, but for a cultural figure, the survival of one's positive image or reputation is arguably as important post-mortem as it was in life, perhaps even more so when considering the importance of one's legacy. Mass media coverage of Jackson's death thus operates in recuperative mode, reducing the offensive impact of his troubled final years in an effort to repair Jackson's damaged image for the sake of his legacy.[30]

By focusing on the singer's achievements, talents, and past successes, media coverage of his death reminds us of the Jackson we want to remember—the less complicated, less problematic Jackson. Writing in *The Village Voice* following Jackson's death, Greg Tate comments that:

> The unfortunate blessing of his departure is that we can now all go back to loving him as we first found him, without shame, despair, or complication ... Now that some of us oldheads can have our Michael Jackson back, we feel liberated to be more gentle toward his spirit, releasing him from our outright rancor for scarring up whichever pretrial, pre-chalk-complexion incarnation of him first tickled our fancies. Michael not being in the world as a Kabuki ghost makes it even easier

---

[28]   Ibid., 12.

[29]   Downey, "Evolution," 42. See also Kruse, "Motivational Factors," 21.

[30]   Benoit, *Accounts, Excuses, and Apologies*, 77.

to get through all those late-career movie-budget clips where he already looks headed for the outdoor. Perhaps it's a blessing in disguise both for him and for us that he finally got shoved through it.[31]

Here, Tate simultaneously reflects media and popular sentiment about Jackson following his passing. As troublesome as Jackson's popular image had become in the last 20 years, his death allows audiences to embrace that nearly magical, significantly less complicated figure of "ABC" and *Thriller*. Mass media treatment of Jackson following his death facilitates the audience relationship that Tate posits, or at least creates an environment conducive to such a response. Indeed, through social networking sites and other electronic means, audiences expressed their reactions to Jackson's death in a way that underscores the growing interrelation between traditional mass media forms such as print and broadcasting, and online social media.

The Role of Social Media

Writing in 1964, Marshall McLuhan noted that "no medium has its meaning or existence alone, but only in constant interplay with other media."[32] As media technologies become increasingly interactive and participatory, McLuhan's words appear ever more prescient. As a multimedia event, Jackson's death showed the changing relationship between traditional and new media forms while contributing to the reparation of Jackson's image.

On the day of Jackson's passing, new media in some senses eclipsed the role of traditional mass media outlets. Indeed, it was not a news agency or even cable news that broke the Jackson story, but the Web-based celebrity gossip outlet TMZ. Monitoring online news consumption worldwide, Akamai's Net Usage Index reported a 50 percent increase in Web traffic to news sites the day that Jackson died.[33] CNN's website, for example, experienced a fivefold increase in traffic, logging 20 million visitors during the hour that the story broke, while Yahoo! News set a record for traffic on that site with 15.1 million visitors.[34] In fact, as news

---

[31]   Greg Tate, "Michael Jackson: The Man in Our Mirror," *The Village Voice*, July 1, 2009. [Online]. Available at: www.villagevoice.com/2009-07-01/news/michael-jackson-the-man-in-our-mirror/ [accessed: April 17, 2010].

[32]   Marshall McLuhan, *Understanding Media: The Extensions of Man* (New York: McGraw Hill, 1964), 39.

[33]   Jake Coyle, "News of Jackson's Death First Spread Online," *USA Today*, June 26, 2009. [Online]. Available at: www.usatoday.com/tech/webguide/internetlife/2009–06–26-jackson-online_N.htm [accessed: July 14, 2010].

[34]   Adam Ostrow, "Michael Jackson's Massive Impact (on Google, Facebook, and Yahoo)," *Mashable*, June 26, 2009. [Online]. Available at: http://mashable.com/2009/06/26/michael-jackson-web-impact/ [accessed: July 13, 2010]. Also see Linnie Rawlinson and

of Jackson's death spread, the heavy increase in Internet usage led to site crashes across the Web. The 1.8 million visits and 650 edits to Jackson's Wikipedia entry caused a temporary outage on that site.[35] Google read the onslaught of searches for "Michael Jackson" as a security threat, informing users "your query looks similar to automated requests from a computer virus or spyware application."[36] Other sites including the *Los Angeles Times* and TMZ also experienced site crashes due to visitors flocking to their sites in droves, while the average load time for news sites including ABC and CBS slowed from four seconds to nine.[37]

Even more indicative of Jackson's posthumous status in the digital world was the drastic increase in digital sales of his back catalog. Digital sales of Jackson's albums totaled 12,355,000, approximately 16 percent of all digital sales for 2009—the same percentage by which digital sales increased overall in that year.[38] As a means of contextualizing those figures, Jackson's digital album sales in 2009 total more than individual sales of each of his solo albums since their initial release, excepting *Thriller*.[39]

Most significantly, Jackson's death underscored Web 2.0s function as a social networking medium. As with the websites cited above, Twitter and AOL's Instant Messenger service also experienced outages due to increased activity. Twitter activity related to Jackson's death peaked at 78 tweets per second (over 4,500 per minute, 279,000 per hour.)[40] Facebook users posted status updates at triple the average rate, and by July 6, 2009, Michael Jackson's official Facebook page became the most popular on the site.[41]In addition to flocking to watch Jackson's

---

Nick Hunt, "Jackson Dies, Almost Takes Internet with Him," *CNN.com*, June 26, 2009. [Online]. Available at: www.cnn.com/2009/TECH/06/26/michael.jackson.internet/index. html [accessed: April 17, 2010].

[35]   See Phoebe Ayers, "Jackson's Death, New Data Center, More," *The Wikipedia Signpost*, June 29, 2009. [Online]. Available at: http://en.wikipedia.org/wiki/ Wikipedia:Wikipedia_Signpost/2009–06–29/News_and_notes [accessed: April 17, 2010]; also Nicki Dugan, "Losing Michael Jackson," *Yodel Anecdotal* (blog), June 26, 2009 (12:27 p.m.), http://ycorpblog.com/2009/06/26/losing-michael-jackson/.

[36]   See Maggie Shiels, "Web Slows after Jackson's Death," *BBC News Online*, June 26, 2006. [Online]. Available at: http://news.bbc.co.uk/2/hi/technology/8120324.stm [accessed: April 17, 2010].

[37]   See Rawlinson and Hunt, "Jackson Dies, Almost Takes Internet with Him."

[38]   See Nielsen Company, *The Nielsen Company 2009 Year-End Music Report*.

[39]   See the RIAA's certifications for Jackson sales at www.riaa.com/ goldandplatinumdata.php?table=SEARCH_RESULTS&artist=Michael percent20Jackson &format=ALBUM&go=Search&perPage=100.

[40]   Elsa Kim, Sam Gilbert, Michael J. Edwards, and Erhardt Graeff, "Detecting Sadness in 140 Characters: Sentiment Analysis and Mourning Michael Jackson on Twitter," 2009. [Online]. Available at: www.webecologyproject.org/2009/08/detecting-sadness-in-140-characters/, 40 [accessed: January 30, 2010].

[41]   See Richi Jennings, "Dead: Michael Jackson, Facebook, Twitter and PerezHilton.com (R.I.P.)," *IT Blogwatch*, June 26, 2009. [Online]. Available at: http://blogs.computerworld.

music videos on YouTube, that site also became a means for scores of fans to upload videos sharing their personal reactions to Jackson's death and tributes to his legacy.

The use of social and online media to spread news stories is not particularly new. It is however, a growing trend, of which Jackson's death may be considered the pinnacle. A study by the Pew Internet and American Life Project found that the Internet is now the third most popular news source in America, behind local and national television news.[42] Of those who seek news online, 37 percent are active participants, engaging in news creation, commentary, and dissemination on blogs, social networking sites, commenting on online news stories and contributing original material to online news sites.[43] Specific figures for online participants on the day Jackson died are not available, although one can reasonably assume there was an increase given that day's abnormally high levels of Internet and social networking usage.

Just as Jackson dominated mainstream and traditional media coverage for weeks following his death, blog posts, podcasts, tweets, Facebook updates, and YouTube videos dedicated to Jackson consumed Web activity in the summer of 2009. Also similar to traditional mass media's coverage of Jackson's death, the sentiments expressed on blogs, social networking sites, and other online venues were overwhelmingly positive. An analysis of 2,331,066 tweets from July 24, 2009 (the day preceding Jackson's death) to July 6, 2009 did find negative or ambivalent sentiments, but 75 percent of these tweets expressed sadness over the singer's passing.[44] For example, Kim et al. cite illustrative tweets such as "Michael Jackson's death is a sad loss … thoughts and prays [*sic*] go out to his family" and "Shocked by Michael Jackson's death. Such a sad, sad day."[45] In addition to sharing their personal reactions and tributes, fans utilized social media to redefine Jackson's image in a positive light. Nearly one year after Jackson's death, fans mobilized on Facebook in an effort to persuade methodshop.com to permanently remove their running archive of user-submitted Michael Jackson jokes.[46]

---

com/michael_jackson_facebook_twitter_and_perezhilton_com_died_r_i_p [accessed: July 10, 2010]. See also Nick O'Neil, "Michael Jackson Officially Becomes the Most Popular Person on Facebook," July 6, 2009. [Online]. Available at: www.allfacebook.com/2009/07/michael-jackson-facebook/ [accessed: July 13, 2010].

[42]   Kristen Purcell, et al., "Understanding the Participatory News Consumer," *Pew Internet & American Life Project*, March 1, 2010. [Online]. Available at: www.pewinternet.org/Reports/2010/Online-News.aspx?r=1, 31 [accessed: July 14, 2010].

[43]   Ibid.

[44]   Ibid.

[45]   Ibid., 11.

[46]   "Fans Use Social Media to Take Down Michael Jackson Jokes Page," *methodshop*, June 15, 2010. [Online]. Available at: www.methodshop.com/picts/jacko/index.shtml [accessed: July 25, 2010].

Other pages dedicated to Michael Jackson jokes remain, and certainly, the Internet is not absent any criticism of Jackson. Within Facebook for example, there exist groups such as "I hate Michael Jackson," "THE WORLD IS A SAFER PLACE NOW THAT MICHAEL JACKSON IS DEAD" and "Michael Jackson is dead. Get over it."[47] Notably, these are the only blatantly anti-Jackson groups on Facebook, out of approximately 540 groups associated with Jackson on the social networking site. Following the methodshop.com takedown, one Facebook group developed "to end the hate groups on Facebook regarding Michael [Jackson]."[48] The majority of the other 537 Michael Jackson Facebook groups serve as tributes to Jackson's life and art, mirroring mass media's use of bolstering to emphasize Jackson's positive attributes rather than discuss the more controversial aspects of his life and career. In both of these ways, a contingent of audiences is very actively working to restore Jackson's image through via online social media.

Although Jackson's death is not the first news story to spark a wave of reaction in the online world, it is the first news event to do so on such a profound scale. It was, as Associated Press writer Jake Coyle noted, "a where-were-you moment in a digital age."[49] In contrast to the Kennedy assassination that Coyle alludes to, however, citizens now had unprecedented access to produce as well as consume media as a means of expressing their personal reactions and processing the death of this cultural icon. The deluge of Internet activity following Jackson's death also contributed to the recuperation of his cultural reputation, alongside the abundance of coverage in traditional mass media outlets.

In contrast to coverage in traditional media outlets, however, reactions to Jackson's death expressed via social media generate from individuals rather than institutions. Yet taken in the aggregate, they perform a similar function and provide an indication of cultural sentiment. Recall Madonna's assertion at the 2009 MTV Video Music Awards that "*we* had abandoned him. That *we* had allowed this magnificent creature ... to slip through the cracks ... *we* were all busy passing judgment."[50] As much as Jackson's death provided an opportunity for traditional mass media to reconcile their relationship with the singer, his death provided a similar opportunity for individuals. In effect, social media allowed individuals to enact en masse their own acts of apology regarding Jackson, facilitating the cultural shift in opinion from ambivalence and distaste to admiration and respect.

---

47   See   www.facebook.com/pages/I-hate-Michael-Jackson/95234337181?ref=mf#!/
pages/I-hate-Michael-Jackson/95234337181?v=wall&story_fbid=114023066031;   www.
facebook.com/profile.php?id=516932513&v=wall&story_fbid=107219185999904#!/
group.php?gid=103472904398&ref=ts and www.facebook.com/profile.php?id=516932513
&v=wall&story_fbid=107219185999904#!/pages/Omg-Michael-Jackson-is-Dead-Get-
over-It/141888652505911?ref=ts.

48   See "MJ Supporters against Hate & Racism," Facebook. [Online]. Available at:
www.facebook.com/group.php?gid=100757199965467 [accessed: July 26, 2010].

49   See Coyle, "News of Jackson's Death First Spread Online."

50   Author emphasis.

Conclusion

Over the course of the last two decades, it often seemed that Michael Jackson would never regain the cultural stature he once enjoyed. Too much had happened in his personal and professional life—an artistic decline, eccentric public behavior, a drastically altered appearance, and two sets of child molestation allegations. Yet with his passing, Jackson suddenly reclaimed his throne and his cultural relevance, aided by traditional and new forms media coverage of his death. Although these media texts are not the sole, nor even most determinant, factor in the recuperation of Michael Jackson's image, they provide a permanent and public record documenting the striking shift in Michael Jackson's cultural reputation.

Viewing media coverage of Jackson's death through the lens of apologetic discourse is illustrative not only of the shift in his public image, but also in the growing complexities of apologetic discourse. Downey argues that "the [mid-century] proliferation of mass media and the power of the press to mold and define reality" significantly reshaped the very nature of apologetic discourse.[51] Now in the age of cable news, the 24-hour news cycle, the immediacy of social media and an arguably heightened obsession with celebrity culture, mass mediated apologetic discourse is even more multifaceted, particularly within the relationship between audiences and media. At a time when social media often scoop mainstream outlets, when the Internet is an increasingly popular news source in America and when new media challenge the old guard, our interactions and relationships with media, both new and old, are increasingly complex. We are now able to immediately and simultaneously engage with media texts as both consumers and producers. In the case of Jackson's death, old media worked in tandem with new, user-centered media to reinforce and preserve Jackson's recuperated public image and reputation. In light of this, analyzing coverage of Jackson's death through the lens of apology and image repair provides perspective in relation to how audiences' increasingly complex relationships with media institutions and technologies can reshape the very nature of apologetic discourse.

---

[51] Downey, "Evolution," 55.

Bibliography

Allan, Elizabeth J. "Constructing Women's Status: Policy Discourses of University Women's Commission Reports." *Harvard Educational Review* 72, no. 1 (2003): 44–72.

Alloway, Lawrence. *Topics in American Art since 1945*. New York: Norton, 1975.

Altman, Rick. "An Introduction to Theory of Genre Analysis." In *The American Film Musical*, 1–15. Bloomington, IN: Indiana University Press, 1987.

Appiah, Anthony. "Identity, Authenticity, Survival: Multiculturalism Societies and Social Reproduction." In *Multiculturalism: Examining the Politics of Recognition*, edited by Amy Gutmann, 149–64. Princeton: Princeton University Press, 1994.

Augé, Marc. *Non-Places: An Introduction to an Anthropology of Supermodernity*. London: Verso Press, 1995.

Awkward, Michael. *Negotiating Difference: Race, Gender, and the Politics of Positionality*. Chicago: University of Chicago Press, 1995.

Ayers, Phoebe. "Jackson's Death, New Data Center, More." *The Wikipedia Signpost*. June 29, 2009. [Online]. Available at: http://en.wikipedia.org/wiki/Wikipedia:Wikipedia_Signpost/2009-06-29/News_and_notes [accessed: April 17, 2010].

Babington, Bruce, and Peter William Evans. *Blue Skies and Silver Linings: Aspects of the Hollywood Musical*. Dover: Manchester University Press, 1985.

Bakhtin, Mikhail M. *Art and Answerability*. Edited by Michael Holquist and Vadim Liapunov. Translated by Vadim Liapunov. Austin: University of Texas Press, 1990.

———. *The Dialogic Imagination*. Edited by Michael Holquist. Austin: University of Texas Press, 1990.

———. *Rabelais and His World*. Translated by Hélène Iswolsky. Bloomington, IN: Indiana University Press, 1984.

Baldwin, James. "Freaks and the American Ideal of Manhood." *Playboy* 32, no. 1 (1985): 150–260.

———. "Here Be Dragons." In *The Price of the Ticket*. New York: St. Martin's Press, 1985.

Barnum, P.T. *The Life of P.T. Barnum, Written by Himself*. 1855. Champaign: University of Illinois Press, 2000.

Barrie, James M. *Peter Pan*. Edited by Amy Billone. New York: Barnes and Noble Classics, 2005.

Barthes, Roland. *Image-Music-Text*. New York: Hill and Wang, 1977.

———. *Mythologies*. Translated by Annette Lavers. New York: Hill & Wang, 1972.

———. "That Old Thing, Art ... ." In *Pop Art: The Critical Dialogue*, edited by Carol Anne Mahsun. Ann Arbor: UMI Research Press, 1989.

Bartolomeo, Joey, Bill Hewitt, Bob Meadows, Michelle Tan, Alex Tresniowski, Charlotte Triggs, Kristen Mascia, Lisa Ingrassia, Alicia Dennis, Rennie Dyball, Danielle Dubin, and Chuck Arnold. "The Accused." *People*, July 13, 2009, 87–8.

Baudrillard, Jean. *Cool Memories: 1980–1985*. Translated by Chris Turner. London: Verso, 1990.

———. "The Ecstasy of Communication." In *The Anti-Aesthetic: Essays on Postmodern Culture*, edited by Hal Foster, 126–34. New York: New Press, 1998.

———. *Simulacra and Simulation*. Translated by Sheila Faria Glaser. Ann Arbor: University of Michigan Press, 1994.

Bauman, Richard. "Performance." In *Folklore, Cultural Performances, and Popular Entertainments: A Communication Centered Handbook*, edited by Richard Bauman, 41–9. New York: Oxford University Press, 1992.

Benjamin, Walter. "Rhetoric of the Image." In *Image, Music, Text*, edited and translated by Stephen Heath, 32–51. New York: Hill & Wang, 1977.

———. *Walter Benjamin Selected Writings 1935–1938*. Cambridge, MA: Harvard University Press, 2002.

———. "The Work of Art in the Age of Mechanical Reproduction." In *Film Theory and Criticism: Introductory Readings*, 5th ed., edited by Leo Braudy and Marshall Cohen, 731–51. New York: Oxford University Press, 1999.

Bennett, Lerone. *The Shaping of Black American Thought: The Struggles and Triumphs of African-Americans, 1619–1990s*. Chicago: Johnson, 1975.

Benoit, William L. *Accounts, Excuses, and Apologies: A Theory of Image Restoration Strategies*. Albany: State University of New York Press, 1995a.

———. "Another Visit to the Theory of Image Restoration Strategies." *Communication Quarterly* 48, no. 1 (2000): 40–44.

———. "Hugh Grant's Image Restoration Discourse: An Actor Apologizes." *Communication Quarterly* 45 (1997): 251–67.

———. "Richard M. Nixon's Rhetorical Strategies in His Public Statements on Watergate." *Southern Speech Communication Journal* 47 (1982):192–211.

———. "Sears' Repair of Its Auto Service Image: Image Restoration Discourse in the Corporate Sector." *Communication Studies* 46 (1995b): 89–105.

Benoit, William L., and Susan L. Brinson. "AT&T: Apologies Are Not Enough." *Communication Quarterly* 42 (1994): 75–88.

———. "Queen Elizabeth's Image Repair Discourse: Insensitive Royal or Compassionate Queen?" *Public Relations Review* 25 (1999): 145–56.

Benoit, William L., and Anne Czerwinski. "A Critical Analysis of USAir's Image Repair Discourse." *Business Communication Quarterly* 60 (1997): 38–57.

Benoit, William L., and Shirley Drew. "Appropriateness and Effectiveness of Image Repair Strategies." *Communication Reports* 10, no. 2 (1997): 153–63.

Benoit, William L., and Robert Hanczor. "The Tonya Harding Controversy: An Analysis of Image Repair Strategies." *Communication Quarterly* 42 (1994): 416–33.

Benoit, Willaim L., and Dawn M. Nill. "Oliver Stone's Defense of JFK." *Communication Quarterly* 46 (1998): 127–43.

Benoit, Willaim L., Paul Gullifor, and Daniel Panici. "President Reagan's Defensive Discourse on the Iran-Contra Affair." *Communication Studies* 42, no. 3 (1991): 272–94.

Bhabha, Homi. *The Location of Culture*. Oxford: Routledge, 1994.

Bingham, Dennis. *Whose Lives Are They Anyway?: The Biopic as Contemporary Film Genre*. New Brunswick: Rutgers University Press, 2010.

Björnberg, Alf. "Structural Relationships of Music and Images in Music Video." *Popular Music* 13, no. 1 (1994).

Blaine, Diane. "Necrophilia, Pedophilia, or Both?: The Sexualized Rhetoric of the Jon Benet Ramsey Case." In *Sexual Rhetoric: Media Perspectives on Sexuality, Gender and Identity*, edited by Meta Carstarphen and Susan Savoina, 21–61. Westport: Greenwood, 2006.

Blaney, Joseph R., and William L. Benoit. *The Clinton Scandals and the Politics of Image Restoration*. Westport: Praeger, 2001.

Blaney, Joseph R., William L. Benoit, and LeAnn M. Brazeal. "Blowout! Firestone's Image Restoration Campaign." *Public Relations Research* 28 (2002): 379–92.

Bobo, Jacqueline. "Black Women's Response to the Color Purple." *Black Women as Cultural Readers*. New York: Columbia University Press, 1995.

Boteach, Rabbi Shmuley. *The Michael Jackson Tapes: A Tragic Icon Reveals His Soul in Intimate Conversation*. New York: Vanguard Press, 2009.

Bowman, Michael. "Toward a Curriculum in Performance Studies." In *The Future of Performance Studies*, edited by Sheron J. Dailey, 189–94. Annadale, VA: National Communication Association, 1988.

Bradshaw, Melissa. "Devouring the Diva: Martyrdom as Feminist Backlash in *The Rose*." *Camera Obscura* 21 (2008): 69–87.

Braudy, Leo. *The Frenzy of Renown*. New York: Oxford University Press, 1986.

Breznican, Anthony."Erratic Behavior, Appearance Again Cast Doubts on Michael Jackson's Image and Career." December 2, 2002. [Online]. Available at: http://media.www.elvaq.com/media/storage/paper925/news/2002/12/02/ Entertainment/Erratic. Behavior. Appearance.Again.Cast.Doubts; On.MichaelJackson0146s.Image.And-2533623.shtml [accessed: April 17, 2002].

Brinson, Susan L., and William L. Benoit. "The Tarnished Star: Restoring Texaco's Damaged Public Image." *Communication Quarterly* 12 (1999): 483–510.

Brook, John A. "Freud and Splitting." *The International Review of Psycho-Analysis* 19 (1992): 335–50.

Brueggemann, Brenda Jo., Rosemarie Garland Thomson, and Sharon L. Snyder, eds. *Disability Studies: Enabling the Humanities*. New York: Modern Language Association, 2002.

Bruhm, Steven. "Michael Jackson: Queen Funk." In *Queering the Gothic*, edited by William Hughes and Andrew Smith, 158–76. Manchester: Manchester University Press, 2009.

Bruhm, Steven, and Natasha Hurley. Introduction to *Curiouser: On the Queerness of Children*, edited by Steven Bruhm and Natasha Hurley, ix–xxxviii. Minneapolis: University of Minnesota Press, 2004.

Buber, Martin. *Between Man and Man*. New York: Routledge, 1947.———. *I and Thou*. New York: Scribner and Sons, 1958.

Bukatman, Scott. *Terminal Identity: The Virtual Subject in Postmodern Science Fiction*. New York: New York University, 1992.

Burke, Kenneth. *A Rhetoric of Motives*. New York: George Braziller, 1955.

Burnett, Robert and Burt Deivert. "*Black or White*: Michael Jackson's Video as a Mirror of Popular Culture." *Popular Music and Society* 19, no. 3 (1995): 19–40.

Burns, Judith P., and Michael S. Bruner. "Revisiting the Theory of Image Restoration Strategies." *Communication Quarterly* 48, no. 1 (2000): 27–9.

Butler, Judith. "Appearances Aside." In *Prejudicial Appearances: The Logic of American Antidiscrimination Law*, edited by Robert C. Post, Judith Butler, Thomas C. Grey, and Reva B. Siegel, 73–84. Durham, NC: Duke University Press, 2001.

———. *Bodies that Matter: On the Discursive Limits of "Sex."* London: Routledge, 1993.

———. "Imitation and Gender Insubordination." In *Inside/Out: Lesbian Theories, Gay Theories*, edited by Diana Fuss, 13–31. New York: Routledge, 1991.

———. "Performative Acts and Gender Constitution: An Essay in Phenomenology and Feminist Theory." In *Performing Feminisms: Feminist Critical Theory and Theatre*, edited by Sue-Ellen Case, 270–82. Baltimore: Johns Hopkins University Press, 1990.Butler, Sherry Devereaux. "The Apologia, 1971 Genre." *Southern Speech Communication Journal* 37, no. 3 (1972): 281–9.

Calinescu, Matei. *Five Faces of Modernity: Modernism, Avant-Garde, Decadence, Kitsch, Postmodernism*. Durham, NC: Duke University Press, 1987.

Cashmore, Ellis. *The Black Culture Industry*. New York: Routledge, 1997.

Chambers, Iain. *Urban Rhythms: Pop Music and Popular Culture*. London: Macmillan, 1985.

Condon, Jane. *A Half Step Behind: Japanese Women of the '80s*. New York: Dodd, Mead, 1985.

Cook, Nicholas. "Credit Where It's Due: Madonna's 'Material Girl'." In *Analysing Musical Multimedia*, 147–73. Oxford: Clarendon Press, 1998.

Corliss, Richard. "He's Still a Thriller." *Time*, November 9, 2009.

———. "Let's Go to the Feelies; Michael Jackson and George Lucas Give Disney a 3-D Dream," *Time*, September 22, 1986.

————. "Michael Jackson: The Death of Peter Pan." *Time*, June 26, 2009. [Online]. Available at: www.time.com/time/arts/article/0,8599,1907344,00.html.

————. "Superstar: 1978–1989." *Time Magazine Special Commemorative Edition: Michael Jackson 1958–2009*, July 7, 2009.

Covach, John. "Popular Music, Unpopular Musicology." In *Rethinking Music*, edited by Nicholas Cook and Mark Everist, 452–70. Oxford: Oxford University Press, 1999.

Covington, Richard. "Where Michael Jackson Meets Louis XIV." *Art News* (November 2008): 102–104.

Coyle, Jake. "News of Jackson's Death First Spread Online." *USA Today*, June 26, 2009. [Online]. Available at: www.usatoday.com/tech/webguide/internetlife/2009-06-26-jackson-online_N.htm. [accessed: July 14, 2010].

Crary, Jonathan. *Suspensions of Perception: Attention, Spectacle, and Modern Culture*. Cambridge, MA: MIT Press, 2001.

Csicsery-Ronay, Jr., Istvan. "Antimancer: Cybernetics and Art in Gibson's *Count Zero*." *Science Fiction Studies*, 22, no. 1 (1995). [Online]. Available at: www.depauw.edu/sfs/backissues/65/icr65art.htm.

————. "Cyberpunk and Neuromanticism." In *Storming the Reality Studio: A Casebook of Cyberpunk and Postmodernism Science Fiction*, edited by Larry McCaffery, 182–93. Durham, NC: Duke University Press, 1991.

Custen, George F. *Bio/Pics: How Hollywood Constructed Public History*. New Brunswick: Rutgers University Press, 1992.

————. "The Mechanical Life in the Age of Human Reproduction: American Biopics, 1961–1980." *Biography* 23, no. 1 (2000): 127–59.

Daily, Michael Saul. "Jacko Whacks Biz, Calls Sony Boss Racist." *The Daily News*, July 7, 2010. [Online]. Available at: www.nydailynews.com/archives/news/2002/07/07/2002-07-07_jacko_whacks_biz_calls_sony_.html [accessed: April 17, 2010].

Dargis, Manohla. "Michael Jackson's This Is It (2009)," *New York Times*, October 29, 2009, C1.

Davis, Kathy. "Surgical Passing: Or Why Jackson Nose Makes 'Us' Uneasy." *Feminist Theory* 4, no. 1 (2003): 73–92.

Davis, Robert Con, and Ronald Schleifer, eds. Contemporary Literary Criticism: Literary and Cultural Studies, 4th ed. New York: Longman, 1998.

de Certeau, Michel. *The Practice of Everyday Life*. Translated by Steven Rendall. Berkeley: University of California, 1984.

de Lauretis, Teresa. "Difference Embodied: Reflections on Black Skin, White Masks." *Parallax* 8 (2002): 54–68.

Debord, Guy. *The Society of the Spectacle*. Translated by Donald Nicholson-Smith. New York: Zone Books, 1995.

Desjardins, Mary. "The Incredible Shrinking Star: Todd Haynes and the Case History of Karen Carpenter." *Camera Obscura* 19 (2004): 22–55.

Dikovitskaya, Margaret. *Visual Culture and the Study of the Visual after the Cultural Turn*. Cambridge, MA: MIT Press, 2005.

Donoghue, Denis. *William Butler Yeats*. New York: Viking, 1971.

Doris, Sara. *Pop Art and the Contest over American Culture*. Cambridge: Cambridge University Press, 2007.

Douglas, Mary. *Purity and Danger*. New York: Routledge, 2002.

Downey, Sharon. D. "The Evolution of the Rhetorical Genre of Apologia." *Western Journal of Communication* 57, no. 1 (1993): 42–64.

Du Bois, W.E.B. *Darkwater: Voices from within the Veil*. New York: Schocken Books, 1969.

———. *The Souls of Black Folk*. Introduction by David Levering Lewis. New York: Modern Library, 2003.

Dugan, Nicki. "Losing Michael Jackson." *Yodel Anecdotal* (blog), June 26, 2009 (12:27), 371–81. New York: Routledge, 1999.

———. *White*. London: Routledge, 1997.

Dyer, Richard. "Entertainment and Utopia." In *The Cultural Studies Reader*, ed. Simon During. New York: Routledge, 1999.

———. *Heavenly Bodies: Film Stars and Society*. New York: Routledge, 2004.

———. *Stars*. London: British Film Institute Publishing, 1998.

Dykstra, Bram. *Idols of Perversity*. New York: Oxford University Press, 1986.

Eco, Umberto. *Travels in Hyperreality*. Trans. William Weaver. San Diego: Harcourt, 1986.

Eisenstein, Sergei. *Film Form: Essays in Film Theory*. Edited and translated by Jay Leyda. San Diego: Harcourt, 1949.

English, Whitney and Natalie Finn. "It's Going to Be a Disaster: Associate Says Jackson Was Too Weak for Major Comeback." *Eonline*, 2009. [Online]. Available at: www.eonline.com/uberblog/b133691_its_going_be_disaster_associate_says.html.

Enri, John. "Queer Figurations in the Media: Critical Reflections on the Michael Jackson Sex Scandal." *Critical Studies in Mass Communication* 15 (1998): 158–80.

Fanon, Frantz. *Black Skin, White Masks*. Translated by Charles Lam Markmann. New York: Grove Press, 1967.

———. *The Wretched of the Earth*. Translated by Constance Farrington. New York: Grove Press, 1963.

Farber, Leora. "Skin Aesthetics." *Theory, Culture, & Society* 23 (1998), 247–50.

Fast, Susan. "Difference that Exceeded Understanding: Remembering Michael Jackson (1958–2009)." *Popular Music and Society* 33, no. 2 (2010): 259–66.

Foster, Hal. *Recodings: Art, Spectacle, Cultural Politics*. New York: The New Press, 1985.

Foucault, Michel. "The Discourse of Language." In *The Routledge Language and Cultural Theory Reader*, edited by Lucy Burke, Tony Crowley, and Alan Girvin. New York: Routledge, 2000.

———. *The History of Sexuality, Vol. 1, An Introduction*. Translated by Robert Hurley (1977). New York: Vintage Books, 1990.

Frankenberg, Ruth, ed. *Displacing Whiteness: Essays in Social and Cultural Criticism*. Durham, NC: Duke University Press, 1997.

Frith, Simon. *Performing Rites: On the Value of Popular Music*. Cambridge, MA: Harvard University Press, 1996.

Fuchs, Cynthia. "Michael Jackson's Penis." In *Cruising the Performative: Interventions into the Representation of Ethnicity, Nationality, and Sexuality*, edited by Sue-Ellen Case, Philip Brett, and Susan Leigh Foster, 13–33. Bloomington, IN: Indiana University Press, 1995.

Fuss, Diana. *Essentially Speaking: Feminism, Nature and Difference*. NewYork: Routledge, 1989.

———. "Interior Colonies: Frantz Fanon and the Politics of Identification." *Diacritics* 21, no. 2/3 (1994): 19–43.

Gaiman, Neil. Introduction to *The Stars My Destination*, by Alfred Bester. New York: Vintage Books, 1996.

Gans, Herbert J. *Popular Culture and High Culture: An Analysis and Evaluation of Taste*. New York: Basic Books, 1974.

Garber, Marjorie. *Bisexuality and the Eroticism of Everyday Life*. New York: Routledge, 1995.

———. *Vested Interests: Cross-Dressing and Cultural Anxiety*. New York: Routledge, 1997.

Garland Thomson, Rosemarie. *Extraordinary Bodies: Figuring Physical Disability in American Culture and Literature*. New York: Columbia University Press, 1997.

———. *Freakery: Cultural Spectacles of the Extraordinary Body*. New York: Columbia University Press, 1996.

Gershon, Peter Robert. "Music Videos and Television Commercials: A Comparison of Production Styles." PhD Diss., University of Michigan, 1991.

Gibson, William. *Count Zero*. New York: Ace Books, 1986.

———. *Neuromancer*. New York: Ace Books, 1984.

———. *Virtual Light*. New York: Bantam Books, 1993.

Giddens, Anthony. *The Consequences of Modernity*. Stanford: Stanford University Press, 1990.

Giles, David. *Illusions of Immortality: A Psychology of Fame and Celebrity*. New York: St. Martin's Press, 2000.

Gilroy, Paul. "'Get Up, Get into It and Get Involved' – Soul, Civil Rights, and Black Power." *Cultural Theory and Popular Culture: A Reader*, edited by John Storey, 80–90. Harlow, England: Prentice Hall, 1998.

Gómez-Barris, Macarena, and Herman Gray. " Michael Jackson, Television, and Post-Op Disasters." *Television & New Media* 7, no. 1 (2006): 40–51.

Goodman, Fred. "Michael Jackson's Meltdown." *Rolling Stone*, August 8, 2002.

Goodwin, Andrew. *Dancing in the Distraction Factory: Music Television and Popular Culture*. Minneapolis: University of Minnesota Press, 1992.

Gordon, Lewis. "A Questioning Body of Laughter and Tears: Reading Black Skin, White Masks Through the Cat and Mouse of Reason and a Misguided Theodicy." *Parallax* 8, no. 2 (2002): 10–29.

Gorer, Geoffrey. *Death, Grief and Mourning in Contemporary Britain.* Garden City, NY: Doubleday, 1965.

Graham-Smith, Greg. "Habeas Corpus: Bodies of Evidence and Performed Litigiousness: The Spectacle of Michael Jackson's Trial." *Communication: South African Journal for Communication Theory and Research* 34, no. 2 (2008): 278–89.

Green, James. *Beyond the Good Death: The Anthropology of Modern Dying.* Philadelphia: Pennsylvania University Press, 2008.

Greenwald, John. "Japanese Prejudice and Black Sambo." *Time*, June 24, 2001. [Online]. Available at: www.time.com/time/magazine/article/0,9171,149882,00.html [accessed: January 20, 2012].

Gunning, Tom. "Aesthetics of Astonishment: Early Film and the (In)Credulous Spectator." In *Viewing Positions: Ways of Seeing Film*, edited by Linda Williams, 114–133. New Brunswick: Rutgers University Press, 1995.

———. "The Cinema of Attraction[s]: Early Film, Its Spectator and the Avant-Garde." In *Early Film*, edited by Thomas Elsaesser and Adam Barker, 56–62. London: British Film Institute, 1989.

Hacking, Ian. "The Making and Molding of Child Abuse." *Critical Inquiry* 17, no. 2 (1991): 253–88.

Hall, Donald E. *Reading Sexualities: Hermeneutic Theory and the Future of Queer Studies.* New York: Routledge, 2009.

Hall, Stuart. "Cultural Identity and Diaspora." In *Colonial Discourse and Postcolonial Theory: A Reader*, edited by Patricia Williams and Laura Chrisman, 392–402. New York: Columbia University Press, 1994.

———. "What is this "Black" in Black Popular Culture?" In *Black Studies Reader*, edited by Jacqueline Bobo, Cynthia Hudley, and Claudine Michel, 255–64. New York: Routledge, 2004.

Hamera, Judith, ed. *Opening Acts: Performance in/as Communication and Cultural Studies.* Thousand Oaks: Sage Publications, 2006.

Hamilton, Richard. "Letter to Peter and Alison Smithson, 1957." In *Theories and Documents of Contemporary Art: A Sourcebook of Artist's Writings*, edited by Kristine Stiles and Peter Selz, 296–7. Berkeley and Los Angeles: University of California Press, 1996.

Hammonds, Evelynn. "Black (W)holes and the Geometry of Black Female Sexuality." In *The Black Studies Reader*, ed. Jacqueline Bobo, Cynthia Hudley, and Claudine Michel, 301–15. New York: Routledge. 2004.

Haraway, Donna. "A Cyborg Manifesto: Science, Technology, and Socialist-Feminism in the Late Twentieth Century." In *Contemporary Literary Criticism*, edited by Robert Con Davis and Ronald Schleifer, 696–727. New York: Longman, 1998.

Haring, Keith. *Keith Haring's Journals.* London: Viking Penguin, 1996.

Hesse-Biber, Sharlene Janice. *Am I Thin Enough Yet?* Oxford: Oxford University Press, 1997.

Hiatt, Brian. "What Went Wrong." *Rolling Stone: A Tribute to Michael Jackson*, July 30, 2009.

Hinerman, Stephen. "(Don't) Leave Me Alone: Tabloid Narrative and the Michael Jackson Child Abuse Scandal." *The Celebrity Culture Reader*, edited by P. David Marshall, 454–69. New York: Routledge, 2006.

Hockaday. Mary. "Michael Jackson coverage," *BBC News – The Editors* (blog), June 29, 2009 (6:30 p.m.). [Online]. Available at: www.bbc.co.uk/blogs/theeditors/2009/06/michael_jackson_coverage.html.

Hollinger, Veronica. "Cybernetic Deconstructions: Cyberpunk and Postmodernism." *Mosaic* 23, no. 2 (1990): 29–44.

Holmes, Su and Sean Redmond. *Framing Celebrity: New Directions in Celebrity Culture*. New York: Routledge, 2006.

hooks, bell. *Outlaw Culture Resisting Representation*. New York: Routledge, 1994.

———. *Yearning: Race, Gender, and Cultural Politics*. Boston: South End Press, 1990.

Ignatow, Gabriel. *Transnational Identity Politics and the Environment*. Lanham: Lexington Books, 2007.

Jackson, Michael. *Moonwalk*. New York: Doubleday, 1988.

Jameson, Fredric. *Archaeologies of the Future: The Desire Called Utopia and Other Science Fictions*. New York: Verso, 2005.

———. *The Political Unconscious: Narrative as a Socially Symbolic Art*. Ithaca: Cornell University Press, 1981.

———. "Postmodernism and Consumer Society." In *The Norton Anthology of Theory and Criticism*, edited by Vincent Leitch, 1960–74. New York: W.W. Norton & Company, 2001.

———. *Postmodernism, or, the Cultural Logic of Late Capitalism*. Durham, NC: Duke University Press, 1991.Jefferson, Margo. *On Michael Jackson*. New York: Pantheon Books, 2006.

Jennings, Richi. "Dead: Michael Jackson, Facebook, Twitter and PerezHilton.com (R.I.P.)." *IT Blogwatch*, June 26, 2009. [Online]. Available at: http://blogs.computerworld.com/michael_jackson_facebook_twitter_and_perezhilton_com_died_r_i_p [accessed: July 10, 2010].

Johnson, E. Patrick and Mae G. Henderson, eds. *Black Queer Studies: A Critical Anthology*. Durham, NC: Duke University Press, 2005.

Johnson, Richard. "Exemplary Differences: Mourning (and Not Mourning) a Princess." In *Framing Celebrity: New Directions in Celebrity Culture*, edited by Su Homes and Sean Redmond, 510–29. New York: Routledge, 2006.

Johnson, Victoria. "The Politics of Morphing: Michael Jackson as Science Fiction Border Text." *The Velvet Light Trap* 32 (1993): 58–65.

Jones, Jel D. Lewis. *Michael Jackson, the King of Pop: The Big Picture: The Music! The Man! The Legend! The Interviews: An Anthology*. Phoenix, AZ: Amber Books Publishing, 2005.

Jones, Meredith. "Mutton Cut Up as Lamb: Mothers, Daughters and Cosmetic Surgery Continuum." *Continuum: Journal of Media & Cultural Studies* 18, no. 4 (2004): 525–39.

Josef, Ralina Landwehr. "Tyra Banks is Fat: Reading (Post-)Racism and (Post-) Feminism in the New Millennium." *Critical Studies in Media Communication* 26, no. 3 (2009): 237–54.

Joy, Morny. "Mindfulness of the Selves: Therapeutic Interventions in a Time of Dis-solution." In *Healing Deconstruction: Postmodern Thought in Buddhism and Christianity*, edited by David Loy, 267–78. Atlanta: Scholars, 1996.

Julius, Anthony. *Transgressions: The Offences of Art*. Chicago: University of Chicago Press, 2002.

Karlyn, Kathleen Rowe. "Comedy, Melodrama, and Gender: Theorizing the Genres of Laughter." In *Classical Hollywood Comedy*, edited by Henry Jenkins and Kristine Karnick, 39–59. New York: Routledge, 1995.

———. *The Unruly Woman: Gender and the Genres of Laughter*. Austin: University of Texas Press, 1995.

Kee, Joan. "The Curious Case of Contemporary Ink Painting." *Art Journal* (Fall 2010): 88–113.

Kelsky, Karen. *Women on the Verge: Japanese Women, Western Dreams*. Durham, NC: Duke University, 2001.

Kenny, Robert. *Teaching TV Production in a Digital World*. New York: Libraries Unlimited, 2004.

Kern, Louis J. "Terminal Notions of What We May Become: Synthflesh, Cyberreality, and the Post-Human Body." In *Simulacrum America: The USA and the Popular Media*, edited by Elizabeth Kraus and Carolin Auer, 95–105. Rochester: Camden House, 2000.

Kim, Elsa, Sam Gilbert, Michael J. Edwards, and Erhardt Graeff. "Detecting Sadness in 140 Characters: Sentiment Analysis and Mourning Michael Jackson on Twitter." 2009. [Online]. Available at: www.webecologyproject. org/2009/08/detecting-sadness-in-140-characters/, 40 [accessed: January 30, 2010].

Kincaid, James. *Erotic Innocence*. Durham, NC: Duke University Press, 1998.

Kinder Carr, Carolyn. *Americans: Paintings and Photographs from the National Portrait Gallery*. Washington, D.C. New York: Watson-Guptill, 2003.

Kolata, Gina. "Doctor Says Michael Jackson Has a Skin Disease." *New York Times*, February 13, 1993.

Koons, Jeff. *Jeff Koons: Easyfun – Ethereal*. With interview by David Sylvester. Berlin and New York: Deutsche Guggenheim and the Solomon R. Guggenheim Foundation, 2000.

————. *The Jeff Koons Handbook*. With introductory essay by Robert Rosenblum, "Notes on Jeff Koons." London: Thames and Hudson in association with the Anthony d'Offay Gallery, 1992.

Kozloff, Max. "Popular Culture, Metaphysical Disgust and the New Vulgarians." In *Pop Art: The Critical Dialogue*, edited by Carol Anne Mahsun, 17–22. Ann Arbor: UMI Research Press, 1989.

Kroker, Arthur, and David Cook. "Television and the Triumph of Culture." In *Storming the Reality Studio: A Casebook of Cyberpunk and Postmodernism Science Fiction*, edited by Larry McCaffery, 229–38. Durham, NC: Duke University Press.

Kron, Joan. "Michael Jackson's Dermatologist and Former Plastic Surgeon Talk." *Allure: The Beauty Expert*, 2009.

Kruse, Noreen W. "Motivational Factors in Non-Denial Apologia." *Central States Speech Journal* 28, no. 1 (1977): 13–25.

————. "The Scope of Apologetic Discourse: Establishing Generic Parameters." *Southern Speech Communication Journal*, 43 (1981): 278–91.

Kuppers, Petra. *Disability and Contemporary Performance: Bodies on the Edge*. New York: Routledge, 2003.

Lacan, Jacques. "The Mirror Stage as Formative of the *I* Function as Revealed in Psychoanalytic Experience." In *Ecrits: A Selection*, translated by Bruce Fink, 93–100. London: Norton, 2002.

Lacayo, Richard. "Deformed by Surgery. Warped by Fame. The Sad End of an American Icon." *Time*, June 26, 2009, 48–50.

Langellier, Kristen M., and Elizabeth Bell. "The Performance Turn: Poiesis and Praxis in Postmodern Times." In *A Century of Transformation: Studies in Honor of the 100th Anniversary of the Eastern Communication Association*, edited by James W. Chesebro. Oxford: Oxford University Press, 2009.

Lévinas, Emmanuel. *Time and the Other*. Translated by Richard A. Cohen. Pittsburgh, PA: Duquesne University Press, 1987.

Lévy, Bernard-Henri, "The Three Stations of the Cross in Michael Jackson's Calvary," *The Huffington Post* (2009).

Light, Alan. "Jackson's Dangerous Game." *Rolling Stone*, April 1, 1993.

Lott, Eric. *Love and Theft: Blackface Minstrelsy and the American Working Class*. New York: Oxford University Press U.S., 1995.

Loy, David. *A Buddhist History of the West: Studies in Lack*. Albany: State University, 2002.

————. *The Great Awakening: A Buddhist Social Theory*. Boston: Wisdom, 2003.

————. *Lack and Transcendence: The Problem of Death and Life in Psychotherapy, Existentialism, and Buddhism*. New Jersey: Humanities, 1996.

Lyotard, Jean-François. *The Postmodern Condition: A Report on Knowledge*. Translated by Geoff Bennington and Brian Massumi. Minneapolis: University of Minnesota Press, 1984.

McCaffery, Larry. Preface to *Storming the Reality Studio: A Casebook of Cyberpunk and Postmodernism Science Fiction*, edited by Larry McCaffery, 1–16. Durham, NC: Duke University Press, 1991.

McClary, Susan. *Feminine Endings: Music, Gender, and Sexuality*. Minneapolis: University of Minnesota Press, 1991.

McIlwain, Charlton. *Death in Black and White: Death, Ritual, and Family Ecology*. Cresskill, NJ: Hampton, 2003.

McLuhan, Marshall. *Understanding Media: The Extensions of Man*. New York: McGraw Hill, 1964.

McRuer, Robert. *Cultural Signs of Queerness and Disability*. New York: New York University Press, 2006.

Marcus, Greil. *Lipstick Traces: A Secret History of the Twentieth Century*. Cambridge, MA: Harvard University Press, 1989.

Marshall, P. David. *Celebrity and Power: Fame in Contemporary Culture*. Minneapolis, London: Minnesota University Press, 1997.

———. *The Celebrity Culture Reader*. New York: Routledge, 2006.

Marx, Karl. *Critique of Hegel's "Philosophy of Right."* Translated by Annette Jolin and Joseph O'Malley. Cambridge: Cambridge University Press, 1977.

Mason, Penelope. *History of Japanese Art*. Upper Saddle River, New Jersey: Prentice Hall, 2005.

Mayo Clinic. "Research, M.F. f. M.E. a." Mayo Clinic: Medical Education and Research. [Online]. Available at: www.mayoclinic.com/health/vitiligo/DS00586 [accessed: January 3, 2009].

Melcher, C., et al., eds. *The "National Enquirer": Thirty Years of Unforgettable Images*. New York: Melcher Media, 2002.

Mercer, Kobena. "Monster Metaphors: Notes on Michael Jackson's Thriller," in *Sound and Vision: The Music Video Reader*, edited by Simon Frith, Andrew Goodwin, and Lawrence Grossberg, 80–93. New York: Routledge, 1993.

Michael by the Editors of Rolling Stone. New York: HarperCollins, 2009.

Michael Jackson: A Tribute to the King of Pop, 1958–2009: Platinum Edition Collector's Vault. Atlanta: Whitman Publishing, 2009.

Morgan, Jessica, and Octavio Zaya. "Essays on Candice Breitz." In *Multiple Exposure*. Exhibition catalogue. Léon: Museo de Arte Contemporáneo de Castilla, 2007.

Morrison, Toni. *Playing in the Dark: Whiteness and the Literary Imagination*. Cambridge, MA: Harvard University Press, 1993.

———. "Unspeakable Things Unspoken: The Afro-American Presence in Literature." Presentation, Tanner Lecturers on Human Value, University of Michigan, October, 1988.

Mulvey, Laura. "Changes." *Discourse* (Fall 1985): 11–30.

Muñoz, José. *Cruising Utopia: The Then and There of Queer Futurity*. New York: New York University Press, 2009.

Nelson, Jeffrey. "The Defense of Billie Jean King." *Western Journal of Communication* 48, no. 1 (1984): 92–102.

Nielsen Company. *The Nielsen Company 2009 Year-End Music Report*. Nielsen, 2009.

Nunn, Trevor. "Michael Jackson's Peter Pan Obsession." *TimesOnline*, July 5, 2009. [Online]. Available at: http://entertainment.timesonline. co.uk/tol/arts_and_entertainment/stage/theatre/article6634042. ece?token=null&offset=0&page=1 [accessed: May, 2010].

Ochs, Donovan. *Consolatory Rhetoric*. Columbia: South Carolina University Press, 1993.

O'Neil, Nick. "Michael Jackson Officially Becomes the Most Popular Person on Facebook." [Online]. Available at: //www.allfacebook.com/2009/07/michael-jackson-facebook/ [accessed: July 13, 2010].

Orth, Maureen. "Losing his Grip?" *Vanity Fair*, April 2003. [Online]. Available at: www.mjfiles.com/allegations/losing-grip-maureen-orth/ [accessed: July 20, 2010].

Ostrow, Adam. "Michael Jackson's Massive Impact (on Google, Facebook, and Yahoo)." [Online]. Available at: http://mashable.com/2009/06/26/michael-jackson-web-impact/ [accessed: July 13, 2010].

Po, Huang. *The Zen Teaching of Huang Po: On the Transmission of Mind*. Translated by John Blofeld. New York: Grove, 1958.

Pollock, Della. "Memory, Remembering, and the Histories of Change." In *Sage Handbook of Performance Studies*, edited by D. Soyini Madison and Judith Hamera, 87–105. Thousand Oaks, CA: Sage, 2006.

Purcell, Kristen, Lee Rainie, Amy Mitchell, Tom Rosenstiel, and Kenny Olmstead. "Understanding the Participatory News Consumer." *Pew Internet & American Life Project*, March 1, 2010. [Online]. Available at: www.pewinternet.org/ Reports/2010/Online-News.aspx?r=1 [accessed: July 14, 2010].

Rawlinson, Linnie, and Nick Hunt. "Jackson Dies, Almost Takes Internet with Him." *CNN.com*, June 26, 2009. [Online]. Available at: www.cnn.com/2009/ TECH/06/26/michael.jackson.internet/index.html [accessed: April 17, 2010].

Revel, Judith. "Identity, Nature, Life: Three Biopolitical Deconstructions." *Theory, Culture & Society* 26, no. 6 (2009): 45–54.

Robertson, Jessica. (June 25, 2009). "'Idol' Judge Calls Michael Jackson the 'Greatest Entertainer of All Time." *Spinner*, June 25, 2009. [Online]. Available at: www.spinner.com/2009/06/25/idol-judge-calls-michael-jackson-the-greatest-entertainer-of/ [accessed: April 17, 2010].

Rojek, Chris. *Celebrity*. London: Reaktion Books, 2001.

Rosenfield, Laurence W. "A Case Study in Speech Criticism: The Nixon-Truman Analog." *Speech Monographs* 35, no. 4 (1968): 435–50.

Rosenstone, Robert. "In Praise of the Biopic." In *Lights, Camera, History: Portraying the Past in Film*, edited by Richard Francaviglia and Jerry Rodnitzky, 11–29. College Station, TX: Texas A&M University Press, 2007.

Ross, Marlon B. "Beyond the Closet as Raceless Paradigm." In *Black Queer Studies: A Critical Anthology*, edited by Patrick E. Johnson and Mae G. Henderson. Durham, NC: Duke University Press, 2005.

Ryan, Halford Ross. "Kategoria and Apologia: On their Rhetorical Criticism as a Speech Set." *Quarterly Journal of Speech* 68 (1982): 254–61.

Salecl, Renata. *Sexuation*. Durham, NC: Duke University Press, 2000.

Savan, Leslie. "Commercials Go Rock." In *Sound and Vision: The Music Video Reader*, edited by Simon Frith, Andrew Goodwin, and Lawrence Grossberg, 85–90. New York: Routledge, 1993.

Sedgwick, Eve Kosofsky. *Tendencies*, edited by Michèle Aina Barale et al. Durham, NC: Duke University Press, 1993.

Sheffield, Robert. "Rock's 50 Greatest Meltdowns." *Rolling Stone*, 2002.

Shiels, Maggie. "Web Slows after Jackson's Death." *BBC News*, June 26, 2009. [Online]. Available at: http://news.bbc.co.uk/2/hi/technology/8120324.stm [accessed: April 17, 2010].

Shildrick, Margrit. "The Disabled Body, Genealogy, and Undecidability." *Cultural Studies* 19, no. 6 (2005): 755–70.

Shohat, Ella and Robert Stam. *Unthinking Eurocentrism: Multiculturalism and the Media*. New York: Routledge, 1994.

Siebers, Tobin. *The Body Aesthetic: From Fine Art to Body Modification*. Ann Arbor: University of Michigan Press, 2000.

———. "Disability as Masquerade." *Literature and Medicine* 23, no. 1 (2004): 1–22.

Silberman, Seth. "Presenting Michael Jackson." *Social Semiotics* 17, no. 4 (December 2007): 417–40.

Slusser, George. "Literary MTV." In *Storming the Reality Studio: A Casebook of Cyberpunk and Postmodernism Science Fiction*, edited by Larry McCaffery, 334–42. Durham, NC: Duke University Press, 1991.

Smith, Martin and Patrick Kiger. *Poplorica: A Popular History of the Fads, Mavericks, Inventions, and Lore That Shaped Modern America*. New York: Collins, 1994.

Somaiya, Ravi, "Michael Jackson, Celebrated and Sold," *New York Times*, October 10, 2011, C1.

Spitzack, Carole. "The Spectacle of Anorexia Nervosa." *Text and Performance Quarterly* 13, no. 1 (1993): 1–20.

Sterling, Bruce. Preface to *Mirrorshades: The Cyberpunk Anthology*, edited by Bruce Sterling, ix–xvi. New York: Ace Books, 1986.

———. *Schismatrix Plus*. New York: Ace Books, 1996.

Steuever, Hank. "Moonwalker in Neverland." *Washington Post*, December 11, 2000, C1.

Stockton, Kathryn Bond. *The Queer Child, or, Growing Sideways in the Twentieth Century*. Durham, NC: Duke University Press, 2009.

Stonequist, Everett V. "The Problem of *the Marginal Man*." *American Journal of Sociology* 41, no. 1 (1935): 1–12.

Strine, Mary S. "Articulating Performance/Performativity: Disciplinary Tasks and the Contingencies of Practice." In *Communication: Views from the Helm for the 21st Century*, edited by Judith. S. Trent, 312–17. Boston: Allyn & Bacon, 1998.

Sullivan, Andrew. "Thinking about Michael." *The Atlantic*, June 25, 2009. [Online]. Available at: http://andrewsullivan.theatlantic.com/the_daily_dish/2009/06/thinking-about-michael.html [accessed: August 9, 2010].

Taraborrelli, John Randall. *Michael Jackson: The Magic, the Madness, the Whole Story, 1958–2009*. 1991. Reprint, New York: Grand Central Publishing, 2009.

Tate, Greg. "'I'm White!' What's Wrong with Michael Jackson." *The Village Voice*, September 22, 1987.

———. "Michael Jackson: The Man in Our Mirror." *The Village Voice*, July 1, 2009. [Online]. Available at: www.villagevoice.com/2009-07-01/news/michael-jackson-the-man-in-our-mirror/ [accessed: April 17, 2010].

Tavuchis, Nicholas. *Mea Culpa: A Sociology of Apology and Reconciliation*. Stanford: Stanford University Press, 1991.

Thompson, Krista. "The Sound of Light: Reflections on Art History in the Visual Culture of Hip-Hop." *The Art Bulletin* (December 2009): 481–505.

Turner, Victor. "Frame, Flow and Reflection: Ritual and Drama as Public Liminality." *Japanese Journal of Religious Studies* 6, no. 4 (1979): 465–99.

Vineyard, Jennifer. "Michael Jackson Calls Baby-Dangling Incident a 'Terrible Mistake'." November 20, 2002. [Online]. Available at: www.mtv.com/news/articles/1458799/20021120/jackson_michael.jhtml [accessed: April 17, 2010].

Walker, Mike. "Tiger Woods: Michael Jackson was the greatest entertainer ever." *Golf.com*, June 30, 2009. [Online]. Available at: http://blogs.golf.com/presstent/2009/06/woods-michael-jackson-was-greatest-entertainer-ever.html [accessed: April 17, 2010].

Ware, B.L., and Wil A. Linkugel. "They Spoke in Defense of Themselves: On the Generic Criticism of Apologia." *Quarterly Journal of Speech* 59 (1973): 273–83.

Wasko, Janet. *How Hollywood Works*. London: Sage, 2003.

Wegner, Phillip. *Imaginary Communities: Utopia, the Nation, and the Spatial Histories of Modernity*. Berkeley: University of California Press, 2002.

West, Cornel. *Keeping Faith: Philosophy and Race in America*. New York: Routledge, 1993.

———. "The New Cultural Politics of Difference." In *The Cultural Studies Reader*, edited by Simon During, 256–67. New York: Routledge, 1999.

———. *Race Matters*. New York: Vintage Press, 2001.

Whiteley, Sheila. "Celebrity: The Killing Fields of Popular Music." In *Framing Celebrity: New Directions in Celebrity Culture*, edited by Su Holmes and Sean Redmond, 329–42. New York: Routledge, 2006.

Wiener, Michael, ed. *Japan's Minorities: The Illusion of Homogeneity*. New York: Routledge, 2009.

Wilkinson, Peter. "Is the King of Pop Going Broke?" *Rolling Stone*, 2002a.

———. "Jacko's Money Woes Deepen." *Rolling Stone*, 2002b.

———. "The Truth about Jackson's Money." *Rolling Stone*, 2003.

Winterman, Denise. "Thrills and Spills and Record Breaks." *BBC News Magazine*, November 30, 2007. [Online]. Available at: http://news.bbc.co.uk/1/hi/magazine/7117000.stm [accessed: November, 2007].

Yamada, Amy. *Trash*. Translated by Sonya Johnson. New York: Kodansha International, 1994.

Yancy, George, ed. *What White Looks Like: African-American Philosophers on the Whiteness Question*. New York: Routledge, 2004.

———. "Whiteness and the Return of the Black Body." *Journal of Speculative Philosophy* 19, no. 4 (2005): 215–41.

Yuan, David. "The Celebrity Freak: Michael Jackson's Grotesque Glory." In *Freakery: Cultural Spectacles of the Extraordinary Body*, edited by Rosemarie Garland Thomson, 368–84. New York: New York University Press, 1997.

Žižek, Slavoj. *The Fragile Absolute, or, Why is the Christian Legacy Worth Fighting For?* London: Verso, 2000.

Index